GAY DADS

QUALITATIVE STUDIES IN PSYCHOLOGY

This series showcases the power and possibility of qualitative work in psychology. Books feature detailed and vivid accounts of qualitative psychology research using a variety of methods, including participant observation and field work, discursive and textual analyses, and critical cultural history. They probe vital issues of theory, implementation, interpretation, representation, and ethics that qualitative workers confront. The series mission is to enlarge and refine the repertoire of qualitative approaches to psychology.

GENERAL EDITORS
Michelle Fine and Jeanne Marecek

Gay Dads

Transitions to Adoptive Fatherhood

Abbie E. Goldberg

NEW YORK UNIVERSITY PRESS
New York and London

NEW YORK UNIVERSITY PRESS
New York and London
www.nyupress.org

References to Internet websites (URLs) were accurate at the time of writing. Neither the author nor New York University Press is responsible for URLs that may have expired or changed since the manuscript was prepared.

Library of Congress Cataloging-in-Publication Data
Goldberg, Abbie E.
Gay dads : transitions to adoptive fatherhood / Abbie E. Goldberg.
p. cm. -- (Qualitative studies in psychology)
Includes bibliographical references and index.
ISBN 978-0-8147-3223-6 (cl : alk. paper) -- ISBN 978-0-8147-3224-3 (pb : alk. paper) -- ISBN 978-0-8147-0815-6 (ebook) -- ISBN 978-0-8147-0829-3 (ebook)
1. Gay fathers. 2. Gay fathers--Family relationships. I. Title.
HQ76.13.G65 2012
306.874'208664--dc23
2011052281

New York University Press books are printed on acid-free paper, and their binding materials are chosen for strength and durability. We strive to use environmentally responsible suppliers and materials to the greatest extent possible in publishing our books.

Manufactured in the United States of America
c 10 9 8 7 6 5 4 3 2 1
p 10 9 8 7 6 5 4 3 2 1

Contents

ACKNOWLEDGMENTS

Writing this book was a journey. Before I even began the writing process, I engaged in five years of participant interviews. I did not do all of these interviews by myself—I had a team of fantastic graduate research assistants who assisted me. I am deeply grateful for the sensitivity, care, and discipline of my doctoral students Jordan Downing, Lori Kinkler, April Moyer, Hannah Richardson, and Christine Sauck, all of whom interviewed participants. These same graduate students also helped to transcribe the open-ended interviews, a process which took several years. This book would have never come to fruition without their collaborative and disciplined work ethic. Many hardworking undergraduate research assistants also provided transcription assistance. Special thanks are owed to those undergraduate students who put in several years of service to the Transition to Adoptive Parenthood Project. These "longtimers" put in many hours transcribing the interviews, editing them, and sharing their ideas about them with me. I know that my research assistants will recognize and recall with much fondness the voices featured in this book.

I am also indebted to my superb mentors and colleagues, most notably, Katherine R. Allen and Maureen Perry-Jenkins. Both women nurtured my intellectual development, provided me with support and guidance, and on more than one occasion gave me the "rah-rah!" I needed to continue. In addition, they have also been wonderful friends and collaborators. I am also very grateful to have such excellent friends and collaborators in Dana Berkowitz, Mark Gianino, Kate Kuvalanka, Ramona Oswald, Lori E. Ross, Stephen Russell, and JuliAnna Smith. I have found an "academic family" in these individuals, all of whom study or have collaborated with me on research related to sexual diversity, social justice, or gay-parent families. Without them I would be an island.

I am also deeply grateful to my funders, who recognized the potential of this work and provided the resources to help make it happen. Clark University, the National Institute of Child Health and Human Development, and the American Psychological Association all provided funding that enabled me to conduct this particular study on gay fathers' transition to adoptive parenthood. I am fortunate to have received funding from the Williams Institute, the Gay and Lesbian Medical Association, the Alfred P. Sloan Foundation, the Society for the Psychological Study of Social Issues, and the Spencer Foundation to conduct further follow-ups of this group of men.

I am also filled with gratitude that I have such a wonderfully supportive group of colleagues at Clark University. Michael Addis, Esteban Cardemil, James Cordova, and Wendy Grolnick all read many drafts of my initial grant proposals on this topic. They—and the psychology department at as a whole—have always been supportive and encouraging of my research on this topic, for which I am so appreciative.

My journey in writing this book was deeply enriched by the editorial guidance of Jeanne Marecek and Michelle Fine, the series editors, and Jennifer Hammer, my editor at NYU Press. They provided important critical feedback at every stage of the manuscript. I could not have asked for more dedicated and thoughtful editors. Their wise insights and ability to see the bigger picture truly facilitated a finer finished product. I also thank the two external reviewers for engaging with my manuscript so fully and for offering valuable and constructive feedback.

I am thankful, beyond words, to the men in this study. They shared their stories, struggles, heartaches, joys, successes, and insights. They let us into their lives and enabled us to learn from them. I am so moved by their willingness—and often excitement—to let us share with them the intimate and often challenging experience of transitioning to parenthood. This book is for them, and all the gay fathers who preceded them and who will follow them.

They say that all work and no play makes Jack a dull boy, and they are right. I am grateful to my inner circle of family and friends who have helped me to maintain a balance between work and play. I share all my successes with them, because they have been my biggest supporters—in particular, my parents, who taught me that I could achieve anything, and my brothers, who let me believe that.

Finally, I cannot begin to express how grateful I am for the love and support of my immediate family. Owen, my husband and partner, has ensured that I have time to write and work, while also filling my life with so much light that I am regularly drawn out of my literal and symbolic "office." I have him to thank for everything. Alex, my daughter, is the firefly at the center of that light. She has redefined my life and my understanding of what is important, and for that I am deeply grateful.

INTRODUCTION

Gay Parenthood in Context

Carter, a 37-year-old teacher, and Patrick, a 41-year-old professor, lived in a midwestern suburb. They had been together for approximately 10 years at the time they began to consider parenthood. Before meeting Patrick, Carter had been unsure of whether he would be able to become a parent. He felt that he might have "abandoned that dream" when he came out. In contrast, Patrick had never considered *not* becoming a parent: "As a gay person there are so many things you can't do and you just have to work around it. It is just one of those things. I knew that if I want[ed] to have a family, that is just what I am going to have to do." Meeting Patrick and being exposed to other gay parents led Carter to rethink his initial hesitations about gay parenthood. After 10 years together, and a move into a larger house in a family-friendly neighborhood, the couple finally felt ready to take the plunge. They had a large, supportive network of family and friends and therefore felt well supported in their quest to become parents.

In deciding what route to take to parenthood, both men briefly considered surrogacy but then concluded, largely based on cost, that it did not make sense. Their interest in an infant, which had initially led them to consider the surrogacy option, influenced their decision to pursue a private domestic adoption. They were also drawn to the philosophy of openness and honesty inherent in open adoption, which is characterized by contact pre- and/or post-placement between the adoptive and birth parents. As Patrick observed, "It is obvious that there is no mom in the picture. We just decided that open adoption was a good way for children to know where they came from." Both men described actively researching various adoption agencies, because they hoped to circumvent, or at least minimize their exposure to, heterosexism in the adoption process. As Carter recalled, some of the agencies in their area made them feel somewhat uncomfortable, in that "we were being asked to be a little on the deceitful side and that was not what we were willing to do to start a family." Both Carter and Patrick were firm that they were unwilling to closet themselves in order to adopt a child. This meant that the process of finding an agency that would work with them took many months—a cost that they preferred to incur rather than sacrifice their personal integrity.

Both White themselves, Carter and Patrick ultimately adopted Arianna, a biracial female infant. They were thrilled with their daughter—and so were their families. As Carter laughed, "My mom doesn't call to talk to us anymore. It's 'How's my granddaughter?' I'm like, 'I'm fine, Mom, thanks for asking.'" Interestingly, some of their friends responded less positively—particularly their gay male friends, all of whom were nonparents. As Carter observed, "For them, it's so far from their realm of reality to even want a kid that they don't understand why we did this." He added, "[We now] kind of connect with some of our coworkers [more] than some of our friends." Both men noted shifts in their support networks in that they spent less time with their nonparent friends (who were mostly gay), and more time with their friends who were parents (and who were often heterosexual). Their social support network had therefore become increasingly straight—and their lives, as they put it, "more mainstream." They were aware of the irony that, at the same point that their sexuality was suddenly more on display in that they were more readily recognized as a couple, as opposed to just "buddies," in the presence of a child, they suddenly felt "less gay than before," in that parenthood, not their sexuality, was the defining feature of their identity. Further, although both men had described themselves as "workaholics" prior to parenthood, and were highly identified with their careers, parenthood caused them to "seriously rethink [their] commitment to work," such that their work lives now took a backseat to their roles as parents.

* * *

Brazil allows gay unions.
— *Financial Times*, May 6, 2011

Legal exemptions allow Australian religious groups to discriminate
against gays.
— *Associated Press*, May 4, 2011

U.S. gay couples banned from adopting Russian children.
— *Moscow Times*, July 22, 2010

Hollywood paints an updated portrait of the American family.
— *Philadelphia Inquirer*, July 22, 2010

As these news headlines illustrate, gay rights in general and gay parenthood
in particular are prominent topics on the social and political agenda. The
marriage and adoption rights of sexual minorities are being fiercely debated
across the globe, a reality that is reflected in the extensive media cover-
age devoted to these topics. In addition to receiving more attention in the
news, the lives of gay parents and their children are also increasingly being
depicted on television and in the movies. The TV show *Modern Family* pre-
miered on ABC in September 2009—the first network show to feature two
gay men raising an infant. And Focus Features released the film *The Kids Are
All Right* in the summer of 2010; although not the first film to depict gay parents, it was unique both in profiling a lesbian-mother family formed through
alternative insemination, and in its use of A-list actors. The fact that gay parents are the focus of political, media, and entertainment attention reflects a
new reality wherein they are recognized, albeit not universally accepted, as
members of society. It also points to the need for social science research to
document, and to provide greater insight into, the lived experiences of gay
parents and their place in the broader discourse about families. Analysis of
gay-parent families' experiences and perspectives has the capacity to challenge and reconfigure our basic ideas about families.

This book responds to the increased interest in gay parents, and gay
fathers specifically, by examining the perspectives of gay men who became
parents through adoption. It takes up the lively political and lived contradictions of this historic juncture: indeed, the virulent assault on gay rights
and gay parenting occur at the very moment that there is an explosion of
new family forms, including gay-father families. Through its exploration of
the experiences of gay fathers in today's society, this book exposes the centrality of heteronormativity in the institutions governing and the discourses

surrounding families. Further, by examining how gay fathers themselves wrestle with and respond to dominant ideas about families and gender, it pushes us toward a more nuanced understanding of how families and family life operate more broadly. It also encourages us to develop a deeper awareness of our own most basic assumptions about family, parenthood, gender, and sexuality, and how our daily actions and interactions have the potential to either uphold or resist dominant heteronormative discourses and institutions. Indeed, on a most basic level, exploration of the experiences of gay adoptive fathers has the capacity to stretch and enrich our national understanding of the sexuality, gender, and race contours of "family."

How Did We Get Here? A Look at Families through the Past Few Decades

How did we get to a place where films and TV shows depicting gay-parent families are described in a *Philadelphia Inquirer* article as "represent[ing] America's evolving social arrangements" and "repainting the portrait of the American family"? (Rickey, 2010). An answer to this question requires some discussion of the broader changes in family life and social relationships that have occurred in the United States over the past six decades (Cherlin, 2010; Thornton & DeMarco, 2001). Sociological and demographic data tell us that employment rates among women have increased dramatically since the 1960s, especially among White women (Cohen & Bianchi, 1999). The marriage and baby booms after World War II were followed by subsequent declines in marriage and childbearing rates (Fitch & Ruggles, 2000), and divorce rates accelerated sharply in the 1960s and 1970s (Cherlin, 1992). The 1960s and 1970s were also characterized by rapid increases in premarital sex and cohabitation (Bumpass & Lu, 2000) and innovations in medical technology, such as the birth control pill and other effective contraceptives (Thornton & Young-DeMarco, 2001).

Attitudes and values about gender roles and family life in the United States shifted alongside these behavioral changes. National surveys have documented substantial and persistent trends toward the endorsement of gender equality in families since the 1960s. Americans are increasingly likely to desire less differentiation of male and female roles, and to view maternal employment as benign as opposed to harmful for children and families (Thornton, 1989; Thornton & Young-DeMarco, 2001). A long-term trend towards tolerance of a diversity of personal and family behaviors is also evident, as exemplified by increased acceptance of divorce, premarital sex, cohabitation, remaining single, and choosing to be child-free (Thornton, 1989; Thornton &

Young-DeMarco, 2001). On average, Americans have also become increasingly tolerant of nontraditional approaches to family formation over the past several decades. National surveys indicate that Americans show increasingly favorable attitudes toward adoption (Evan B. Donaldson Adoption Institute, 2002) and reproductive technologies (Evan B. Donaldson Adoption Institute, 2002; Kindregan, 2008) as a means of becoming a parent.

These behavioral and attitudinal shifts have led bodies such as the United States Supreme Court to contend that "the demographic changes of the past century make it difficult to speak of an average American family" (*Troxel v. Granville*, 2000, p. 63). Yet while it is difficult to dispute the existence of these changes, Americans differ widely in their opinions and interpretations of them. There is considerable debate among both the general public and scholars as to whether they are indicative of "family decline and disintegration," or whether such changes should be interpreted as evidence that "the family is merely changing rather than declining" (Thornton & Young-DeMarco, 2001, p. 1011). Regardless of the actual observable changes in family life that are occurring, idealized notions of the family as nuclear, heterosexual, and biologically related continue to dominate contemporary popular media and public discourses (Chambers, 2000); these notions necessarily have implications for the lived experiences of gay fathers and their families.

Homosexuality: Political Movements and Changes in Attitudes

Alongside these large-scale shifts in behaviors and values relevant to family life, historical changes in gay identity politics and attitudes about homosexuality have also occurred. Such changes provide the historical backdrop for the way the current generation of gay fathers understands and approaches their roles and identities. They also provide the backdrop for our knowledge of how contemporary society responds to gay fathers.

The gay and lesbian revolution of the 1960s and 1970s has been described as the "stepchild of all the radical social and political movements of the decade—the student movement and the New Left, the anti-war movement, radical feminism, the Black Panthers, hippies and yippies" (Miller, 2006, p. 339). The early gay liberation movement was characterized by an atmosphere of openness and pride, increased organizing efforts, and, by extension, the influx of gay men and lesbians into the cities or "gay ghettos." Karen Heller, citing a 1989 *San Francisco Examiner* article by Richard Ramirez, estimated that one-third of San Francisco's gay male population had migrated to the city between 1974 and 1978 (Heller, 1993). In this new atmosphere of openness, the nature of gay male sex also shifted: "It was as if years of repression had suddenly shed its skin, as if every gay man were 16 again and all the men about whom he had ever fantasized . . . were suddenly available for a smile" (Miller, 2006, p. 393). In other words, as the 1970s wore on, gay male sex—which in previous decades had often been quick and anonymous, out of necessity or fear—was increasingly becoming casual and anonymous out of choice.

Then, in the 1980s, the first cases of AIDS were diagnosed. Gay men were disproportionally represented among these early cases, which led to AIDS initially being dubbed the "gay disease" or the "gay cancer." The syndicated columnist (and eventual presidential candidate) Pat Buchanan wrote in a 1983 column that "the sexual revolution has begun to devour its children," described gay men as a "community that is a common carrier of danger-ous, communicable, sometimes fatal diseases," and pronounced AIDS to be "nature's revenge" (Miller, 2006, p. 421). The deaths of millions of gay men from AIDS prompted widespread mobilization by the gay commu-nity, which became increasingly recognized as a political force during the 1980s and 1990s. In fact, in 1988, the Human Rights Campaign Fund, which gives money to political candidates who support gay rights and AIDS issues, became the ninth-largest PAC in the country (Bernstein, 2002; Miller, 2006). As bars and cruising areas became less central to the social life of the gay community, new types of organizations and institutions began to take their place, such as 12-step groups, gay churches and synagogues, gay choruses, and gay athletic clubs. In addition, as the perceived need to be in the "cen-ter of the action" declined, gay men began to disperse beyond the confines of gay ghettos, with many settling in the neighboring suburbs. The 1990s marked a period during which gay men were "no longer leaving their home-towns to establish separate identities and live in urban enclaves," but were "choosing to be part of the American mainstream" (Seidman, 2002, p. 3). Indeed, the journalist Frances FitzGerald visited the Castro (a neighborhood in San Francisco that had been very densely populated with gay men during the 1970s) in 1985 and observed that it was "still a gay neighborhood, but it had lost its 'gender eccentricities.' It was a neighborhood much like the other white, middle-class neighborhoods surrounding the downtown. . . . It [was] stable and domesticated" (as cited in Miller, 2006, p. 417). About the social changes that followed the advent of AIDS, the journalist Neil Miller writes:

 Many of the social changes in the lives of gay men might have occurred anyway if AIDS hadn't come along. The aging of the "baby boom" genera-tion, the more conservative social climate, the gradual lessening of social hostility toward homosexuals, an increasing sense of self-confidence and self-esteem, were all factors in pushing gay values more toward . . . "stability and domesticity." . . . But the arrival of AIDS unquestionably accelerated the process, individually and collectively. (2006, p. 420)

As more and more gay men became sick from AIDS, the importance of recognizing ties (e.g., between lovers) became more apparent, as dying men's assets and possessions were often given to their parents and other members of their family of origin (Bernstein, 2002; Miller, 2006). Therefore, during the 1980s and 1990s, there was an increased push for domestic partner legislation and bereavement leave, which became central priorities for the movement. By the late 1990s, a number of cities ranging from Minneapolis to Seattle to New York permitted same-sex couples to register their partnerships, and more than 3,500 businesses or institutions of higher education offered some form of domestic partner benefit (Miller, 2006; Seidman, 2002). During the 1990s, considerable steps toward legal and social integration were made (Seidman, 2002; Stychin, 2005). Efforts to secure other rights—such as partner relationship recognition—continued to build steam during the late 1990s and early 2000s. In 2000, Vermont became the first state to offer civil unions to same-sex partners. In 2003, Massachusetts became the first state to grant civil marriage to same-sex partners.

Society's attitudes about homosexuality have shifted alongside these changes in the gay political movement. Up until the early 1970s, the American Psychiatric Association classified homosexuality as a mental illness in its *Diagnostic and Statistical Manual* (*DSM*) (Sullivan, 2003). In the 1970s, gay activists began to protest this designation, and it was removed from subsequent revisions of the *DSM*. Survey data suggest that attitudes began to shift toward greater tolerance of homosexuality during this time period. The National Opinion Research Center's General Social Survey indicated that between 1972 and 1994, the percentage of people who believed that homosexuality was "not wrong" increased from 19% to 31%, and, with the exception of the late 1980s, when the number of deaths from AIDS was at a peak in the United States, the trend has been in the direction of increasing tolerance over time (Sullivan, 2003; Sullivan & Wodarski, 2002). By the early 1990s, the *New York Times*, reflecting this trend toward tolerance, began to feature almost daily articles on various aspects of gay/lesbian life (Miller, 2006). By 1998, the percentage of respondents who believed that homosexuality was "not wrong" had risen to 34% (Sullivan, 2003). Survey data gathered by the Pew Research Center indicate that in 2006, 36% of Americans believed that homosexuality is something that people are born with, up from 20% in 1985 (Pew Research Center, 2006). Other national survey data suggest that even more tolerant attitudes toward homosexuality in American society have taken hold today. A 2010 Gallup poll found that 52% of Americans considered homosexual relations morally acceptable, up from 40% in 2001 (Saad, 2008, 2010). The news that Americans' acceptance of gay relations crossed the 50% threshold inspired excitement among pro-gay advocates, who claimed this as a noteworthy victory for the gay rights movement (Biesen, 2010).

The Emergence of Gay Fatherhood

What are the implications of these social changes for gay parenthood? During the 1970s and 1980s, the gay community was political, politicized, and often regarded as entirely separate from—indeed, an alternative to—the "straight world." There was little acknowledgment of gay men's "procreative consciousness" (Berkowitz & Marsiglio, 2007). In fact, gay men were often stereotyped as uninterested in children and as "antifamily" (Stacey, 1996).[1] In the 1990s, increasing acceptance of homosexuality, coupled with increased options for becoming parents in the context of same-sex relationships, led to a rise in the number of intentional gay-father households.[2] These numbers increased even more sharply during the beginning of the twenty-first century, when adoption, fostering, and surrogacy became more widely available to gay men. Estimates based on U.S. census data suggest that about 1 in 20 male same-sex couples and 1 in 5 female same-sex couples were raising children in 1990. In 2000, these numbers had risen to 1 in 5 male same-sex couples and 1 in 3 female same-sex couples (Gates & Ost, 2004).

Yet even though attitudes toward homosexuality are becoming more tolerant on average, many Americans continue to hold ambivalent or hostile attitudes, particularly where matters of parenting are concerned (Stein, 2005). In 2006, only 42% of Americans favored allowing lesbians and gay men to adopt, up from 38% in 1999 (Pew Research Center, 2006). Religious and politically conservative persons are particularly likely to have negative attitudes about homosexuality, and to believe that gay persons should not be allowed to adopt children (Brodzinsky, Patterson, & Vaziri, 2002; Logan & Sellick, 2007; Whitley, 2009). For example, politically conservative and religiously oriented organizations like the Family Research Council believe that "since reproduction requires a male and a female, society will always depend upon heterosexual marriage to provide the 'seedbed' of future generations. The evidence indicates that homosexual or lesbian households are not a suitable environment for children" (Family Research Council, 2011). Gay men, then, pursue adoptive parenthood in a climate that is both complex and contested.

In addition to contending with broader social attitudes about ho
ality, gay men also confront dominant, sometimes conflicting, ide
gender and parenthood. Gay men who become adoptive fathers in
text of same-sex committed relationships are typically doing so without a
female co-parent. They often encounter powerful ideologies regarding the
importance of female parents to child development, as well as complicated
and sometimes contradictory ideals regarding fatherhood (Goldberg, 2010a).
Old stereotypes of fathers as primarily breadwinners and as less involved in
the care of their children continue to prevail (Blankenhorn, 1995), yet at the
same time, a new fatherhood ideal is emerging (Coltrane, 1996; Henwood &
Procter, 2003). Changes in societal attitudes toward gender and increases in
women's employment have contributed to greater expectations for fathers'
involvement with their children—not just as breadwinners and playmates but
also as equal co-parents (Coltrane, 1996; Henwood & Procter, 2003). As men
in relationships with other men, gay fathers and fathers-to-be must negotiate
these competing ideals as they create and enact their roles as parents.

Studying Gay Adoptive Fathers: Theoretical Perspectives ✗ start

This book explores the perspectives and experiences of 70 gay men (35 adoptive couples) who were first interviewed while they were actively seeking to
adopt, and then again after they became parents—3–4 months post-adoptive placement—in order to provide a picture over time of how their lives
changed when they became parents. It offers insight into how these men
decided to become parents in the context of various competing discourses
about whether gay men can parent; how they reconfigured their roles as
partners and workers once they became parents amid contradictory ideals
of masculinity and fatherhood; how they viewed their changing relationships
with friends, family members, and the larger society during the transition
to parenthood; and how they managed their families' visibility and multiple minority statuses in the context of their larger communities. Although
the sample of men is relatively racially homogenous (82.5% White) and well
educated, half the men adopted transracially, allowing for variability in the
number and type of intersecting minority statuses with which families contended. Moreover, the sample of couples is geographically diverse, allowing
for variability in the kinds of challenges and barriers they faced in their quest
to adopt, and once they became parents.[3] This book focuses on gay men who
adopted their children, as opposed to men who became parents through
surrogacy, for several reasons. First, adoption represents the more common route to parenthood for male same-sex couples who are intentionally

pursuing parenthood. Further, surrogacy is typically pursued by only a narrow subset of gay men: those who have considerable financial resources (the
average cost of surrogacy in the United States is over $100,000; see Goldberg,
2010a).[4] Also, gay men who adopt must navigate multiple ways in which
their families are different from the dominant notion of "family," in that they
are nonheterosexual and their children are not biologically related to them
(and may be racially different from them as well).

This book is about how gay fathers both shape and are shaped by their
broader social context. As we will see, by embarking on and enacting fatherhood, the gay men in this study can be viewed as disrupting heteronormativity, an act that may lead them to (re)define gender and family for themselves,
their families, their friends, and their communities. To examine these men's
stories, we need a framework that situates them in the larger sociohistorical
and political context and that acknowledges the multiple and often competing discourses and ideologies that shape their identities, behavior, and func-
tioning. This study draws from social constructionist and queer theoretical
perspectives to frame its research questions, data analysis, and the overall
approach in this book.

A social constructionist perspective views both families and gender as
socially and materially constructed. From this perspective, the meaning of
family is not "objective," and it is constantly being (re)defined and (re)nego-
tiated in different contexts (Stacey, 2006). Similarly, gender can be conceptualized as not merely a defining, stable characteristic of individuals (i.e., a
personality characteristic or role), but rather as something that is created,
defined, and maintained through daily interactions (West & Zimmerman,
1987). From a social constructionist perspective, gender is deeply embedded
in the social processes of daily life and social organizations, and is therefore
constructed at both the micro-level (family) and macro-level (laws, ideology, culture) (Ridgeway & Correll, 2004; Risman, 2004). Queer theorists also
view gender, sexual orientation, and family as fluid and contested. That is,
there are many ways to "do gender," to "do sexual orientation," and to "do
family." Queer theory, however, is distinct from social constructionism in
that it situates heteronormativity at the center of analysis (Oswald, Blume,
& Marks, 2005). Heteronormativity has been described as "the mundane,
everyday ways that heterosexuality is privileged and taken for granted as
normal and natural" (Martin, 2009, p. 190). It can perhaps be even more
precisely defined as "an ideology that promotes gender conventionality, heterosexuality, and family traditionalism as the correct way for people to be"
(Oswald, Blume, & Marks, 2005, p. 143). Queer theory attends to the inter-
dependence of gender, sexuality, and family in relation to heteronormativity,

and to how heteronormativity is produced through discourse—that i
talk and action of everyday life. Queer theory can be used to challenge several binaries embedded in heteronormativity: "real" males and "real" females
versus gender deviants; "natural" sexuality versus "unnatural" sexuality;
and "real" families versus "pseudo" families. Sexual minorities, because of
their marginalized status in society, are in a unique position to engage in
"queering processes"—that is, to engage in acts and put forward ideas that
challenge such binaries and therefore expand our ideas about gender, family
structure, and sexual orientation. Alternately, some gay men, despite their
marginalized status, may choose to focus their efforts not on "queering" the
status quo, but on adapting and conforming to the existing heteronormative
structures in which they and their families live.

From both of these theoretical perspectives, gay-father families contest
and expose traditional conceptualizations of family and highlight the ways
"family" and "parenthood" are subjectively interpreted (Stacey, 2006). By
actively disentangling both heterosexuality and biology from parenthood,
gay adoptive fathers destabilize several key assumptions about family, such
as the notion that all families are created through heterosexual reproduction
and the notion that all families are biologically related. The very fact that
men are parenting with male, not female, co-parents is a fundamental challenge to traditional notions of "motherhood" and "fatherhood." Men's same-
sex relational context by definition precludes the enactment of traditional
heterosexual mother and father roles, and in turn upends basic assumptions
about the meaning of "family" and "parenthood" (Goldberg, 2010b). Their
unique relational and social context may lead gay adoptive fathers to act
or construct meaning in ways that dislodge or challenge traditional family
relations (e.g., the notion of a "mother" and "father" role) and gender relations, including their intimate partner relationships and their relationships
with their children. Indeed, men's marginalized status as *gay* men parenting
with *another man* arguably allows them greater freedom to create meaningful and personally satisfying parental roles and identities.[5] To the extent that
the gay men in this study describe parenting desires that are not predicated
on biological relatedness to one's child, and act in ways that defy traditional
notions of masculinity (e.g., as tied heavily to breadwinning), they invite us
to reexamine our implicit associations about families and gender, what is a
"masculine" man," and the unspoken dominance of heteronormativity in our
most basic ideas about family processes.

Gay men are, of course, exposed to the same societal and cultural ideologies about family, gender, and parental roles as heterosexual women and
men, such as those of women as caretakers and nurturers, and of men as

breadwinners and playmates. Gay adoptive fathers necessarily negotiate parenthood within a societal system that is fundamentally gendered, and one in which women and men (and mothers and fathers) are assumed to have different and complementary qualities, roles, and responsibilities (Blankenhorn, 1995). Women as mothers are presumed to be nurturing, caring, and self-sacrificing, whereas men as fathers are presumed to be more practical, less emotional, and strongly committed to paid employment (Connell & Messerschmidt, 2005). Thus, at the same time that gay adoptive fathers may construct and enact meanings in ways that resist heteronormativity and gendered relations, they are not insulated from or immune to heteronormative gender norms and ideals. They may *alternately* or *simultaneously* draw from or derive meaning from normative conceptualizations of family, fatherhood, and parenthood even as they create their own "nontraditional" families. It is overly simplistic to assume that all gay parents, as "family outlaws" (Calhoun, 1997), actively and purposefully transform traditional notions of family. Such an approach precludes exploration of how the choices, behaviors, relationships, and roles of gay fathers may be accommodating or assimilating rather than resistant and revisionist in nature (Goldberg, 2009a). By extension, it is possible that some gay men, realizing their marginalized status as *gay* fathers, feel additional pressure to conform to traditional notions of fatherhood and family because they do not want to expose themselves and their children to additional criticism or attack. Or, alternatively, some gay men may simply long for the type of parenting arrangements that heterosexual couples have long enjoyed, and may not be particularly interested or attuned to the ways they do, or do not, challenge heteronormativity.

The societal system within which gay adoptive fathers negotiate parenthood is, of course, not only gendered but also heterosexist. Gay men become parents in a societal climate that often denigrates their sexual orientation and choice of partners in both symbolic and practical ways. In most states, gay men's commitment to their partners is undermined by the absence of laws that recognize and protect their unions. Their commitment to their children is similarly undermined by the lack of legal protection for both parents. Gay men who wish to adopt may also encounter discrimination and opposition at other, more localized levels. They may confront adoption agencies that refuse to work with them or that perpetuate more subtle types of discrimination; or they may face a lack of support from family members and friends. Gay men's experience of parenthood, and, specifically, the degree to which gay men resist and accommodate to dominant cultural and societal norms (such as the societal presumption that family members should look alike), may be shaped by the broader sociopolitical/

legal climate and the degree to which gay men perceive their relationships and families as being under attack.

The men's experiences of negotiating heteronormativity, and their ability or willingness to challenge heteronormative discourses and practices, are likely influenced not only by broader legal/structural factors but also by the social, geographic, and financial resources they have available to them. For example, a fairly affluent gay man living in an urban and progressive area may feel more comfortable challenging heterosexist treatment by adoption agencies than a gay man who lives in a conservative area of the country and is not financially privileged, and therefore has fewer adoption options available to him. Likewise, a gay man with a large social support network may be more willing and able to resist family members' gendered and heteronormative assumptions regarding child rearing than a gay man who, lacking extensive social ties, feels he must conform to these stereotypes in order to be accepted by his family of origin. By examining how the gay men in this study create and maintain their families in the context of broader norms and ideologies that uphold heteronormativity, we can gain an understanding of how, and the conditions under which, heteronormativity can be resisted and alternative notions of gender and family realized—and, likewise, how, and under what conditions, gay men yield to or internalize heteronorms (Oswald, Kuvalanka, Blume, & Berkowitz, 2009).

Gay fathers are but one example of individuals who are parenting "against the grain," and their struggles and creativity are in some ways reflective of the types of experiences and possibilities engaged by new family forms (e.g., single-parent families, adoptive families, multiracial families, and grandparent-headed families). The men in this study can be seen as "innovating" family and parenthood through their resourceful family-building efforts, their creative parenting practices, and their ability to carve out new political and personal possibilities for themselves and others, thereby illuminating what is possible in terms of family life. In short, the increasing presence of gay adoptive fathers in society has the capacity to revision dominant understandings of family, including who is "seen" and recognized as family.

Finding the Men

Community, state, and legal contexts necessarily shape the experiences of gay men who adopt. Gay men who reside in states that do not allow gay men to co-adopt their children openly, for example, may face a broader set of challenges and barriers than do men who live in states characterized by more flexible adoption laws. Gay men who live in urban communities with a visible gay community may have a different experience in seeking to adopt and then raising their child than do men who live in rural communities with a limited gay presence. My interest in the social geography of men's lives, and how men's experiences and perspectives might be shaped by both immediate and more distal contextual factors, led me to seek out a geographically diverse sample.

I used U.S. census data to identify states with a high percentage of lesbians and gay men (Gates & Ost, 2004) and made an effort to contact adoption agencies in those states. More than 30 agencies agreed to provide information to their clients—that is, prospective adoptive parents—typically in the form of a brochure that invited them to participate in a study of the transition to adoptive parenthood. Clients were asked to contact me for more information about the study. For the larger study from which this sample is drawn, both same-sex couples and heterosexual couples were invited to participate. Inclusion criteria for the larger study were that couples must be adopting their first child, and both partners must be becoming parents for the first time. Because some same-sex couples may not be "out" to agencies about their sexual orientation, I also enlisted the help of large gay/lesbian organizations such as the Human Rights Campaign (HRC) to aid me in disseminating study information. For example, the HRC posted study information on their FamilyNet Listserv, which is sent to 15,000 people per month.

I did not extend my recruitment efforts beyond the United States for several reasons. First, the nature of adoption—including the procedures for adopting, the regulations surrounding adoption, and the role of adoption in society—varies significantly across cultures. Second, the nature of adoption by *gay men* in particular necessarily varies cross-culturally. Because of these differences, and my uncertainty about how I would synthesize and effectively compare findings from such different international contexts, I limited my study to residents of the United States. The findings of the current study must be viewed within this particular cultural context. This study therefore focuses on a particular cross section of adult men in the United States who are actively engaged with, and transforming, the landscape of the American family, at a politically contentious moment in gay human rights history.

Doing the Study

To gain insight into how gay men experience and perceive the transition to adoptive parenthood, and, more broadly, how they wrestle with and navigate heteronormative and sometimes conflicting discourses regarding parenthood, family, and gender, I conducted in-depth, semi-structured interviews (with open-ended questions) with 70 men (35 gay male couples)—both before they became parents, while they were waiting to be placed with a child (Time 1), and after they became parents, 3–4 months after adoptive placement (Time 2).[6] Because of the geographically diverse nature of the sample, all participants took part in telephone interviews, which lasted about 1.5 hours on average (usually ranging from 1 to 2.5 hours). At the time of the pre-adoptive (Time 1) interview, the majority of couples had completed their home study, an in-depth evaluation of the pre-adoptive parents.[7] In addition to participating in individual interviews, both partners also completed a questionnaire packet at Time 1, which they mailed back to me in separate, postage-paid envelopes. After these initial interviews, I maintained regular contact with participants. Checking in periodically with them by phone and e-mail enabled me to learn quickly of a child placement, and so to schedule the post-adoptive placement interview (Time 2). At Time 2, both partners again completed an individual interview and a questionnaire packet.

Semi-structured interviews, which I would later analyze using theoretically grounded coding strategies, seemed most appropriate given how little is known about gay men's parenthood experiences, as well as the nuances and complexity of the issues I was interested in studying. Open-ended interviews allowed me to tailor my questions and follow-up queries to the men's specific experiences and social locations. For example, I asked different questions and follow-up inquiries depending on whether the men had adopted transracially, had adopted via public adoption versus private adoption, and were able to legally adopt their child.[8]

I was determined to interview gay men both before they had adopted and after they had become parents, given my interest in how their ideas and experiences pertaining to family, gender, and parenthood might change after they were placed with a living, breathing child. Further, I set out to interview gay male couples, as opposed to single gay men, because I was aware that for these couples, parenthood renders their sexual orientation more visible in that they are now navigating the world as "two men and a baby." In turn, I sought to document how these men simultaneously made families and managed an "invigorated visibility" as gay couples. I also wanted to interview members of couples because of my interest in how relational processes (such as the division of paid and unpaid labor) were renegotiated during the transition to parenthood. Finally, as noted, I felt that it was important to seek out a geographically diverse sample because I was interested in gaining insight into how men in different social contexts (in terms of legal barriers, community climate, etc.) negotiated their identities and experiences as gay male parents. This ultimately led me to conduct telephone interviews with all the men, who were spread throughout the United States. In the interest of developing solid rapport with all participants, I spent time on e-mail and the telephone talking to and getting to know them prior to our official "interviews." I also made an effort to leave time for informal chat before, during, and after the actual interview.

All the men were interviewed separately from their partners in order to allow them to speak openly about their own personal perspectives, opinions, and experiences. Interviewing both partners separately was important since partners sometimes had very different perspectives and experiences of particular issues. For example, gay men whose work arrangements differed markedly from their partners' often voiced different challenges and concerns related to their work-family arrangements. Interviewing both partners separately also enabled me to access complicated and sometimes negative emotions that the men might have been unwilling to share had they been interviewed with their partners.[9]

The interview questions asked in the study were often quite personal (see appendix C for the interview questions). For example, I—or sometimes one of my trained graduate research assistants—inquired about participants' personal and family (combined) income, questions that often highlighted the disparity between partners' incomes (or, at the post-placement interview, underscored the fact that only one partner was now "bringing home the bacon"). No participant resisted providing this financial information, but it was clear that it made a few men uncomfortable—particularly when they did not make any money (e.g., because they were a graduate student, or not working because they were caring for the child). Some men responded to these questions with elaborations about how they used to be the primary earner (e.g., before returning to school). Thus sometimes the difficult questions led men into a discussion of masculinity and cultural ideologies of manliness, enabling me to obtain valuable data to which I otherwise would not have had access.

Another line of inquiry that proved somewhat uncomfortable for some participants was questions about how couples chose which partner would adopt as a single parent, among those couples in which partners could not co-adopt. Some of the men seemed uncomfortable with highlighting discrepancies in job status, income, and educational level between themselves and their partners—even though (and perhaps because) the decision of who would adopt often rested on these very discrepancies. Those men with the higher job status, income, and educational level were more attractive "on paper" and therefore chosen to be the adoptive parents. Yet these men, and their lower-status partners, expressed discomfort with the notion that one partner presented—even on the most superficial level—the more "attractive" package. They also seemed to resist the reality that occupational status/money was power, in that it granted the higher earner the legal privilege of completing the official legal adoption. Indeed, this is an example of how, without gender to "naturalize" differences within couples, these men had to navigate the meaning and implications of differences in power and responsibilities within couples—an experience that they generously shared with us, and which provides us with insights about how difference and power may operate more broadly in all couples.

Of note is that our use of telephone interviews, as opposed to in-person interviews, eliminated certain rapport-building devices, such as facial cues. We therefore made considerable efforts to build rapport before, during, and after the interviews with participants. We strived to be sensitive and warm in our interactions with participants; to express our genuine appreciation for their participation, time, and insights; and to convey our congratulations appropriately when they were finally placed with a child (e.g., by sending a card and a gift). We also sent our participants quarterly newsletters that included updates about the research, resources on gay parenting adoption, newsworthy items pertaining to parenting and adoption, and seasonal activities for parents and children. These quarterly newsletters served as a periodic "thank-you" to our participants and, we hope, conveyed to them our ongoing appreciation of their contributions.

Analyzing the Data

Interviews were transcribed and analyzed using qualitative methods, in general, and a thematic analysis, more specifically, because these methods are particularly suited to grounding participants' constructions within their specific sociocultural context (Morrow, 2005). My analysis is grounded in a social constructivist philosophy of science, whereby I view participants' discourse as illustrative of their meaning-making processes, rather than of any presumed objective reality (Gergen, 1985; Ponterotto, 2005). Although I emphasize the emergence of themes throughout this book, I recognize that any analysis of the data involves my own (i.e., the researcher's) constructed interpretation of the participants' responses (Gergen, 1985). Further, I approached the data using a social constructionist and queer theory–informed theoretical framework, which necessarily sensitized me to attend to certain themes and issues and to ignore or minimize others. Thus my choice and use of that theoretical frame inevitably shaped the data and themes that I report.

I engaged in a thematic analysis, which involved carefully sorting through data to identify recurrent themes or patterns (Bogdan & Biklen, 2003). I first engaged in line-by-line analysis of each participant's transcript, attending closely to their statements to generate initial theoretical categories (Charmaz, 2006). During this stage I considered and compared responses across participants, whereby the responses of partners within couples were compared, and the data from Time 1 and Time 2 were compared, both within and across couples (Glaser & Strauss, 1967). At the start of the coding process, I was broadly interested in the ways that the men negotiated their parenting desires and experiences amid broader cultural discourses about gender, family, and parenthood. I was also interested in changes in men's experiences and perceptions across the transition to parenthood. These broad interests framed my selective analysis and coding of the data. I first read and applied initial codes to the transcripts of the first five couples (10 men) and then wrote extensive memos about the transcripts. Careful analysis of these memos led me to identify a number of initial themes. I then read the transcripts of the next five couples, wrote memos about the emergent themes in these transcripts, and then compared their data to those of the first 10 men. This led to further refinement and specification of themes. For example, I consolidated some specific themes into larger, more abstract categories. I repeated this process—that is, reading transcripts, writing in-depth memos, articulating themes, and comparing these themes against already-coded data—until all the data had been coded. Then, using the emerging coding scheme, I reread all the transcripts multiple times, attempting to categorize all the participants' narratives in the existing coding scheme. This process led to further refinement of the emerging categories. For example, some codes were combined with other codes, some were modified or reconceptualized, and others were dropped. This thorough analysis process also led me to identify linkages or connections between categories, as well as to notice both consistency and contradiction within the narrative of an individual participant, and between the narratives of partners within a couple.

At this point, I had a very long list of fairly specific codes. Therefore, I next applied focused coding to the data, using the most significant, meaningful, and substantiated coding categories to sort the data. This led me to further integrate some codes and to discover new connections among the data. Several rounds of focused coding of all the narratives enabled me to refine my descriptive categories further. Also at this stage, I examined the relationships among key categories (Charmaz, 2006). For example, I examined how participant demographics such as race, geographic location, and adoption type might relate to or serve to categorize participant responses. My focused codes, which can be understood as being more conceptual and selective (Charmaz, 2006), became the basis for what I refer to as the themes developed in my analysis. Then I reapplied the coding scheme and made subsequent revisions until all data were accounted for. I organized the findings around the final coding scheme, which consisted of five major sections—that is, the five major chapters in the book.

Throughout the process of writing each chapter, I made minor revisions and additions to the scheme. I also frequently revisited the data to extract quotes that I had previously identified as being exemplars of a particular theme. Thus the process of coding and writing was an iterative one, whereby I consistently compared my writing, the participants' narratives, and the coding scheme against one another, querying and addressing all inconsistencies.

Pseudonyms were assigned to the men and their children to protect their confidentiality. I also took a number of other steps to preserve the confidentiality of the participants while also maintaining the meaning and integrity of the interviews and the reality of participants' lives. For example, while general job titles were typically preserved (e.g., lawyer, physician), those job titles that were more specific were altered somewhat. Efforts were made to ensure that the altered job title was fairly close to the actual job title in terms of level of education required, type of responsibilities involved, and approximate annual income earned. In addition, when introducing participant quotes and stories, I generally discuss participants' geographic location in terms of the U.S. region in which they resided (East, West, South, Midwest) and whether they lived in an urban, rural, or suburban locale. In some instances, however, I identify the specific city and state in which participants resided, because this information provides important contextualizing detail. Of course, while I took steps to protect the confidentiality of participants, those who read this book may very well be able to identify themselves—and their partners. Thus it is impossible to keep participants' responses entirely "secret" from their partners.

The Men in the Study

The men who were interviewed for this study tend to be somewhat older than were the average heterosexual first-time parents (Centers for Disease Control and Prevention, 2009). At the time they were first interviewed, the men's mean (average) age was 38.4 years old (their ages ranged from 30 to 52; SD = 4.5 years).[10] The men largely identified as "exclusively gay/homosexual" (86%); a minority (14%) identified as "predominantly gay/homosexual." (No men identified as bisexual.) The men were generally in fairly long-term relationships: on average, they had been in their current relationships for 8.3 years (relationship length ranged from 1 to 19 years; SD = 3.8 years). At the time of the pre-adoptive placement interview, 55% of the men reported having had a commitment ceremony, and 12% of the men reported having had a civil marriage (not necessarily in their state of residence; only one couple was legally married in their home state). The men were also fairly well educated and affluent: seven of the men (10%) had graduated high school with no further education; five (7%) had an associate's degree or some college; 28 of the men (40%) had completed college; 19 of the men (27%) had a master's degree; and 11 (16%) had a PhD, JD, or MD. Pre-adoption, the men's annual median personal salary was $70,000 ($SD$ = $6,702; range $0–$450,000), and their annual median family (combined) income was $122,800 ($SD$ = $9,463; range $53,000–$510,000).[11]

The men waited for an average of 13.7 months for a child placement (SD = 10.4 months, range 2–60 months). Twenty-four couples pursued private domestic open adoptions (i.e., adoptions in which there is contact between the birth and adoptive parents before or after the adoptive placement); nine couples pursued public domestic adoptions (i.e., they adopted through the child welfare system); and two couples pursued international adoptions (i.e., they adopted from abroad). Twenty-five couples (75%) were placed with newborns or infants, five couples (15%) were placed with toddlers, and five couples (15%) were placed with school-aged children. Twenty couples adopted boys, and 15 couples adopted girls. Most adoptions were transracial for at least one partner.[12] Specifically, 58 of the men (82.5%) were White/Caucasian; five (7%) were Latino; three (4.5%) were Asian; two (3%) were biracial/multiracial; and two (3%) were African American. With regard to the children's races, 17 (49%) were White/Caucasian, seven (20%) were biracial/multiracial; five (14%) were African American; five (14%) were Latino/Latina; and one (3%) was Asian.

In terms of geographic region, 10 couples lived in California; three couples each lived in Washington DC, Washington State, Oregon, and New York; two couples each lived in Texas, Georgia, and Missouri; and one couple each lived in Michigan, North Carolina, Pennsylvania, Delaware, Maryland, Massachusetts, and Vermont. Most of the participants (31 of 35 couples; 89%) lived in counties that are characterized as "large metropolitan areas" (1 million residents or more) by the U.S. Department of Agriculture. Three couples lived in small metropolitan areas (fewer than 1 million residents) and one couple lived in a micropolitan area—that is, a community adjacent to a small metropolitan area. Thus most participants were living in urban metropolitan areas. But living in a metropolitan area does not guarantee, and is not

always associated with, the presence of a large number of gays and/
or gay/lesbian-parent families. According to the U.S. census, only
couples (14%) lived in cities where more than 2% of households reportedly
were comprised of same-sex couples (e.g., San Francisco). Another 14 couples (40%) lived in cities where 1–2% of households were same-sex couples
(e.g., Atlanta). Finally, 16 couples (46%) lived in cities where less than 1% of
households were same-sex couples (e.g., St. Louis); in seven of these cases,
the percentage of same-sex-couple households was less than 0.5%.

Focus of the Book

This book uses data from these 35 gay male adoptive couples to explore how
gay men navigate and respond to heteronormativity in the process of becoming, and then living as, adoptive parents.[13] By showing how they respond
to available sociocultural discourses and also how they drew on their own
creative potential and personal resources, these men's stories provide insight
into the "doing" and "creating" of new family forms and practices against a
backdrop of societal resistance. As this book will illustrate, when gay men
choose to become parents (especially adoptive parents) in the United States
today, they continually encounter societal, legal, and institutional practices,
as well as mundane interpersonal experiences, in which heteronormativity
is either explicit or implicit—and is in some cases enforced by legal stat-
utes. Indeed, gay couples who adopt inescapably come face-to-face with elements of heteronormativity that single gay men, or gay couples not seeking
to adopt, may never encounter. The men in the study, as we will see, sometimes actively confronted and resisted such practices and discourses, perhaps at times prompting or promoting societal change. In other cases, they
conformed to such practices and discourses for the sake of expediency (e.g.,
they did not want to jeopardize their chance of adopting a child) or relational
harmony (e.g., they did not want to jeopardize interpersonal relationships
with family members). Relatedly, they sometimes seemed to draw unself-
consciously on heteronormative meaning systems (e.g., conventional notions
about gender and parenting) to understand their own experiences.

Chapter 1 explores the men's perceptions of their parenting trajectories
and choices, with attention to the historical, social, and geographical backdrop of their decision making. Specifically, it addresses how the men constructed their parenthood desires amid the controversy surrounding gay parenthood, and how they wrestled with the broader heteronormative context in
realizing, and then articulating, their parenting desires. It also explores how
the men decided to pursue adoption over surrogacy—a process that in some

cases was fraught with ambivalence, revealing the power of dominant discourses surrounding biogenetic relationships for some of the men. Another issue it takes up is the process by which the men decided what type of adoption to pursue, and how the heteronormative values, laws, and practices of the surrounding culture constrained their choices. The discussion of these decision-making processes attends to the personal, contextual, and temporal factors that the participants perceived as influencing their decision making. This chapter reveals how all the men contended with salient and interconnected discourses concerning biologism, heteronormativity, and the family. But the men varied in the degree to which they accepted or resisted these discourses. Some men, for example, strongly desired a genetic connection to their child. This desire did not foreclose their decision to pursue adoption, but rather just delayed it. Other men rejected the centrality of biogenetic relatedness in defining family, and embraced more expansive notions of family, implicitly "queering" or challenging heteronormativity. This chapter also illuminates the role of financial privilege in shaping the degree to which men can circumvent heteronormativity. For example, gay men with financial resources were in a better position to pursue and embody certain aspects of the heteronormative ideal (e.g., to adopt a newborn via private adoption) than men with few financial resources.

Chapter 2 explores the formal and informal barriers that the men encountered as they sought to build their families through adoption. It attends to how broader social and legal inequities, such as state laws regarding gay adoption, shaped the path to parenthood of the men in this study, and how they negotiated and responded to these, either through resistance or accommodation. Further, the men's ideas about and valuing of marriage are examined. This chapter considers the degree to which the men viewed marriage as more important once they were parents, insomuch as marriage offered practical and symbolic support for their families; or as unimportant, because, for example, the men had access to other legal supports or because they rejected the institution of marriage as heterosexist. This chapter builds on chapter 1 to illustrate how geographic and economic privilege fundamentally influenced the men's ability to resist or circumvent heteronormativity in the adoption process. It also illustrates how some men used the limited power available to them, regardless of their social locations, to resist heteronormativity.

Chapter 3 examines how the men in the study configured their roles and identities as parents in the context of broad cultural discourses regarding gender, parenthood, and family. The chapter discusses how the men made decisions about the division of work and family responsibilities, and how they felt about those arrangements—with particular attention paid to the experiences of men whose work arrangements violate cultural expectations for masculinity (i.e., they were working part-time or staying at home). Further, it explores how the men reexamined their work roles in light of fatherhood, and the degree to which they felt less committed to work upon becoming a parent. This chapter shows how gay men must navigate and reconcile dominant ideologies surrounding masculinity (which emphasize breadwinning) with their own realities as parents who are "doing it all" (i.e., performing both paid and unpaid labor, which have stereotypically been associated with fathering and mothering, respectively).

Chapter 4 explores the men's changing relationships with their immediate social networks—namely, their family members and friends—during the transition to parenthood. It first examines the men's perceptions of families' and friends' support (or nonsupport) for their parenting efforts, and attends especially to the ways their family members' and friends' concerns reflect broader heteronormative discourses regarding families and gender. It also examines how the men's family and friends responded in diverse ways to the arrival of a child, thereby provoking dramatic shifts, in some cases, in the men's social networks. For example, some men described their family members as becoming increasingly supportive during the transition to parenthood. Sexual orientation suddenly paled in importance next to the significance of their new role as parents. In sum, this chapter reveals how gay men's social networks may both influence and be influenced by gay men's status as parents. It further reveals the potential for network members themselves to actively challenge heteronormativity (e.g., by recognizing and acknowledging their gay family member's family as family).

Chapter 5 examines how the gay adoptive fathers in this study managed their multiple (often visible) differences in the context of societal scrutiny and ignorance. It addresses the extent to which they felt that parenthood made their sexuality more "visible," and the extent to which those who adopted transracially experienced a heightened sense of visibility because their children's race marked them and their families as "definitely adoptive," thereby inviting additional inquiries about their families and sexuality. This chapter shows how gay men may respond to the increasing visibility of their sexual orientation and family status in diverse ways. For example, they may view this visibility as an opportunity to challenge others' ideas about families, or they may resent it because it disrupts their efforts to "blend in" and "go mainstream."

This book as a whole reveals the contexts and ways in which heteronormativity operates, as well as the varied, often creative responses that the men employed in dealing with systemic heteronormativity. It also provides insights into the "doing of" and the "living in" of new family forms, particularly families that have been formed amid sociopolitical opposition. The creativity and resourcefulness that the men exhibit reveal the exciting potential of the "new families"—both those of today and those of the future.

1

Decisions, Decisions

Gay Men Turn toward Parenthood

When I first interviewed Rufus and Trey, they had been waiting for a child placement for just a few months. They were both excited to talk about the adoption process; this was not always the case for couples who had been waiting for many months or even years for a child placement. Both fairly young (Rufus was 37 and Trey was 32), they conveyed a boyish excitement about their impending parenthood. As Rufus exclaimed, "I have always loved kids. . . . I just feel like I have a lot to offer." Both men voiced a long-standing interest in parenthood, and both described themselves as "very family-oriented," although Rufus also acknowledged having temporarily "shelved" his dream of becoming a parent when he came out. He said he had no role models for what gay parenthood might look like, and he therefore admittedly "bought into" common notions about the fundamental incompatibility of gay life and parenthood. Later, in his early 20s, he began to meet gay parents, which helped to shift his thinking about parenthood from "I want to do it" to "I can do it!" It was not long after he met Trey that the two began to talk about children. Rufus explained, "Trey and I have talked about having kids for a long time; we both, I think, came into the relationship hoping that one day we would have a family. That was a point of commonality for us." But it took several years for the couple (who had been together for almost five years at the time of the first interview) to pursue parenthood actively. Their mutual desire for both financial and relationship stability ultimately stalled their parenting efforts. Trey, a dermatologist, was in medical school when the two met, and both men agreed that for financial reasons it would be ideal for Trey to finish school before pursuing parenthood. Both men also wanted to make sure that their relationship was "stable" before pursuing parenthood. Now, Trey said, "we're just, we're ready. I think financially, we're ready, personally, we're ready."

Once they began to consider parenthood seriously, Rufus and Trey faced numerous decisions: Surrogacy or adoption? If adoption, what type? Although both men had ruled out the possibility of surrogacy early in the process for financial reasons, this decision was initially difficult for Rufus, who acknowledged wanting a child to "serve my immortality element," helping to ensure that there would be "a little bit of me in the future." He felt "depressed" by the idea that he would not be "continuing my genes." Trey, in contrast, mused that he never "had that need to have a child that was biologically mine." Ultimately, however, the two men decided jointly to pursue adoption. They then faced the decision of what type of adoption to pursue— private domestic, public domestic, or international. Trey expressed the feeling that although it would be wonderful to adopt an older child from foster care who would especially benefit from a stable home, he ultimately felt committed to raising an infant because he would be able to have an effect on that child from the very beginning of his or her life. Rufus also voiced a strong desire to raise an infant, particularly given that he would not have his own biological children. Their strong desire to raise a child from infancy led the couple to pursue private domestic adoption. Both Trey and Rufus also emphasized their attraction to the philosophy of open adoption. Trey described it as "just a kind of way to make everything out in the open. It seemed very natural to us."

As Rufus and Trey's story illustrates, the pursuit of gay parenthood is complex and involves many decisions along the way. In order to become parents, gay men must first acknowledge their desire to parent, a process that may be impeded by heteronormative assumptions and practical barriers. In many cases, gay men may also desire—and therefore must seek out—a partner who is similarly dedicated to becoming a parent. They must then explore the various routes to parenthood, and, if they are unwilling or unable to pursue surrogacy, explore their feelings about parenting a child who is not biologically related to them, and before pursuing adoptive parenthood, make peace with any feelings of loss related to not passing on their genes. Finally, gay men who decide to adopt must then decide what type of adoption to pursue, taking into account such considerations as finances and moral/philosophical beliefs. As this chapter reveals, gay men inevitably confront and wrestle with the importance of biological and genetic relations and heterosexuality to dominant notions of family, and, in turn, with stereotypes regarding the incompatibility of homosexuality and parenthood (Stacey, 1996). The men's narratives highlight the varied ways that gay men may resist or challenge the dominant discourses regarding family—as well as the ways they may ultimately internalize them.

* * *

Men who decide to become parents in the context of same-sex relationships engage in a different decision-making process from that of their heterosexual counterparts. Whereas parenthood is culturally accessible, socially valued, and even expected among heterosexual married men and women, gay men who wish to parent are subject to societal scrutiny and questioning. Gay men who seek to adopt, far from being applauded for their desire to make a difference in a young child's life (as heterosexual adoptive parents often are), are vulnerable to suspicion regarding their motives (Hicks, 2006a). Further, the households of gay male couples who seek to adopt are often presumed deficient by virtue of the fact that they typically lack a live-in female parental figure (Hicks, 2006b). Indeed, men are generally stereotyped as being less effective nurturers and caretakers than women (Coltrane, 1996; Quinn, 2009), and thus the presence of *two* men is not necessarily viewed as better than one (Stacey & Biblarz, 2001). Such judgments are routinely made by both the broader society and adoption agencies and create a challenging climate for gay male couples who wish to become adoptive parents, who must navigate an interrelated set of assumptions regarding gender, family, and sexuality that are biased against them (Oswald, Kuvalanka, Blume, & Berkowitz, 2009).

Invidious stereotypes about gay men's motivations to parent and about their parental fitness are offset by a societal climate in which gay parenting is becoming increasingly possible and accepted, although still debated. The gay men who became parents in the United States in the 1980s and even the 1990s were to some extent pioneers who had few visible role models of gay fathers (Gianino, 2008; Mallon, 2004). Today, gay men in the United States are surrounded by more examples of gay parenthood than ever before, and therefore may be more likely to imagine parenthood as a possibility for themselves (Berkowitz & Marsiglio, 2007).

As noted earlier, the average age of the men whom I interviewed was 38; most men were born in the late 1960s, meaning that they entered adolescence and young adulthood—and began to "come out"—in the early 1980s. Although there were some gay men pursuing parenthood in the context of same-sex relationships in the 1980s, this was far more common among lesbians. Indeed, the 1980s are sometimes referred to as the time of the "lesbian baby boom" (Chauncey, 2005). This "boom" originated in urban, more progressive cities such as Washington DC and San Francisco, where "maybe baby" groups and conferences were increasingly being held for lesbians considering parenthood (Armstrong, 2002; Chauncey, 2005). Before this time, there were gay and lesbian parents, but most had given birth to or adopted their children in the context of heterosexual relationships and later came out as gay. The lesbian baby boom of the 1980s ushered in a new era of sexual minorities—mainly women—who were intentionally pursuing parenthood as "out" gay lesbians and gay men, often in the context of same-sex relationships.

The majority of the men in the study were somewhat aware of lesbians pursuing parenthood at the time that they came out, but few knew any gay men who had become or were becoming parents in the context of same-sex relationships. It was not until the mid to late 1990s and early 2000s that gay parenthood became increasingly visible and accessible, in part due to the Internet revolution (Planck, 2006).[1] Exploring how the gay men in this book came to realize their desire to parent, whether this desire was present when they came out, and whether they felt compelled to give up or suppress such desires in light of the perceived incompatibility of gayness and parenthood, sheds light on both the power of heteronormative structures in shaping men's desire to parent—and their awareness of this desire—as well as men's potential for resisting heteronormative domination. As we will see, gay men are affected by and must grapple with dominant discourses regarding kinship, gender, and sexuality. In turn, their decision making regarding parenthood and adoption reflects these discourses, as well as their personal ideals, various practical constraints such as geographic location and financial resources, and broader historical and geographic factors.

Reconciling One's Sexuality and One's Parental Aspirations

I asked the men in the study how they came to want to be a parent. Through the process of explaining how they became aware of their desire to parent, many of them highlighted their own coming out as a crucial event in which they juxtaposed their own parental aspirations against their imagined future as a gay man. The men were diverse in the degree to which they internalized societal imperatives regarding the impossibility of gay parenthood, and, in turn, the degree to which they felt that they had—albeit temporarily—forestalled their own parenting desires upon coming out.

"When I Came Out, I (Temporarily) Gave Up That Dream"

One-third of the men whom I interviewed (24 men, including four couples) acknowledged that they did not think parenthood was possible when they came out. These men were often interested in becoming parents, but the absence of gay-parent role models, and the broader social inaccessibility of gay fatherhood, led them to "kind of give up on ever becoming a parent." Because gay fathers were thoroughly marginalized from mainstream depictions of American family life, these men's private desires for fatherhood seemed unrealistic and unachievable (Berkowitz & Marsiglio, 2007; Gianino, 2008). As Rufus, the 37-year-old White computer programmer who lived in a city in the South and whose story opened this chapter, revealed, "I think when I was younger and I was coming out I thought, 'Oh, that's it, I'm never gonna have kids.' I mean, I had no role models." Likewise, Carter, a 37-year old White teacher who resided in a midwestern suburb, explained, "It is something that I have always *wanted* to do, but I didn't think that as a gay man, it was something that I was going to be *able* to do."

Societal depictions of homosexuality and family as fundamentally incompatible—and of heterosexual sex as the necessary precursor to parenthood—continued to prevail in the early 1980s, leading some of these men to experience their own coming out as synonymous with relinquishing their prospective parent identity (deBoer, 2009; Mallon, 2004; Weston, 1991). Bill, a 38-year-old White director of programs who lived in a city on the West Coast, recalled, "When I came out, I mourned the possibility of [parenthood]. Part of my coming out process was, okay, I can't have children, and accepting that possibility, accepting that I'm enough without having to have a family." Bill and others perceived themselves as having to make a choice between coming out and becoming a parent. While they realized that coming out was imperative to their own identity, integrity, and well-being, they "mourned" the loss of their parenthood aspirations, revealing the power of heteronormative structures in shaping men's sense of possibilities.

In several cases, the men recognized that their not becoming parents would also be a loss for their parents, who often longed to become grandparents. Carlos, a 30-year-old Latino sales representative who lived in a city on the West Coast, reflected:

> Growing up Mexican, it was hammered into you that your family comes first, family is most important in life. I had to come to terms with what it means to be homosexual [when I came out]. I didn't know how or if [parenthood] would happen. I was worried I would be a disappointment to my parents.

Clearly compounding Carlos's personal sense of loss about the prospect of not becoming a parent was a concern about failing to live up to his family's—and his ethnic community's—norms and expectations. He described himself as deviant, and therefore a potential disappointment, on two levels: first, in that he was gay, and second, in that he would presumably not become a parent. For Carlos, coming out to his parents was additionally complicated by the fact that in being gay, he was presumably also violating a cultural norm regarding the importance of having and raising children.

Ultimately, of course, these men came to believe that they could become parents. They typically attributed this shift to social and political progress, including changing attitudes toward gay people, as well as concrete changes, such as laws permitting adoption by same-sex couples in their own or other states. As the sociologist Judith Stacey (2006) has surmised, "The increasing visibility of gay and lesbian parenthood arouses widespread expectations, hopes, and fears that public acceptance of homosexuality will cause its incidence to increase" (p. 28). Echoing this notion, Sam, a 36-year-old White financial analyst who had come out in his early teens in the early 1980s, reflected, "[When I came out], I didn't feel like it was part of gay life, but the world has changed dramatically and now we're in the position like we feel we can do it comfortably." Similarly, Vaughn, a 39-year-old White consultant who resided in a rural area in the Northeast, explained how his ability to imagine himself as a parent was facilitated by the societal changes that had occurred over the past several decades, such as advances in gay civil rights, and increases in the number of gay-parent families:

> [Being a parent] is one of those things I never thought I'd be able to do. Like in my 20s, I wanted to be a parent, but I knew that I couldn't—I would have to sleep with women! (*laughs*) I suppose there were gay people with children back then, I just didn't know any. Definitely things have changed. . . . Vermont [now allows] civil unions, and now Massachusetts has marriage . . . and just in the past couple of years a lot has changed.

In a few cases, the men had to overcome their own internalized homophobia to realize that not only could they parent, but they could be *good* parents. In explaining why it took him a while to match his partner Kevin's commitment to parenthood, Brendan, a 43-year-old White graduate student living in a midwestern city, explained:

> A lot of it was stuff that I hadn't analyzed about myself, like my doubts. Would I be a good parent? A lot of it is society and what's drummed into you in terms of being gay or whatever. Then I just started thinking, I could do as good of a job as these people, if not better. I think a lot of it was looking at things from a different perspective. I didn't have a light bulb moment where I said, "I want to adopt. I'd be a great parent." It was a process.

The men's recognition that they could in fact pursue parenthood was often accompanied by feelings of relief and excitement. As Brendan suggested, they often enjoyed a newfound sense of entitlement to parent as they overcame internalized doubts about their capacity to parent—a process that was facilitated by actively confronting and resisting heteronormative discourses that fueled societal stereotypes about gay parenting (Colberg, 1997; deBoer, 2009). In some cases, they positioned themselves (as Brendan did) as just as good as, "if not better" than, heterosexual parents, a strategy that may serve to further distance themselves from stereotypes of gay men as inadequate and insufficient caregivers.

"I Always Wanted to Be a Parent"

Just under one-third of the men (21 men, including two couples) emphasized that they had always wanted to become a parent, and noted that coming out as gay had not lessened their desire or their intention to parent. Unlike the previous group of men, they did not internalize heteronormative discourses; instead, they resisted them. These men described having come of age in an era where they knew few, if any, gay male parents, but they emphasized that this fact had not dissuaded them from what they described as an "innate" and "unshakeable" longing to parent. These men knew when they came out that they would face many social and legal obstacles to parenting but never thought of giving up their "life goal" of becoming fathers. Harvey, a 41-year-old Asian American sales representative who lived in a West Coast city, articulated:

> I always knew I wanted to be a parent, but when you're in a society where you can't get married, it just sort of makes it a lot harder. Of course, when

you come out, you know that *everything* is going to be hard! I mean, you have to look at your whole life as there being obstacles and there always will be obstacles. But I just knew I would [become a parent], and it was just a matter of time and then finding the right partner who also wanted to have a child, too.

Harvey resisted both ideological and structural barriers to parenthood. He demonstrated his commitment and intention to parent—even though he knew it would be hard. In this way, he viewed the act of resisting heteronormativity as something that he necessarily must do as a gay man. He was undeterred from pursuing parenthood—even though, on a practical level, he was unsure of how and when it would happen. Other men, too, voiced that while they always knew that they would become a parent, they were not always sure exactly *how* they would become a parent. Yet they felt certain that "something would work out." Stan, a 32-year-old White college professor who lived in a city on the West Coast, reflected:

It's something that I've always wanted to do. I sort of just always assumed that I would be [a parent]. It just never really occurred to me to *not* be a parent. The only question was, you know, how to go about making that happen, and the vehicle through which I would become a parent. I never had a question about whether or not I would but I definitely had a question about how it would happen, when it would happen, all of that.

That almost one-third of the men whom I interviewed emphasized such a long-standing, unshakeable faith in their eventual parenthood is remarkable given their exposure to overwhelmingly negative societal attitudes about gay parenting, at least during their early years, and their awareness of the many structural and legal barriers that they might face in becoming parents. What facilitated their ability and willingness to pursue parenthood? As highlighted by these narratives, a strong conviction in the importance of pursuing one's goals, even in the face of obstacles, may be operative. In addition, support from their families may have facilitated these men's resistance to societal heteronormativity. In several cases, the men explicitly noted that their families' support had helped to counteract the negative messages they received from society about their inability to parent, and served to sustain them even as they struggled with their own self-doubts. Trey, the 32-year-old White dermatologist, explained, "I feel like I've been very lucky and very supported throughout my life, with my family and friends, and so I just never really thought [becoming a parent] was going to be a problem."

"I Never Thought of Becoming a Parent until Recently"

The remaining third of the men emphasized that they did not have any interest in parenthood until adulthood. They articulated that when they came out, parenthood was "just not on [their] mind," and therefore they did not experience any real or imagined loss of a childhood dream of becoming a father. Rather, during their coming out period they were "caught up in figuring out what it meant to be gay" and were "hanging out in the gay scene, where there typically weren't a lot of parents." Their interest in parenting did not emerge until they were in their late 20s and 30s, when parenting as a gay man gradually became something that was both psychologically and socially accessible to them. Roger, a 36-year-old White small business owner living in an East Coast city, explained:

> It was definitely something Derek—he was the one initially more interested in [parenthood] from the get-go. There was a time earlier on when I wasn't convinced that I wanted to be a parent, and I'd say I felt that way until about maybe five years ago. I feel like I had a very delayed—not delayed adolescence, but I just didn't do all the things I wanted to do at a young age in my life. I didn't really come of age until about 30, so I was just—I went around being a young person for a long time and didn't see myself being tied down. But being in our relationship, especially, made me settle down and made me refocus my priorities in terms of what mattered to me.

For Roger, then, "coming of age" later in life (i.e., around the age of 30) forestalled any serious consideration of parenthood until recently, as he spent much of his 20s enjoying a single-oriented gay lifestyle that he felt he had missed before he was "out." Entering into a committed relationship with Derek caused him to reevaluate his priorities and to consider other long-term commitments such as becoming a parent.

The Timing of Parenthood

For gay men, parenthood is highly intentional. The intentional nature of gay parenthood in general, and parenthood by adoption in particular, meant that the men whom I interviewed were quite deliberate in considering the timing of parenthood.[2] Notably, as the men described it, their choice of when to become a parent was often heavily informed by societal discourses that emphasize relationship stability—and, indeed, marriage—as a prerequisite to children (Friedman, 2007; Huston & Melz, 2004). Their decision making about the timing of parenthood was also influenced by middle-class discourses that emphasize the importance of achieving career/financial stability before assuming the responsibility of raising children (Evans et al., 2009; Rabun & Oswald, 2009). Notably, most men mentioned multiple factors as affecting their decision making about the timing of parenthood; thus there is overlap among the categories described below.

One Partner Was Not Ready Previously

For 15 of the men (including three couples), the timing of parenthood was determined by one partner's lack of readiness to parent. Until recently, one partner had been strongly committed to parenthood whereas the other had been less certain. Sometimes, this lack of readiness was related to fears about parenthood that, over time, began to dissolve. In other cases, men did not have particular fears about parenthood but simply lacked the emotional readiness or desire to parent until recently. Will, a 37-year-old White marketing manager who resided in a city on the West coast, recounted:

> When I met Charlie seven years ago, you know, obviously I didn't start saying, "Let's adopt a kid" (*laughs*), but after we had been together for a while, I sort of started toying with the idea. He is four years younger and had come out later than I had. I think he was less excited about the idea at first. So we would just sort of talk about it, and it was clear to me that it was just not something he really wanted to think about at that point. A couple years later, we talked about it a little bit more and, you know, he started to feel like, "Yeah, it is something I would like to do." He said, "Just not yet, maybe down the road." So it was a little over a year ago he started bringing it up himself. I think it just took a while for him to feel ready.

Will and Charlie differed sharply in their interest in parenthood when they first became a couple, with Will expressing a much stronger and more immediate desire to pursue it. Yet after several years of quietly contemplating parenthood, and intermittently "picking it up and putting it down" (Gianino, 2008), Charlie came to a point where he was willing and able to commit himself to pursuing parenthood with Will.

Similarly, Miles, a 40-year-old White consultant living in a Massachusetts suburb, recalled:

> We started out earlier in our life together, you know, as most married couples do, and couples in general, they start talking about having kids. And

I really wanted to. Paul was terrified of the idea, and then slowly the idea grew on him, and he became very eager.

Miles contextualized the process of discussing the possibility of children as something "most married couples do"—he and Paul (who were not legally married) included. His description is striking in that he clearly conceptualized discussions about children as a normative milestone in long-term relationships—including those of same-sex couples (or, at least, his own current relationship). His nonchalance in discussing this process reveals that he does not regard it as atypical for gay men, and, this, in turn, speaks to the "new normalcy" of gay parenthood (Seidman, 2002; Stacey, 2006). Historical factors, such as the passage of pro gay marriage and adoption legislation, as well as increasingly tolerant attitudes regarding homosexuality, have created a climate where lesbians and gay men are increasingly likely to view parenthood as an option—and one that is worth pursuing even in the face of structural obstacles. And yet it is important not to overstate the ways that "gay is the new black" (Gross, 2009). In other words, "gay" is not unanimously regarded as acceptable or even normal across the United States. Individuals' social locations necessarily affect their views of the "normalcy" and accessibility of gay parenthood; indeed, Miles and Paul lived in Massachusetts, which is known for its progressive politics and laws pertaining to homosexuality. Gay men in less progressive areas might be less likely to view their desire to parent as normative or to view the prospect of adoption as feasible. The "new normalcy" of gay fatherhood is therefore most present in urban or progressive areas of the United States. It is certainly not, at this point, a national sentiment.

Met a Man Who Also Wanted to Parent

For 14 of the men (including three couples), the timing of parenthood was determined by having finally met "the one." These men expressed that they were pursuing parenthood now because they had finally met someone who wanted to become a parent as much as they did. In many cases, men noted that they had been in previous relationships that had not worked out because their partners' enthusiasm for parenting did not match their own. Some men, too, recalled the challenges of dating different men when in reality "any guy who didn't want to be a parent was a deal breaker." After "wasting time" with men who had no interest in parenting, these men realized the importance of discussing their dream of becoming a parent up-front, to preclude further dead-end relationships. Discussing their desire to parent "became a first-date sort of thing." This led them to find someone who was equally as interested in and ready for parenthood as they were. Finding this person was described as a "huge relief," particularly after meeting and in some cases dating many gay men who enjoyed the "urban gay lifestyle" and for whom parenthood was a foreign, and perhaps even unimaginable, concept. Derek, a 32-year-old White software consultant living in an East Coast city, recalled:

> We started talking about having children, that was the first conversation that Roger and I had when we first met each other. Because you know, you don't really want to get involved with [just anyone] if you know that you want to have kids and you know, I guess we knew that. At the time [we met], it seemed like so many—there were gay men that didn't really want to have kids. I didn't really want to be with [those men]—it's like, [there's] the kind of gay man that doesn't want to have kids, and the kind that does.

Derek and others alluded to this notion that there were two different types of gay men: those who were interested in parenthood, and those who were not. Men who were uninterested in parenthood were described as focused on club culture, art openings, and dinner parties—and as firmly situated in, and committed to maintaining, an urban lifestyle. Men who were interested in parenthood were indirectly painted as suburban and home- and family-oriented. Such descriptions are notable in that they serve to signify and uphold certain binaries within the gay community, such that one "type" of gay is presumed to be more "(hetero)normative" than the other (Kurdek, 2005; Seidman, 2002). As Seidman (2002) and Jackson (2006) have argued, gay men who are "gender conventional, committed to romantic-companionate and family values, uncritically patriotic and detached from a subculture" represent the new "gay normal," whereby gay becomes normal without overly unsettling heteronormative ideals (Jackson, 2006, p. 112). Further, this discursive formation—that is, of one "type" of gay as more "heteronormative" than the other—has the effect of actually redrawing the boundaries of normative (i.e., the "good homosexual" or "normal gay" is distinguished from the "dangerous homosexual" or the "bad citizen"; Jackson, 2006). It also serves to reify a false binary between parent types and party types by concealing from view, for example, suburban heterosexuals who do not want children and urban gay men who do. Thus, far from deconstructing this false binary, some of the men's descriptions seemed to rigidify and actually "shore up" heteronormativity—as well as homonormativity.

Relationship Stability

For 14 of the men (including two couples), it was reaching a certain level of security and stability in their current relationships that enabled them to move forward with their parenthood pursuits. These men emphasized that they had wanted to wait until their relationships felt "stable" and "committed" before bringing children into their lives. They were emphatic about wanting to establish a strong relational foundation on which a family could be built. As Trey, 32, explained, "Rufus and I both feel really great about our relationship and we've worked hard to make it something that we're both really excited about and committed to and we feel 100% comfortable that it's going to last forever. That was an important issue for me in thinking about kids—just making sure that I was in a relationship [that would last]."

Some men noted that they had been through "bumps" in their relationships that they had wanted to resolve before pursuing parenthood. They did not wish to begin a family with their partners until they were satisfied that they were in healthy, committed, and long-lasting relationships. The years they spent building their relationship, working out conflicts, and developing a sense of togetherness with their partners, were viewed as instrumental to establishing a solid relational foundation, and they looked forward to the future with confidence and excitement.

Interestingly, five of these 14 men (including one couple) noted that they also did not feel comfortable moving forward with their adoption plans until they had a formal commitment ceremony that symbolized their mutual dedication to each other. For these men, it was not enough to simply feel stable and committed in their relationships; it felt necessary to declare this commitment formally and ceremoniously. Having a commitment ceremony "set the stage for the adoption." Chris, a 45-year-old White research scientist living in an urban area on the West Coast, explained, "We felt that it was important that you have a commitment and a bond with each other before you take another thing on like a kid." His partner, Eric, a 40-year-old Latino marketing executive, elaborated:

> I think we wanted to do [the commitment ceremony] sooner, but we tend to move slowly. We talked about it. I think if we were to do it again we would've done [the adoption] sooner, maybe a little after the commitment ceremony. But that was actually part of the reason why we *had* a commitment ceremony. I told Chris that we should have a commitment if we're going to have a child. We should clearly get married. That's just the model that I know.

Here, Eric indicates that his feelings about the importance of marriage before children are rooted in, and reflect, broader societal norms (Friedman, 2007; Murdock, 1960) and possibly his own experience as the child of two heterosexual married parents in a Latino, Roman Catholic family. Although his relationship lies outside the heterosexual "model," he nevertheless feels compelled to approximate this model as closely as possible. His statement "That's just the model that I know" implies he is conscious of the ways in which his choices and values, while enacted in a homosexual context, are affected by heteronormative discourses and norms. Like Miles and his partner, Paul, discussed above, Eric and Chris appear to situate their relationships within, and view their relationships as accommodating to, broader heteronormative structures and discourses. They do not question the heterosexual model—perhaps because they see no reason to. As the sociologist Jeffrey Weeks (2008) has argued, many gay people simply long to enjoy the same rights and opportunities as heterosexual people. Such pursuit and enactment of "normalcy" can be viewed, Weeks asserts, as "assimilation into the status quo" (p. 792). He further notes, however, that "at a deeper level, surely, what we see here is the wish for recognition for what you are and want to be, for validation, not absorption, a voting with our feet for the ordinary virtues of care, love, mutual responsibility. We should never underestimate the importance of being ordinary. It has helped transform the LGBT community and the wider world" (p. 792).

Job/Career Stability

Almost one-third of the men (21 men, including seven couples) emphasized that they had not wanted to pursue parenthood until they or their partners had achieved some degree of job or career stability, reflecting middle-class ideals regarding the prerequisites for parental readiness (Rabun & Oswald, 2009). Some men simply felt a need to establish themselves in their careers before pursuing parenthood, and thus delayed parenthood until they felt that they had reached a satisfactory level of achievement in their jobs. Others named more concrete milestones that they had wished to accomplish before starting the adoption process (e.g., a promotion).

Some men noted that their parenthood plans were put on hold because one partner was making a career change. In some cases, this involved a move, necessitating that couples become geographically settled before initiating the adoption process. In a few cases, such career changes were prompted by general job dissatisfaction. In other cases, however, men noted that they or their partners had actually altered their career trajectories in preparation for parenthood—that is, they felt that their prior jobs were incompatible with parenting and had therefore pursued positions that promised to be more family friendly—as well as more gay friendly. Gregory, a 40-year-old White man who resided in a suburb in the South, and who had worked as a lawyer until he recently decided to go back to school, recalled:

> I was in private practice when we started talking about it. I was working a ton and it was especially—I couldn't be completely out at work. So some of the delay was just timing, and then we knew at some point that I was going to get out of practice. It just wasn't a good fit for me. So one of the motivations for trying to get into graduate school instead of practicing law and moving out here was we could finally go down that road [to adopt]. I didn't want to be a parent and be a full-time, you know, just working six days a week in a firm that wasn't going to acknowledge my family in any way. There were a lot of pieces to the puzzle.

Gregory sought a career change that would allow him to better align his interests, priorities, and values with the needs, requirements, and philosophy of his employer. For him, finding a job that he perceived as reasonable and validating was a crucial prerequisite to building a family. Although the experience of having his sexuality silenced at his job was tolerable (but unpleasant) prior to considering parenthood, the prospect of working hard at a company "that wasn't going to acknowledge my family in any way" prompted Gregory to pursue another career path once he began to consider parenthood. Gregory's willingness to continue to endure heterosexism was challenged by the reality of starting a family, which would presumably render his sexuality more salient. Impending parenthood prompted him to confront and resist heteronormative domination, illustrating how the consideration and pursuit of parenthood may cause shifts in the ways that gay men manage and navigate their sexuality in their larger communities.

Financial Stability

For 13 of the men (including two couples), financial stability was viewed as a prerequisite for pursuing parenthood, reflecting dominant discourses regarding the necessity of financial preparation for parenthood (Evans et al., 2009), and therefore a middle-class ideology that emphasizes financial security as a requirement for responsible parenthood. Cognizant of the costs associated with both the adoption process in particular and parenthood in general, men wished to be "at a point where [they] could afford it" before launching forward. Toward this end, they had spent the past few years saving their money, paying off debts, and "getting finances in order" in preparation for parenthood.

In a few cases, it was clear that men's definition of "financial stability" implied something far beyond having enough money saved to cover the costs of adoption. A few men expressed their desire to be financially "comfortable"—meaning, they wanted to be assured that they could continue to afford the lifestyle they had grown accustomed to, and that they would be able to handle the additional costs of children easily. As Corey, a 31-year-old White journalist living in a southern city, whose combined family income with his partner, Shane, a sales representative, was close to $120,000, explained:

> We wanted to make sure we were financially stable. There's, you know, a particular lifestyle that we wanted to give our children, so we wanted to achieve the financial goals that we had set forth. We like a nice house, we like a nice neighborhood, we like to be able to do things, and that takes time to get all of those ducks in a row.

The meaning of financial stability—and its importance to starting a family—was clearly subjective. For some, financial stability meant having just enough money to finance the cost of the adoption. For others, it meant saving enough money to cover the adoption as well as the cost of furnishing their child's room and preparing for their arrival. For still others, it meant ensuring that they had enough money so that their current middle- or upper-middle-class lifestyle was not disrupted.

Moving

Eight of the men (including two couples) noted that their plans to pursue parenthood had been put on hold until they had completed a recent move—into a larger house, a more family-friendly neighborhood, or a more gay-friendly locale. These men explained that their previous living quarters were inappropriate for raising a child, either because of the type of home that they were living in (e.g., an apartment); insufficient space for a child (e.g., no extra bedroom); or the type of neighborhood that they were located in (e.g., no families or no gay-parent families). Moving enabled these men to feel that they were finally able to move forward with the adoption process, in that they were finally in an environment that felt conducive to raising children. Xavier, a 39-year-old White software developer whose annual family income was approximately $115,000, observed:

Seattle is easy to raise kids regardless of interracial to same-sex couples or non-married heterosexual couples. . . . We can afford a bigger house here than in New York. We were going to [start the adoption process] in New York but it would have been tight with one bathroom. People do it, it is not impossible, but here we have got a yard and we are in a better neighborhood.

These men viewed their living quarters and geographic location as key contextual factors that would inevitably affect their families' quality of life, and felt compelled to situate themselves in gay-friendly and family-friendly environments before taking steps toward parenthood. These findings echo Sullivan's (2004) findings that more affluent lesbian mothers can choose to—and afford to—live in more progressive, gay-friendly areas; hence the assumption of "geographic choice" (Rabun & Oswald, 2009) reflects middle-class ideologies. Privileged men could afford to be geographically mobile, allowing them to possibly circumvent homophobic neighborhoods and schools.

Other Considerations

About a quarter of the men identified their advancing age as a major factor in why they were pursuing parenthood (i.e., they did not want to be "old" parents). For six men, parenthood simply seemed like the "natural next step," having achieved stability in all other areas of their lives, leaving them to wonder, "What's next?" Finally, for five men, it was witnessing other gay men and lesbians within their social network become parents that prompted them to finally take the plunge into parenthood.

Deciding on a Route to Parenthood: Adoption versus Surrogacy

Although all the couples were actively pursuing adoption at the time I interviewed them pre-parenthood, some had considered surrogacy before deciding to adopt. Indeed, although adoption is the most common route to parenthood for gay male couples, and also the most widely publicized option for gay men (Planck, 2006), it is not the only route. Some gay male couples become parents via surrogacy (Bergman, Rubio, Green, & Padron, 2010), and some pursue other arrangements as a means of fulfilling their parenthood aspirations. For example, one partner may donate sperm to a lesbian couple, with the agreement that all four partners will participate in parenting the child together (Lev, 2004). Although none of the men in the study mentioned the latter option, many men emphasized that they had considered, at least briefly, the possibility of surrogacy. These men were intrigued by and attracted to the possibility that they could have their own genetic offspring, feeling that, as one man expressed, "I think there's something innate in that we want to sort of reproduce ourselves." Thus the fact that they were in same-sex relationships, in which they could not reproduce, did not by itself necessarily quash their longing for a biological child. Dominant family ideology establishes biological relatedness as fundamental to family relationships and critical to defining family (Hayden, 1995). Thus, even though they fall outside of the *heterosexual* nuclear family model, gay men are still exposed to and likely to be influenced by dominant notions of kinship (Ryan & Berkowitz, 2009). Research on childless gay men suggests that some men strongly desire biogenetically related offspring, whereas others espouse a firm commitment to adoption as a means of building their families (Berkowitz & Marsiglio, 2007).

Deterrents to Pursuing Surrogacy

About half the men initially considered surrogacy but decided that adoption was a more promising or more attractive alternative, based on their consideration of a range of factors. These factors serve to highlight the complexity of parental decision making among gay men and how various structural and ideological forces may ultimately constrain or inform their decision to adopt. Some men referenced multiple factors as implicated in their decision making, whereas others highlighted a single factor that led them away from surrogacy and toward adoption.

COST

A quarter of the men (18 men, including seven couples) mentioned the cost of surrogacy as a major deterrent to pursuing this route. Although surrogacy is an option for gay men in theory, it is quite expensive (e.g., $100,000–$150,000, on average, in the United States), making it a practical impossibility for the majority of gay men—even those who are financially comfortable (Goldberg, 2010a).[3] For example, Frank, a White physician, and his partner, Cooper, a multiracial physician assistant, earned a combined income of $300,000. Yet Frank described cost as the major deterrent to pursuing surrogacy, and the factor that led him and Cooper to explore adoption:

> The idea of having a biological child is really interesting to me, or really appealing to me. And so, I had been thinking that "that's an option, that's

a real option." We knew someone who had done it, a couple who had done it. But a few things have happened since that. One, we had an eye-opening realization of the cost of surrogacy versus adoption. And I, I really hate that that's a factor in it, but it is. And so, I think that forced me to spend a lot more time exploring the adoption route, that I just hadn't done before. And now I love the idea of it, actually, really love the idea of adoption.

Here, Frank suggests that although he had initially been quite attracted to the possibility of surrogacy, once he began to explore the option of adoption, he came to "love the idea of [it]." Many men in the study expressed similar sentiments, noting that the more they came to learn about adoption, the more it felt like a viable, attractive, and meaningful option to them. In turn, the prospect of not having a child that was genetically related to them became less important over time. This theme echoes prior research on lesbian couples who chose adoption after unsuccessfully attempting to conceive via alternative insemination, who also described a process of gradually becoming more excited after adoption as they "let go" of the idea of having a biogenetically related child (Goldberg, Downing, & Richardson, 2009). Their actions simultaneously highlight the salience of biogenetic relatedness to notions about family—even among sexual minorities, who themselves cannot reproduce in the context of same-sex relationships—and underscore the potential for sexual minorities to not be thwarted or immobilized by discourses that privilege biological ties.

ETHICAL/MORAL CONCERNS

Fifteen men (including three couples) expressed moral or ethical concerns that had led them to reject surrogacy as an option. Specifically, seven of these 15 men noted that surrogacy seemed "really selfish" to them, given that there were already so many children on the planet who were in need of homes. Spending money to create a child, when there were already children available for adoption, "just seemed wrong." For example, after briefly considering surrogacy, Daniel, a 38-year-old White graduate student who was pursuing a public adoption in a rural area of the Northeast, noted that he and his partner, Vaughn, came to feel that "there's a lot of children out there that need to have families that don't have families, so we want to find a child who normally wouldn't have a good household to live in or that we can bring home and give them the best experience that we can." Luis, a 45-year-old Latino surgeon who was pursuing a private domestic adoption in an urban area of the Northeast, described a similar situation:

And then the surrogacy thing for us—you know financially, we would have been able to do it but it just sort of . . . We both have this opinion of, if we really believe in the whole idea that we were created this way and there's a plan there, we just sort of felt that we know that there are children out there that are going to need homes. It just makes a lot more sense that we be the family to accept that child, or you know, to receive that child into the world, and we just thought that it would make a better story.

For Luis and others, pursuing surrogacy ultimately felt out of step with their spiritual beliefs and moral philosophy. Adoption was more consonant with their sense of a grander "plan," whereby they would "receive" the child that was meant for them. Additionally, becoming parents through adoption was perceived to be an easier and possibly more acceptable "story," to tell their child and others, about how their child came to be with them.

TOO COMPLEX AND DIFFICULT

Eight men (four couples) reported having taken concrete steps toward pursuing surrogacy before pursuing adoption. Although these men expressed that they had initially been highly motivated to pursue surrogacy, they found that it involved "too many hurdles" and was "too complex," leading them to view adoption as the easier route, both emotionally and logistically. Stan, the 32-year-old White college professor, recounted this story of his and his partner Dean's frustrated surrogacy efforts:

We've had two friends approach us and say they wanted to carry kids for us. We got pretty far along in both of those processes. In one case, we were at the point of making the arrangements with the insurance companies and going to the first ovarian reserve tests. And then it fell apart because she moved spontaneously. And then in the other case, we were finalizing the contract and negotiating the nuts and bolts. You know, like how many of her counseling sessions are we going to pay for during the process to help her make sense of what's going on and that kind of stuff. And then her husband threatened to leave her if she went through with the process. Yeah, it's been really disgusting. . . . And so, it kind of felt like, really about as close as we could ever get to a miscarriage. And so we've kind of gone through this whole sort of, pretty intense grieving process around that. And we just sort of decided, this doesn't make sense; why are we trying so hard to put together these surrogacy [arrangements] when we could adopt? And we might as well just give that a shot. And so it sort of stopped making sense not to.

Three of these four couples noted that they had women in their lives (a friend in one case, and a sister in two cases) who were willing to donate eggs, but they were unable to find someone who was willing to carry the child. All the women in these scenarios were comfortable with donating eggs but were unwilling to carry the child because of concerns that they would become too bonded with the child, highlighting the very complicated emotional terrain of surrogacy—particularly surrogacy arrangements involving family members (Teman, 2009). One couple, Thomas and Devon, both White and living in an urban area in the South, had been able to secure a commitment from a family member to carry the child, but ultimately decided against pursuing this option as they worried it would create strange and possibly uncomfortable family dynamics. Thomas, 36, explained:

> My sister volunteered. . . . It was an honor to be asked and it was during the middle of when we lost the first baby [due to a failed adoptive placement]. She called . . . and she said, "I just want to let you know that we have talked about it and we really think that this is good option for you guys." To be honest with you, we did think about it . . . but she would be the mother of the child and she would be a big part of the child's life. To me that would be a little weird. I want to make the decisions and Devon wants to make the decisions and I was afraid that. . . . Parenting would be crossed, you know.

The idea of having a female family member donate the eggs and possibly carry the child was in some ways a dream come true, in that it would allow both partners to be genetically related to the child. Yet both Thomas and Devon came to recognize that such a scenario might involve very complicated and potentially demanding family dynamics, and decided that adoption was a more straightforward and less complex option. Even if Devon, Thomas, and Thomas's sister were able to establish a contract about the roles of all parties involved, there was still the potential for family members to treat Devon and Thomas's *sister* as the parents, ousting Thomas from the parental equation. Devon and Thomas were likely aware that even in the presence of two active male co-parents, family members—and society in general—might still be tempted to impose a heteronormative configuration on their family. They resisted this possibility by forgoing their dream of having a biological child and pursuing adoption instead.

Three of the men noted that although they or their partners had initially been drawn to surrogacy, they had come to view surrogacy as a less-than-ideal option, in that only one partner would be genetically related to the child, a scenario that could potentially lead to power imbalances and problematic family dynamics. They therefore favored adoption, which would allow both partners to start out on an equal plane concerning the child. Frank, 39, affirmed:

> We liked the fact that an adopted kid, it's more mutual, in the sense that with surrogacy the child would be genetically part mine or part Cooper's. And how would that affect the family dynamics for this kid, you know? How does that change things in terms of how they feel toward us and [how] we feel toward them and so on and so forth? I wasn't really worried about that, personally; Cooper was worried about that, and so that was another reason [we didn't pursue surrogacy].

Moving On Is Hard to Do

Notably, although most of the men who had considered surrogacy described themselves as fully committed to adoption, the process of moving from considering surrogacy to fully embracing adoption was described as challenging for some men. Seven of the men described the process of turning away from surrogacy and toward adoption as emotionally difficult. Making this shift, they said, required them to engage in a process of self-exploration, which involved probing their motivations for parenthood, their concerns regarding adoption, and their ability to love an adopted child. Daniel, the 38-year-old White graduate student, reflected:

> It wasn't a crisis or anything like that, but it was hard. It took me a while to sort of sit with both [adoption and surrogacy] and think about them. I think that the thing I became most worried about was, I didn't want to be less of a parent of the child because of my own hang-ups about [adoption]. So I wanted to be sure that I could be just as present and as loving and as committed of a parent to an adopted child as I could to my own biological child. That's what I think took me a little while to—but I was really, I was actually patient with myself, in that I sort of gave myself permission to sit with it for a while and to not beat myself up over it too much. I think that I started to go there a few times where I felt like less of a person or worse of a person because of those kinds of feelings. I finally just realized that—I

realized how natural it was to want a biological child and to want that first even, or to prioritize that as something you'd want more.

Rufus, 37, expressed similar types of concerns about adoption as opposed to surrogacy:

> I guess I have some concerns about, you know, raising a child and having it work, and bonding. I have no fear that I won't—well, I don't know, I'd say that . . . I'm sure that I will love the child, but, sometimes, and maybe when it was earlier in the process, I thought, "Oh, I wish I could have a genetic, a child genetically related." I actually, I definitely, I definitely felt that . . . I definitely was depressed by the idea that I'm not continuing my genes. This idea that, I, I don't know, you know, I want a child that will serve my immortality element, I want a child that's a little bit of me and the future.

Both Daniel and Rufus voiced some of their concerns about adoption, including the fear that they would not love an adopted child as much as a biological child, and the fear that they might not immediately attach to an adopted child. They also described continued fantasies of what it would be like to have genetic offspring. These sentiments are similar to those voiced by both lesbian and heterosexual couples who, when faced with an inability to conceive naturally, must decide whether to seek fertility treatments, pursue adoption, or remain child-free (Goldberg, Downing, & Richardson, 2009; van Balen, Verdurmen, & Ketting, 1997). At the same time, Daniel and Rufus—and most of the men who experienced the process of abandoning their consideration of surrogacy as emotionally difficult—viewed themselves as having resolved these concerns and relinquished these fantasies, at least for the time being.

Two men, though, did not view themselves as entirely abandoning the idea of surrogacy. For example, Elliott, a 40-year-old White executive director living in the urban Northeast, affirmed that although he was committed to the adoption process for the immediate future, he remained somewhat attached to the idea of having a biological child. He acknowledged that "there is definitely a part of me that still really wants to have a biological child; it's almost like a sense of failure in a way," and noted that the possibility of pursuing surrogacy in the future was not "completely off the table." These men's status as gay prospective parents, then, did not mean that they were released from or immune to the biological imperative. Although both their sexual orientation and inability to reproduce in the context of a same-sex relationship marked them as "deviant" from traditional notions of family, these factors did not preclude a longing for a biological connection to their offspring. Some gay men may be just as hesitant to relinquish the notion of biological parenthood as heterosexuals, and may struggle with accepting adoption as a legitimate route to parenthood.

Lack of a Need for Biological Connection

About half the men whom I interviewed emphasized that they had never seriously considered surrogacy, simply because they did not have a strong need to be genetically related to their child. These men noted that they were not preoccupied with continuing their "family bloodline," and were confident that they could love a child that was not biologically related to them. James, a 41-year-old White urban planner living in a city on the West Coast, observed:

> Neither of us have, I don't think, any strong ties to our heritage or something like that. We don't need to have a child that is from us. For me it was more of a *gift* to be able to parent. . . . Having a child "naturally" of my own was never an issue or a desire.

Several of these men contrasted their lack of investment in a genetic tie with what they perceived to be heterosexual couples' "preoccupation" with having a biological child. They viewed themselves as more grateful for the "opportunity" to adopt as compared to heterosexual couples, who were typically adopting due to infertility and who were therefore perceived as approaching adoption as a second choice. Timothy, a 41-year-old White sales manager who was pursuing a public adoption with his partner, Jim, in a northeastern suburb, recalled:

> We went to a five-day workshop that [the adoption agency] held. The first class was really just about coming to terms with your sadness around the fact that you weren't able to have a child, so yeah, we ended up hearing it as a group [for people] who adopted as a last resort, which couldn't have been farther from our own experience. For me, it was a celebration, like, "Wow, this is happening!" For me it was like, "Wow, this is a great opportunity!" and really, that wasn't the same place that other people were coming from.

Timothy observed a contrast in perspective between himself and the heterosexual couples attending the adoption seminar, such that he saw adoption as an exciting opportunity and his heterosexual counterparts seemed to view it as an alternative to their preferred route to parenthood. His perception is somewhat consistent with the research literature, which suggests that lesbians and gay men are more likely to be open to and willing to adopt than are heterosexuals (Tyebjee, 2003), who, on average, tend to pursue adoption largely as a result of fertility problems (Goldberg, Downing, & Richardson, 2009). Gay men like Timothy constructed an adoptive family as a "real" family, challenging the hegemonic discourses of family that presume blood relatedness (Dorow & Swiffen, 2009).

Deciding on an Adoption Route

Upon deciding that they were committed to adoption, the men then faced the complex and sometimes-overwhelming decision of deciding which type of adoption to pursue: private domestic adoption (which is typically open);[4] public domestic adoption; or international adoption (Downing, Richardson, Kinkler, & Goldberg, 2009).[5] Their decision-making processes reflect both the power of broader institutionalized barriers and their efforts to resist such barriers. Their decision making also reveals the ways that they often weighed their personal desires, such as the wish for an infant, against practical constraints, such as finances. The men described a variety of reasons for choosing an adoption route. The men who were pursuing domestic private open adoption most frequently cited "desire for an infant" and "the philosophy of open adoption" as their reasons. Desire to secure a female role model/ mother figure via the birth mother was a less frequently cited reason for pursuing this type of adoption. Among public domestic adopters, altruistic reasons, financial considerations, and a preference for an older child were all described as reasons for choosing to go through the child welfare system. Finally, among international adopters, concerns about open adoption and birth-parent involvement, the desire to "save" a child, and the desire for a child of a particular race were cited as reasons.

Factors Influencing Couples' Decision to Choose Private Domestic Adoption

Twenty-four couples (48 men) in the study chose to pursue private domestic open adoptions. The men in these couples articulated a variety of reasons for why they felt this was the most appealing option to them.

DESIRE FOR A NEWBORN

Almost three-quarters of the men who were pursuing private domestic open adoption (i.e., 35 men; 12 couples) explained this decision by emphasizing their strong preference for a newborn. Echoing the sentiments expressed by hetero-sexual adoptive couples in prior studies (Brind, 2008), many of these men felt that adopting an infant was important, as it would ensure that the adoptive parents would be present "from the beginning" and would therefore be able to exert a strong influence on their child's developing mind, values, and personality. "In the absence of nature, I kind of want to max out on nurture," explained Eric, 40. They wished for a "clean slate" and the opportunity to "shape our child ourselves." Raising a child from infancy was often regarded as important in order to develop a "healthy bond" with their child and to avoid potential attachment problems. The men often juxtaposed their desire for an infant with the possibility of adopting an older child, who might not have started their life in "a healthy kind of place" and who may have already been exposed to problematic experiences that would take "years to overcome." Shane, a 32-year-old White sales representative, recalled, "We actually talked about an older child, [but] when we researched a lot about bonding, how important it is, how important the first three months are, we [decided] we would really like to adopt an infant for that reason." Reading, research, and talking with other adoptive parents led Shane and others to internalize the supposed importance of early attachment in child development (Bowlby, 1969), and contributed to their preference for an infant. Shane's emphasis on the extensive research that he and his partner conducted highlights the important role that social workers, the Internet, and other sources of information have in constructing prospective adopters' ideas about and preferences regarding adoption. It also reveals how discourses about adoption are in fact historical and cultural products—not natural, unassailable, and timeless "facts" and "truths," as they are sometimes portrayed to be.

For several men, having an infant was important because it was the closest they could get to having their own biological child. Lacking the reproductive means to have a child in the context of a same-sex relationship, and having ruled out surrogacy for a variety of reasons, these men had chosen to adopt, but not without some sense of loss regarding the biological bond. Raising an adopted child from birth would approximate as closely as possible the experience of having a biological child. In explaining why he so strongly wanted to adopt a newborn, Derek, the 32-year-old White software consultant, revealed:

> I wanted to recreate the natural process of raising a child in the more traditional sense, on every level that I possibly could. I wanted to have as much control of that relationship from day one, and in the case that we're hoping will work out now, from before the birth.

Derek's use of the phrase "traditional sense" is notable, as it suggests that despite the fact that he is not pursuing parenthood in the context of a "traditional" family, he nevertheless values the biological component of "traditional" parenthood—which is often conflated with heterosexuality. Derek and other men constructed their choice of adopting an infant as a strategic compromise between their desire for a biological child and the structural constraints that prevented them from easily pursuing surrogacy.

PHILOSOPHICAL APPEAL

Over half the men pursuing private domestic open adoption (28 men, including seven couples) described having chosen private domestic open adoption because it was the most philosophically appealing to them. They appreciated the values of openness and honesty that are associated with open adoption, which is characterized by initial and/or ongoing exchange of information between birth parents, adoptive parents, and children (Brown, Ryan, & Pushkal, 2007). These men sometimes explained their attraction to open adoption in terms of their experiences as *gay* men, whose ability to be open and honest about their sexuality and relationships was often curtailed. As Derek, 32, reflected, "I guess secrets connote something different for me and, it's just, you hit danger zones, I think, when you don't know everything." Likewise, Nick, a 38-year-old White public relations manager who was living in an urban area on the West Coast, explained:

> [Our agency] gave us a lot of education about open adoption and we just thought it was the best way to go. I think, you know, for us, I mean, we've had different experiences, but growing up gay and having, you know, just knowing what it's like to hide things and not be completely honest about things and how detrimental that can be, I would never want to start off a kid's life like that. And you know, that's what open adoption is all about, is knowing everything really.

The men felt that the openness in open adoption would be potentially valuable in multiple ways. Some men appreciated that their child would grow up in an environment in which there were as few secrets and as little mystery as possible. They felt that open adoption fostered an environment of openness and honesty that would facilitate their child's understanding of adoption as something that is healthy, normal, and nothing to be ashamed of. Darius, a 41-year-old White graduate student in an urban area on the West Coast, shared:

For us, philosophically, it makes sense that it'll probably be easier for a kid to have as little mystery about this whole thing as possible: "This is your mom, she couldn't take care of you, she wanted us to raise you." And you know, the kid can continue to have phone conversations and visits and so on and so forth. It just becomes less of a mystery and less of an odd thing and more of just kind of a normal process of our society. So we liked that for open adoption.

In other cases, the men believed that open adoption was beneficial because they hoped that ongoing contact with birth parents and birth relatives would help to answer their child's ongoing questions about his or her origins in a way that was natural and comfortable. They hoped that having easy and natural access to information about birth parents would facilitate their child's self-esteem and self-understanding, and help to avoid some of the challenges that they associated with closed adoptions.

Finally, some men also mentioned their attraction to the transparency of open adoption. They noted that they were building their families in such a way that it would be obvious that their child was adopted (since two men cannot produce a child) and felt that, in accordance with this transparency, it only made sense to pursue an open adoption. As Drew, 33, said, "It just seemed that having open adoption, [everything is] open and honest and there are no options for us to pretend that we are the biological father." Likewise, Vaughn, 39, expressed:

I'm not a really big believer in secrets. So, part of it, I just feel like, why wouldn't it be open? . . . I mean, I just see this picture of us walking around, it's like okay, here's these two 40-year-old, 40-plus men walking around with a little Black girl. Well, how can you have any secrets there?

Thus the men who pursued open adoption because they were drawn to its philosophy of openness and honesty described many ways that it functionally challenged traditional notions of family. Open adoption contests and expands dominant notions of kinship in that it does not presuppose one family, but allows for the possibility that a child might recognize and form relationships with both his or her birth family and adoptive family. Further, open adoption acknowledges the value of both social and biological ties without asserting the primacy or superiority of biological ties. The men also voiced their awareness that their families would necessarily be recognizable as "deviant"—that is, not biologically related or heterosexual. The reality that their families would be quite visible, and the "truth" of their children's origins would be "guessable," made open adoption seem like the obvious best choice in that it encouraged openness and honesty by and among all members of the adoption triad.

DESIRE FOR A FEMALE ROLE MODEL OR "MOTHER FIGURE"

In some cases, the men's decision making was influenced by societal discourses concerning the necessity of women in children's lives (Risman, 1998), and the men's desire for a built-in role model or "mother figure" for their child. Specifically, eight men (including two couples) described choosing open adoption in part because they desired a maternal figure for their child. They recognized that their child "will never have another mother" and believed that it would be valuable for their child "to identify with that person." In some cases, men specifically referenced the possibility that contact with a birth mother/maternal figure might shield their child, and their families, from stigma and criticism. For example, in explaining the appeal of open adoption, Robbie, a 34-year-old White information technology (IT) manager living in an urban area of the South, explained:

> We looked into [surrogacy], but we really wanted to have a mother figure and that is why we chose open adoption. We know how kids can be and things like that and we really wanted to have a mother figure—not necessarily involved all of the time, but at least a mother figure that could be referred to in situations.

Likewise, Trey, the 32-year-old White dermatologist, asserted:

> We know that whatever child we adopt, we will have friends that come in and say, "Where's your mommy?" We want them to be able to say, "Well, my mommy's here." We don't want kids to say, "You don't have a mom." We want them to be able to say, "Well, yes, I do have a mom and I know her and I know where she lives and I talk to her."

Such statements reflect these men's awareness that their future children might be harassed for not having a mother, particularly in the context of having two fathers, and imply their desire to secure a maternal figure whose existence could be invoked should such harassment occur. The presence of a birth mother would presumably counter multiple types of attacks: attacks on their nonnormative, "pseudo-family" status (insomuch as all "real" families have mothers); attacks on their child's presumably inadequate gender socialization (especially if they were raising a girl); and attacks on the men's, and their child's, sexuality (in that their child would be exposed to *gay* parents). The men's desire to procure female role models as a means of deflecting criticism echoes previous research on lesbian prospective mothers, who expressed wanting "male role models" in part to minimize negative attention regarding their child's lack of a father (Goldberg & Allen, 2007).

But the men's desire for a maternal figure for their child did not always appear to be solely rooted in awareness of societal stigma. In some cases, it appeared to reflect a desire to secure a particular type of gender role modeling—which they felt a woman was most capable of embodying—for their child. Some men articulated a belief that their child would benefit from having access to a female role model, although they were rarely explicit about what exactly they felt a woman could provide that they could not. As Todd, a 46-year-old African American man who worked in marketing, stated simply, "It will be nice to have female contact and the birth mother will provide access to a regular woman."

NO DESIRE TO PURSUE (OR CANNOT PURSUE) ANOTHER TYPE OF ADOPTION

Half the men pursuing private domestic adoption (26 men, including six couples) contrasted this path with their lack of access to international adoption. These men either perceived themselves as being *unable* to adopt internationally as a result of legal regulations barring same-sex male couples from adopting (16 men), or were *unwilling* to adopt internationally, since doing so would require them to closet their relationship with their partners (10 men). In other words, these men either perceived international adoption as a practical impossibility, given the increasing restrictions on single men adopting from abroad, or viewed international adoption as an option, but one that was viable only if they were willing to closet their relationship—which they were not willing to do. They felt that closeting their relationship, even in the service of getting a child, was unacceptable in that it would threaten the integrity of their relationships and the families they were trying to build. They therefore resisted the stipulations imposed by heteronormativity and opted for a route that would allow them to be open about their sexuality and relationship status.

Other men (13 men, including four couples) who were pursuing private domestic open adoption contrasted this path against that of public domestic adoption, which they perceived as having many drawbacks. Most of these men expressed their belief that there was a greater chance of being placed with "mentally challenged and physically challenged kids" in public adoptions—which they wished to avoid. They also pointed to the legal insecurity and risk associated with foster-to-adopt placements as a deterring factor. As Luis, the 45-year-old Latino surgeon, said, "We knew we wanted an infant, and we also didn't want the insecurity of 'Oh my god, we're gonna spend three or four months with this child and then they're going to want it back and take it away.'"

Factors Influencing Couples' Decision to Choose Public Adoption

Nine couples were pursuing a public domestic adoption. The men in these couples described a variety of reasons for pursuing a public domestic adoption, including the desire to help a child in need, the desire to adopt an older child, and financial considerations.

ALTRUISM: THERE ARE CHILDREN IN NEED OF HOMES

The most frequently cited reason (named by 17 men, including five couples) for choosing public adoption was men's perception that public adoption would allow them to adopt the children who were the most in need of healthy, loving, and supportive homes, which they viewed as "just the right thing to do." Dashaun, a 36-year-old African American mental health technician living in a West Coast suburb, asserted, "Theo and I are both loving people. . . . We just know that there are children out there that need a home, and we have one to offer, so why not?" These men often commented that they felt drawn to "go where the greatest need was"—namely, to adopt through the foster care system, as opposed to pursuing a private adoption. As Barry, a 35-year-old IT manager living in a midwestern city, explained:

> Rett worked in residential treatment for quite a while and we were just familiar with the kinds of situations that might lead a kid to be placed into residential treatment. And both of us—I guess just me personally, I want to help where possible. And it seems to me like there's a lot of need in the foster care system for parents, foster and adoptive, and I just wanted to provide that. To be part of the system, I guess, if that makes sense.

Several of these men—all of whom were employed in the helping professions, and worked with youth in some capacity—explicitly stated that they wanted to give a home to a child whose life up to that point had not "been the greatest" and who had been given a "rough deal." These men did not perceive these children's past experiences as a liability. Rather, helping children who had negative early life experiences was emphasized as a key reason for why they were adopting through the child welfare system. These data are consistent with research on some heterosexual couples' motivations for adopting through the child welfare system. Such studies find that a wish to save children from further harm and a desire to take in children who need loving parents represent the top two reasons why heterosexual couples pursue child welfare adoptions (Cole, 2005; Rodger, Cummings, & Leschied, 2006).

PREFERENCE FOR AN OLDER CHILD

In contrast to many of the men who were pursuing private domestic adoptions, eight men (including two couples) emphasized that they chose public adoption specifically because they preferred to adopt an older child, as opposed to an infant. Interestingly, these men often framed their desire for an older child as being related to their sense that they were not very "maternal." Theo, a 40-year-old White man, reflected, "I don't have the strong maternal feelings that a lot of people do. I don't know, I wasn't really excited about changing diapers and picking snot out of children's noses." Timothy, the 41-year-old White sales manager, similarly remarked, "We knew we didn't want an infant. . . . Just, we don't see ourselves as having that real maternal type of skill and experience." These men's narratives echo social discourses that regard men as lacking the maternal skills required to care for an infant (Doucet, 2009; Folgero, 2008; Hicks, 2006a), suggesting that, far from resisting such gendered stereotypes, some of the men appear to have internalized and accepted them as "truth." In a few cases, the men did not describe the work of caring for an infant as explicitly maternal (and therefore inaccessible to them), but simply noted that they had no interest in it. Joshua, a 40-year-old White administrative assistant, explained, "We decided that we really don't need to do the 3:00 am feedings and diaper changes. There's really no reason that we have to experience that part of parenthood; we don't need to be tired all the time." Thus the men's resistance to parenting an infant seemed to stem from both perceptions of themselves as ill equipped at baby care (in part due to their gender) and a personal lack of interest in the types of activities involved in parenting an infant.

FINANCIAL REASONS

Eight men cited financial reasons as a salient factor influencing their decision to pursue public adoption. They were attracted to the fact that adopting a child through the child welfare system was essentially free, in contrast to private domestic and private international adoptions, which they knew could be quite expensive. Although all the men in the study were relatively affluent, the men who pursued public adoption had lower family incomes than did the men who pursued private adoptions (i.e., on average, public adopters' annual family income was $50,000 less than that of private adopters). Thus the men who pursued public adoption had less expendable income. Reflecting this, the men sometimes noted that adopting through the child welfare system allowed them to save the money that they would have spent on private adoption for their child's future, which they viewed as a more intelligent investment. Charlie, a 32-year-old Asian American operations manager living in an urban area on the West Coast, explained the reasoning that led him to choose public adoption over other routes:

> I didn't really think about surrogacy just because it's not important to me that this kid is my blood, but it's [also] like 120 grand. You know, that is a college degree for the kid. We thought and went through [all the options] and international adoptions can cost $15,000 to $30,000. Again, take that $30,000 and how much more could you do for a local kid with that money? Make sure they have a future, rather than going overseas.

NO DESIRE TO PURSUE (OR CANNOT PURSUE) ANOTHER TYPE OF ADOPTION

In addition to citing factors that drove them to choose public adoption, men also described choosing public adoption by default—that is, because they did not want to (or could not) pursue another type. Five men (including one couple) explained that they chose public adoption because they did not want any contact with their child's birth parents. In drastic comparison to couples who were choosing open adoption specifically because birth-mother contact was appealing, these men viewed such contact as threatening or undesirable. And, like some of the men who were pursuing open domestic adoption, three men (including one couple) said that they chose public adoption because of laws and policies restricting them from adopting internationally.

Factors Influencing Couples' Decision to Choose International Adoption

Two couples (four men) were pursuing international adoption. These couples represent a minority of the men whom I interviewed, perhaps in part due to how difficult it is for gay men to adopt internationally: most countries no longer accept applications by single men and explicitly bar gay male couples from adopting (Poncz, 2007). Despite the reality of barriers to international adoption, these men explained a variety of factors that led them to choose this type of adoption.

DESIRE TO RESCUE A CHILD IN NEED

Three men reported being drawn to international adoption because they liked the idea that they would be helping a child from a country with fewer resources, "who were obviously not wanted," and who would otherwise have been raised in an impoverished environment. Such motivations echo those voiced by some heterosexual adoptive parents adopting from abroad, who espouse a "rescue" mentality in explaining their drive to adopt internationally (Dorow, 2006). As Donovan, a 42-year-old Latino engineer stated, "After investigating that route we liked that idea of taking some orphan [from] what is considered a third world country to us anyway."

DESIRE FOR A CHILD OF A SPECIFIC RACE

One couple sought to adopt internationally because of their preference for a Latin American child, given that one partner in the couple was Latino. Both partners were concerned that if they adopted domestically, they would have little chance of getting a Latino child, and, more specifically, they would be placed with an African American child. As Chuck, a 38-year-old White web developer living in Washington DC, explained:

> My partner [Donovan], his mother is from Ecuador, but he has a Hispanic background. And we were looking around just at what was available. And in DC, most of the children they place are African American, and in DC, there's a lot of racial tension and we didn't think that it would be, well, we weren't prepared for that.

Chuck's interest in international adoption was rooted in a personal desire to have their child have a similar background as his partner, and he also juxtaposed this with adopting an African American child, which he thought might be particularly difficult in light of the perceived racial dynamics of his community. In this way, he constructed Latin American as an "acceptable" race, whereas African American was described as unacceptable. Couples—such as Chuck and his partner—who were open to adopting children of other races, but not African American children, can be regarded as only partially challenging traditional notions of family, in that they asserted a willingness to be different—but not too different. Further, it is notable that men like Chuck and his partner used their financial resources to circumvent the possibility of being placed with an African American child. In this way, financial privilege again enabled some men to avoid perceived problems in the adoption system and to facilitate their racial preferences.

Conclusion

Gay men must overcome numerous societal stigmas surrounding their ability and right to parent, including stereotypes about gay men as unworthy of parenting and as "antifamily" (Brinamen & Mitchell, 2008), and assumptions that men in general are less nurturing than women and therefore less competent as primary caregivers (Folgero, 2008). The men whom I interviewed were differentially affected by these broader discourses. Some men internalized them and temporarily gave up on their dream of parenthood until relatively recently, whereas others remained firmly committed to becoming parents, despite coming of age in a climate that was neither practically nor symbolically supportive of gay men's fathering efforts. The increasing visibility and accessibility of parenthood for gay men (Planck, 2006; Stacey, 2006), combined with structural resources such as finances (Berkowitz, 2009; Downing, Richardson, Kinkler, & Goldberg, 2009), enabled them to realize and pursue their parental aspirations once the "stars had aligned"—for example, they found partners who were also committed to parenthood, and they had established some degree of personal, financial, and relationship stability in their lives. The relatively older age at which these men were pursuing parenthood reflects the complex and lengthy series of developmental milestones and transitions that gay men must make prior to becoming a parent: gay men must identify and accept their sexual orientation, find an appropriate partner, decide to parent, and choose a means to parenthood (Friedman, 2007). Yet their older age, as well as the types of reasons they invoked for pursuing parenthood currently, highlight the reality that these gay men are not simply following a "stalled" version of the heteronormative life course. Although some men did acknowledge a desire to be married before becoming a parent, many did not appear to be wedded to a heteronormative template for how and when parenthood should unfold. In fact, some men's narratives hint at ways in which they disrupted the heteronormative life course, as opposed to upholding it.

Reflecting the complex and prolonged nature of their decision-making process, not all men settled on adoption as their route to parenthood right away. As these narratives illustrate, some men were deeply invested in, or at least interested in, the possibility of having a biogenetic relationship to their child. Likely affected by dominant discourses about parenthood and family that presume biogenetic connections as foundational to family ties and attachment, they struggled to imagine themselves parenting an adopted child. Gay men who adopt are building families that deviate in multiple ways from normative conceptions of family, and men may wonder or question— even unconsciously—whether the family bonds they are creating are as solid and "real" as those of heterosexual or biologically created families. The men's complex and sometimes unresolved feelings about biology reflect the reality that deviance from heteronormative standards pertaining to gender, family, and relationships does not preclude or protect against the influence of such standards (Kahn, Holmes, & Brett, 2011). Indeed, individuals who are single and seeking to parent, as well as infertile heterosexual couples who are considering adoption, also navigate the reality that the families they seek to build will differ from the nuclear family standard. Yet gay men are perhaps uniquely positioned (and even advantaged) by the fact that they deviate from the dominant nuclear model in *multiple* ways, possibly freeing them, in some cases, from measuring themselves against—and trying to embody— this template.

About half the men, though, did not espouse to value or prioritize biology in their relationships with children. Armed with the sense that they could "bond with anyone . . . I love my partner and *he's* not related to me!," they described little to no loss associated with the fact that they would bear no genetic resemblance to their future child. Such findings mirror prior research on lesbian adoptive parents, many of whom deny the salience of biology in forming families (Goldberg, Downing, & Richardson, 2009), and are consistent with Weston's (1991) argument that lesbians and gay men may (in part because of rejection from members of their own biological families) be particularly likely to envision and define family in ways that are not predicated on biological relatedness. By rejecting the centrality of biological connectedness to family life, some of the men espoused a perspective that suggests the revisionist potential of gay male parents: by embracing a broader definition of family, and then enacting that definition, they may transform and expand what we know to be "family."

Ultimately, regardless of the degree to which the men prioritized biology in the initial stages of considering parenthood, almost all the men appeared fairly satisfied with their decision to pursue adoption, and with the particular type of adoption they had settled on. Their choice of an adoption type was often influenced by their own personal values and ideals, such as their age preferences for the child and their desire to be "out" in the adoption process. The men who pursued open adoption often described a deep appreciation for the philosophy of honesty and openness inherent in open adoption, which served to undermine fundamental assumptions about kinship by facilitating the child's relationship with both birth and adoptive families. Indeed, the enactment of open adoptions—particularly in households headed by gay men—reworks basic definitions and ideas about family, such as the notion that children can have only one family, and the idea that children cannot recognize their relationships with both biological and adoptive family members. Of course, the men's decision to pursue a particular adoption path was shaped by numerous factors relatively outside of their control, such as state and national adoption laws, as well as cost. Thus not all the men arrived at the adoption path that they would have chosen voluntarily. In this way, the men's parenting decisions were affected, at various stages, by broader systemic inequities (Goldberg, 2010a), which are discussed more in depth in the next chapter.

In sum, the gay men in this study—and perhaps all gay men, to some extent—are clearly influenced by powerful heteronorms in forming families. The men's narratives revealed that all the men were aware of discourses that presupposed the interconnectedness among biological/genetic relatedness, heterosexuality, and parenthood—but the men varied considerably in the degree to which they internalized or resisted these discourses. The men's narratives also showed how their decisions about parenthood route (adoption vs. surrogacy) and adoption route (private domestic, private international, and public domestic) were intricately shaped and constrained by various social contextual factors, including financial stability as well as personal preferences and ideals, such as the desire to raise a child from birth. The men's decisions were also affected by factors specific to them as gay men, such as their awareness of societal discourses surrounding the importance of female involvement in children's lives—which in a few cases influenced men's desire to pursue open adoption over other types of adoption.

The men's stories therefore illustrate that their sexual orientation is only one—albeit one very important—influence in their parenting decisions and trajectories. Intersecting with their sexual orientation are other axes of relative oppression and privilege that influence their path to parenthood. Their male gender, for example, can be viewed as an added barrier to parenthood in light of stereotypes of mothers as essential to child development. Financial privilege represents another axis of relative oppression/privilege that varied among the men. The more affluent men were more likely to pursue private adoption, particularly private domestic open adoption, which increased the likelihood of adopting an infant and therefore mirroring—at least to some extent—the heteronormative nuclear family ideal. Of course, beyond financial privilege, the men's own values appeared to shape the degree to which they seemed to accommodate to, or resist, heteronormative discourses concerning parenthood and family.

2

Navigating Structural and Symbolic Inequalities
on the Path to Parenthood

Adoption Agencies, the Legal System, and Beyond

Lars, a 36-year-old White man, and Joshua, a 40-year-old White man, had
been together for 12 years when they began the process of adopting. They
described a long period of "considering" parenthood before actually pursuing it, because it took several years for Joshua to match Lars's level of commitment and enthusiasm. Various life events, such as family illness, had also
stalled them from initiating the adoption process. When they finally decided
to move forward with adoption (having not even considered surrogacy),
they found it easy to settle on going through the child welfare system. As
Joshua described the decision, "It was a no-brainer [both for] personal and
financial reasons." Both men agreed that there were "plenty of kids out there"
who needed homes, and they were also attracted to the fact that adopting a
child through the child welfare system was "essentially cost-free." With an
average combined annual income of $85,000, Lars and Joshua (who worked
as a human resources officer and an administrative assistant, respectively)
described themselves as financially comfortable but not rich, and unwilling
to make the financial sacrifices necessary to pursue a private adoption.

As residents of suburban North Carolina, both Lars and Joshua acknowledged anxieties regarding how they, as a gay male couple, would be received by the child welfare system. Lars described the process of going for the initial informational session at the Department of Health and Human Services as nerve-wracking: "I was very, I was nervous, I was scared just being there, you know, being there the two of us: 'Oh, we're a gay couple looking to adopt a child in the middle of the South.' It was a complete rollercoaster." Fortunately, Lars and Joshua were matched with a social worker who was supportive and affirming, and whom they viewed as an advocate. Even though North Carolina did not allow same-sex partners to co-adopt, therefore requiring Joshua to adopt as a single parent, the kindness and support of their social worker, Annie, helped to offset the heterosexist treatment they received at the legal level. They were aware that if they had been attempting to adopt in a more rural area of their state, things might not have been so easy. As Lars explained to me:

> Annie said many times that though they work with all the counties in North Carolina, certainly [in] the more rural counties there is no possibility that they will work with a gay single or a gay couple in placing a child with them. She said that the metropolitan areas in the state are sort of the opposite, because there's such a great need in the foster care system.

Yet even as they were matched with a relatively supportive and accepting social worker, Lars and Joshua still encountered heterosexism in the adoption process. Joshua described how some of their written materials and adoption classes had to do with "fertility issues and how you have been impacted by *not being able* to have a child." From their perspective, the materials failed to acknowledge the perspectives of couples who had not experienced infertility or those who approached adoption as their first choice. Also, at the broadest level, Lars and Joshua were forced to contend with the reality that Joshua would be adopting as a single parent. They noted that a nearby county's judge was known for performing second-parent adoptions for same-sex couples, but neither partner was sure whether they had to be a resident of that county to pursue a second-parent adoption there. This "not knowing" caused both men some concern, but understandably evoked more anxiety for Lars, who was discomfited by the possibility of not having any legal ties to his future child.

After the couple had been placed with a toddler-aged boy named Evan, Lars continued to face uncertainty regarding whether he would ultimately be able to adopt the child, since, in the county that was routinely performing second-parent adoptions, "there is some ambiguity as to the legal validity of them. In fact, currently, one of them is being challenged, and the results of this case will determine what will happen with the rest of them and future ones." Such legal insecurity led Lars to develop a more passionate stance regarding the fight for equal relationship recognition rights for same-sex couples, because he was now more sensitive to how the absence of legal protections might affect his son. Lars worried about his child being teased by his peers, and believed that that the symbolic and legal status of marriage might help to minimize his child's exposure to both interpersonal and structural heterosexism. He realized, though, that "there are certain legal rights which we don't have and we try and struggle to get them, but they're just not here at the moment and that's how it is." Yet Lars did not view himself as powerless in the face of such legal inequities. He emphasized that he and Joshua were using all the "legal tools" they had available to them to protect their family, including powers of attorney, health care proxies, and expressed desire of guardianship in case something should happen to Joshua.

Lars and Joshua's story highlights how gay men are vulnerable to heterosexism at many stages and levels of the adoption process. Further, their story exemplifies how adopting a child may serve to influence gay men's perspectives on political issues such as marriage equality, since their lack of legal rights may become more salient in the presence of a child. This chapter explores the men's experiences of seeking out adoption agencies that were willing to work with them; the types of supportive and unsupportive agency practices that the men encountered, and their responses to them; their experiences of navigating legal inequities; and their efforts to protect their families in the absence of marriage equality and legal adoption rights (e.g., their efforts to resist or subvert the legal system by employing those resources available to them).

* * *

Gay men must move beyond both internalized and societal homophobia to realize and pursue their parental aspirations. Upon deciding to become a parent—and, specifically, to adopt—men's journey to parenthood has just begun. Initiating the adoption process brings gay men into direct contact with a wide range of heteronormative institutions and agents, thereby exposing them to a complex and interrelated system of structural barriers. At the most immediate level, adoption agencies may thwart gay men's efforts to become parents by refusing to work with them, which often reflects an explicit and unapologetic commitment to the heteronormative ideal. Agencies may also impede gay men's parenting efforts in more subtle and possibly inadvertent ways—for example, by failing to provide them with appropriate guidance and support during the adoption process. Gay men who are seeking an open adoption may face additional challenges, because birth mothers are more likely to choose heterosexual couples than gay male couples to be the adoptive parents of their child (Brodzinsky, 2003; Goldberg, Downing, & Sauck, 2007). Finally, at the broadest level, state laws also function as powerful barriers to gay men's adoption efforts. Although most states allow individual, unmarried adults (a category that presumably includes gay individuals) to petition to adopt a child, only a limited number of states have demonstrated, via judicial ruling, either an openness to adoption by openly gay *individuals* or an openness to adoption by openly same-sex *couples* (Goldberg, 2010a). The latter states allow both partners to adopt a child together, at the same time; such adoptions are often referred to as co-parent adoptions. In states that are unlikely to grant co-parent adoptions, same-sex couples typically choose one partner to legally adopt, as a single parent, and then the other partner can petition to adopt his or her partner's child via a second-parent adoption.[1] But there are many states where second-parent adoptions are rarely granted to same-sex partners, leading to a situation in which there is one legal parent and one parent who is not legally recognized. Further, regulations governing second-parent adoptions vary within the same jurisdiction and may even be differentially implemented by different judges. That is, some judges choose to interpret the law in a way that favors same-sex couples, thereby resisting the law, and others choose to interpret it in a way that upholds heteronormativity. Moreover, the relationships between gay parents and their children may go unrecognized at the legal level, which functions to undermine family stability on both practical and symbolic levels (Goldberg, 2010a; Herek, 2006).

Adoption Agencies: Negative Experiences and Interactions

Research on lesbian and gay adopters has often highlighted their encounters with discriminatory adoption agencies and social workers (Brooks & Goldberg, 2001; Downs & James, 2006; Goldberg, Downing, & Sauck, 2007; Hicks, 2006a; Matthews & Cramer, 2006; Ross, Epstein, Goldfinger, & Yager, 2008). Consistent with this, many of the men in this study described decidedly negative experiences with adoption agencies. These negative experiences were on a continuum: some agencies displayed extreme, overt forms of heterosexism, such as rejection of gay men as potential clients; whereas others were guilty of less direct, more benign forms of heterosexism, such as classes and paperwork that ignored the unique experiences of same-sex couples, and a lack of knowledge of state laws pertaining to gay adoption.

At the most extreme level, seven men (including one couple) noted that they had encountered agencies that outright refused to work with them upon learning that they were a male couple seeking to adopt. "There are some agencies that won't talk to us, there are people who won't even consider us," asserted Patrick, a 41-year-old White college professor, who resided with his partner, Carter, in a midwestern suburb and who was seeking a private domestic open adoption. In some cases, these men noted that the agencies did not explain their refusal, whereas in other cases they were told that the agency was unable to work with them because of their funding (e.g., they were affiliated with the Catholic Church). Thomas, a 36-year-old White real estate agent who lived in what he described as a predominantly Christian suburb in the South and who was pursuing a private domestic open adoption with his partner, Devon, recalled:

> A lot of the adoption agencies wouldn't even deal with us, you know, an alternative family. We were like, "What?" I didn't know where to begin. A lot of the adoption agencies are Christian-based who really don't want— and you know, they will be blatant . . . saying, "We only handle husband and wife married couples or single women."

The fact that religiously based organizations such as Catholic Charities refused to work with these men was experienced as upsetting and frustrating, as this refusal reflected and reified dominant heteronormative beliefs about gay men's unfitness as parents (Goldberg, Downing, & Sauck, 2007). Further, being cast out by these religiously based agencies had practical consequences, in that these were often the less expensive and closest agencies. Men such as Thomas and his partner had to incur time and financial losses by searching beyond their immediate communities for an agency that was willing to work with them.

In addition to encountering such uncooperative, heterosexist agencies, Thomas and his partner, Devon, as well as one other couple, encountered agencies that claimed to have a "gay quota." These agencies declared that they "only allow[ed] a certain number of gay couples" at a time and apparently did not want to "skew the pool" by taking them on as clients. These men were left with conflicting impressions of and feelings about such agencies. On the one hand, these agencies were presumably gay friendly by virtue of their willingness to work with same-sex couples. Yet at the same time, they seemed more concerned about their public image than with helping prospective parents to adopt.

Four men (including one couple) expressed discomfort with their agencies' implicit or informal "don't ask, don't tell" policy, which meant that their agencies refused to acknowledge formally that they were in fact a couple. These men, who were pursuing both private domestic and public adoptions, were all living in states that did not explicitly allow same-sex partners to co-adopt. For example, Barry, the 35-year-old White IT manager, and his partner, Rett, a White graduate student, were adopting in a midwestern state in which single men, but not same-sex couples, were allowed to adopt. Barry was the "official" adoptive parent (the one "formally" taking the adoption classes and working with the adoption agency), while Rett was described as the "roommate" in the home study. Although Rett attended all the adoption classes and, according to Barry, "it was clear what was going on," the agency had nevertheless warned Barry that "it's a pretty much 'don't ask, don't tell' policy and so in terms of anything official we need to be very discreet about our relationship." This kind of warning, he noted, had served to inhibit open communication between them and the agency. Joshua, the 40-year-old White administrative assistant who was pursuing adoption through the child welfare system in North Carolina with his partner, Lars (whose story was described in the opening to this chapter), mused:

> Open communication, I think, has been the biggest challenge. . . . They're really supportive but I think it's still a little uncomfortable for them to talk about. . . . They don't want to acknowledge it so much. They don't want to draw attention to it. So that's been a little challenging. There's a lot of pregnant pauses and innuendo even when we're having a normal conversation. They might say, "In your situation, because of your special situation." I mean, it's a little bit of euphemism that can be very frustrating.

In Joshua's case, the social workers' failure to be direct and open with him and Lars was perceived as "frustrating." At the same time, he described them as "really supportive." His conflicted feelings likely in part reflect his awareness of his limited options. Joshua's geographic location, and the fact that he was pursuing a public adoption, effectively *required* that he work with his local child welfare agency—unless he wished to relocate or switch to the more expensive option of private adoption. In this way, social, geographic, and financial resources constrained the options that the men had available to them, sometimes requiring that they tolerate various forms of discrimination to adopt successfully. This created internal tensions for them, as they struggled to reconcile the discrepancy between their values and their lived realities. These men desired equal treatment but were forced to endure heterosexism.

Eleven men (including one couple) noted that their adoption agencies' curriculum, classes, or paperwork were geared explicitly or implicitly toward heterosexual couples, and, by extension, were insensitive to issues specific to same-sex couples. These men were from a range of geographic areas, including progressive urban cities densely populated by sexual minorities as well as less progressive areas, and were pursuing a range of adoption types. Four men, for example, noted that their adoption agencies' classes seemed to presume infertility, in that a large proportion of class time was spent focusing on overcoming the "loss" associated with infertility, a heterosexist assumption that excluded the experiences of gay male couples who were unable to have biological children but who were not medically infertile. Dennis, a 40-year-old White small business owner who was pursuing a public adoption in an urban area on the West Coast, recalled, "One of the things that I wrote in my evaluation was that, you know, the curriculum seemed to be really geared toward straight infertile couples. . . . There was nothing about families being different." Likewise, a few of these 11 men noted that their agencies' forms specified a "husband and wife," forcing them to "cross things out" in order to portray their family accurately, an action that also enabled them to resist and challenge the heteronormative assumptions embedded in their agencies' programming. Conscious of their subordinate status in a relationship of power (Ewick & Silbey, 2003), these men engaged in a quiet, subtle act of resistance that would, they hoped, serve to challenge, but not alienate, their agencies.

Several of these men also complained about the books and literature that they were given on adoption, which they regarded as thoroughly focused on the life cycle and experiences of heterosexual couples. For example, Dean, a 30-year-old Asian American man who worked as the assistant director of a nonprofit organization in an urban area on the West Coast, and who was pursuing a private domestic open adoption with his partner, Stan, recalled:

> I remember that when we chose adoption, we had to go to a seminar and read some books, and the literature that we were told to read was just very heterosexist, very isolating. They assumed a lot about who was reading it and I kind of just didn't see myself there, so I was just missing. Then when we went to the seminar, a lot of the conversation, again, assumed infertility between a man and a woman and that wasn't the case for us. So I often-times felt like we were missing in that process.

Indeed, the adoption literature these men read tended to presume that the adopters in question were heterosexual, and often married, thereby failing to acknowledge the legal and social implications of gay men's unique vantage point. The 44-year-old Finn's experience with his agency, for example, led him to feel that "they need to—I wouldn't say specifically have a manual for same-sex couples, but they need to have better references. Because they have a manual they give you, but a lot of that stuff doesn't apply to same-sex couples. This is wholly, totally a different game."

The failure of adoption agencies to acknowledge or include gay men's perspectives and experiences in their classes and materials led some of the men to feel isolated and marginalized. Some men voiced a sense of dampened morale and lack of enthusiasm for the process because of such marginalization. They understood that their agencies' programming would inevitably cover topics and issues that were not relevant to them, such as infertility. At the same time, they wished that their agencies might offer them some materials and resources that would help them to feel less marginalized and more supported in their journey. As we have seen, gay men may also experience loss related to their inability to parent a biological child, but this loss is inevitably contextualized by their status as gay men. In turn, they require tailored programming and resources that address their unique experiences. Of note is that groups other than same-sex couples may also feel "left out" of (heteronormative) adoption programming. For example, single men and women may also need to work through feelings of loss related to not having a biological child. But their feelings may be shaped by their non-partnered status—a reality that may not be acknowledged in the adoption classes and materials offered.

Seven men (including two couples) also noted that their agencies lacked knowledge of the various state laws regarding gay adoption, which the men viewed as a major liability. For example, they were not confident that their agencies would know what to do if the men were matched with a birth mother in a state that did not allow same-sex partners to co-adopt. Thomas, 36, expressed his frustration that the social workers at his agency "do not know state policy or state laws, which has kept us from being shown [to birth mothers] for over a month. There is no literature to help us understand what the policy and state laws are. Their website has no [information about] policies on adoption laws."

Robbie, a 34-year-old IT manager living in an urban area of the South, was also critical of his agency for providing him and his partner, Finn, with what he understood to be misinformation regarding their capacity to adopt from certain states:

It's obvious that they don't have all the facts and details . . . just about same-sex adoption, because everything that we—we've had to find out through the grapevine from people we've talked to that have gone through same-sex adoption. They should be able to give us information and lead us. So we're paying them the money, but they really don't understand the situations and what the nuances and differences were for us. For instance, [they told us], "Oh, well, you can't adopt in Mississippi." And I said, "Well that's not the case, you can too." I said, "Our friends did it and didn't have any problems. They just had an attorney from Arkansas come in and they did it." And we got the same thing about Utah and, you know, they really didn't know the law, they didn't know which states could and couldn't.

Robbie and others expressed dismay and frustration over their agencies' ignorance of the various state laws pertaining to gay adoption—ignorance that seemed to indicate the agencies' lack of concern for or attention to their lesbian/gay clients. These examples highlight the ways that heteronormativity can act insidiously: by failing to understand the implications of state laws and agency policies for their lesbian/gay clients, agencies perpetuate, reify, and reproduce heteronormative practices and structures.

Heteronormative ideology encompasses interrelated norms regarding gender (conventionality), (hetero)sexuality, and family (traditionalism) (Oswald, Blume, & Marks, 2005; Oswald, Kuvalanka, Blume, & Berkowitz, 2009). Indeed, some of the men who described being marginalized or stigmatized based on their sexuality in their encounters with adoption agencies and social workers also described confronting sexism in the adoption process. For example, three men, all of whom were adopting through the child welfare system with their partners, were informed by social workers that there was little to no chance that they would be placed with an infant because they were men. The unspoken presumption seemed to be that men are less capable of caring for an infant than were women, or that infants need female caretakers (Doucet, 2009; Hicks, 2006a). Barry, the 35-year-old White man who was adopting in the Midwest with his partner, Rett, attested:

They had a lot of apprehension about placing an infant with a single male. . . . [My social worker] described us as a single-male home and the agency licensing worker's response was something like, "Oh," and then there's a pause. Then she said, "You know, I—I probably shouldn't have reacted that way. I wouldn't have if it were a single woman." And our worker was like, "No, you probably shouldn't have. But I understand your concern, you want what's best for the child."

Thus, according to Barry, *both* social workers appeared to presume fundamental differences between men and women as caretakers—differences that
clearly favored women's "innate" capacities over men's. Echoing this example,
Hicks (2006a) interviewed social workers in foster care and adoption agencies in the United Kingdom and found that some social workers acknowledged a prejudice against male caregivers in general—that is, they emphasized that their hesitation to place children in the homes of gay men was not
rooted in homophobia, but rather in gender bias. Gay men who encounter
workers who are obviously hesitant to place children with them because of
their gender may be frustrated by such bias but feel helpless to confront it
directly, because they lack power in the process already and may be apprehensive about "creating waves" and potentially alienating workers (Goldberg,
Downing, & Sauck, 2007). They may also be fearful of seeming too dismis-
sive of the importance of maternal figures in child development (Goldberg &
Allen, 2007), as this may be read as evidence of their lack of attention to the
"best interest of the child" (Clarke, 2001), which in turn may invite attacks
on gay men's parenting capacities. These examples highlight the processes
through which heteronorms are upheld: fears of retribution may keep gay
men from challenging social workers' stereotypes about gender, and in turn,
workers' attitudes—and the broader heteronormative structures that keep
them in place—go unchecked.

Some of the men encountered a different form of gender bias: the assumption that, as men, they were ill equipped to raise female children. Three men
(including one couple), all of whom were adopting through the child welfare
system, were told that they were unlikely to get a female child. As men, they
were not only assumed to lack female "instinct" for child rearing (Doucet,
2009), but their male bodies and male socialization apparently rendered
them incapable of properly raising a daughter. The 36-year-old Lars, whose
story was profiled in the opening to this chapter, revealed:

> I think our social worker said that it's almost guaranteed that we would get
> a boy. She said that in North Carolina it is unlikely, to the extent of being
> impossible, that a girl would be placed in a household of two men. And
> though I feel the need to have a daughter, I have to admit that none of the
> experiences of being a girl do I have, so I'd be lost, I think.

Although he did in fact desire a daughter, Lars ultimately felt compelled
to "admit" that because he lacked female socialization, he would likely "be
lost" in raising a girl. In this way, he seems to have resigned himself to, and
possibly internalized, the notion that women are innately better equipped

to raise female children. Adoption agencies are indeed powerful institutions that have the capacity to undermine men's parental confidence as well as to reinforce and perpetuate gendered and heteronormative notions of parenting. Further, as stated, some men's fear of confronting these gendered stereotypes indirectly perpetuates this conventional wisdom. It is intriguing to consider how these types of gendered norms may be operating in agencies' placement of children in other types of families as well. For example, it is worth considering whether the valuing of same-gender placements applies primarily to single-male adopters rather than single-female adopters. Single-female adopters may, by virtue of their female socialization and presumed maternal "instincts," be viewed as equipped to parent a child of either gender, whereas single-male adopters, like gay male couples, may be presumed to be "crippled" by their male socialization, and only barely capable of parenting a son. Here, single women's gender may help to compensate for their non-(hetero)normative family structure, whereas single men may be doubly marginalized by virtue of their gender and family structure.

Adoption Agencies: Positive Experiences and Interactions

Importantly, many of the men in the study were working with adoption agencies or individual social workers whom they perceived as validating of and supportive to them as same-sex couples. In many cases, the men had conducted extensive research in an attempt to identify a respected and gay-friendly agency—efforts that they realized were specific to their situation as a gay adoptive couple. "We shopped around until we found an agency we felt comfortable with, and a straight couple doesn't really have to do that," stated Nolan, a 36-year-old White man. The men were aware of their disadvantaged status and sought to utilize the resources available to them to actively resist and ideally circumvent heterosexism. They scrutinized agency websites, examining them for evidence that they were open to, or opposed to, working with same-sex couples. They called agencies and lawyers, inquiring about their willingness and expertise in working with same-sex couples, and asking them for references of other lesbian/gay clients. They visited adoption agencies' offices, scanning the walls for pictures of same-sex-couple clients and inspecting their materials for evidence of bias and heterosexism. And finally, they relied on the advice and previous experience of friends and acquaintances in selecting an adoption agency, with the goal of "hopefully avoiding some of the pitfalls just by following the lead of some other people who were trailblazing." Like the gay adoptive fathers studied by the clinical social worker Mark Gianino (2008), the men particularly sought the input of other same-sex couples who had been through the adoption process. These friends frequently saved them time and energy by providing referrals to gay-affirming agencies, lawyers, and adoption facilitators. Kevin, a psychologist, and his partner, Brendan, a graduate student, who were pursuing an open adoption in the Midwest, found their adoption facilitator through their friends Lisa and Joan, a lesbian couple. Kevin, 40, explained:

> Brendan's friends, Lisa and Joan, were working with her. Lisa said, "We started working with this woman. I think you'll like her. She's very gay friendly." It was a direct referral. It was great. I don't know how we would have gone about trying to figure all that out. I'm sure we would have done it but it would have been very time consuming. It made it tons easier. It was like stamp of approval firsthand. Mary has been great.

The men identified a range of specific qualities and practices of their agencies that they perceived as helpful and validating to them as same-sex couples. Nine men (including one couple) emphasized their agency's inclusive attitude toward them and their partners. They noted that their agencies treated them the same as heterosexual couples—that is, they saw no distinction in the treatment and support that their agencies provided them with compared to heterosexual clients. They were very grateful for the simple fact of being treated "like any other couple" and as "equal to heterosexual couples." Will, a 37-year-old White man, stated, "They treat everyone at the same level, give the respect and responsibility that all couples [deserve], and they're eager and wanting to help you achieve your goal, which is being placed with the best and proper placement that they can achieve." Likewise, Henry, a 45-year-old biracial man who lived in an urban area of the Northeast and who was pursuing an open adoption, appreciated the fact that the staff members at the agency that he and his partner, Luis, ultimately decided to work with did not single them out, but simply made an effort to communicate the agency's inclusiveness. Henry recalled:

> They never mentioned anything like—I think that in the seminar they said, "If you're a straight or a gay couple . . . ," and it was very inclusive. They used the word [to] get [it] out there. We went to other seminars where they asked us to wait afterward and said, "You're going to have a really, really hard time."

Interestingly, one of the agencies Henry recalled as less than encouraging with respect to their sexual orientation was also described as having "narrow" ideas related to race. Henry stated, "Obviously Luis is Latin American. I'm half-Spanish but I look [light]. They kind of implied that I wasn't Spanish enough [to be placed with a Latino child]. That was kind of like—it took us aback."

In contrast, nine men (including two couples) emphasized that they particularly appreciated their agencies' efforts to be sensitive to them *as* same-sex couples. To these men, it was important not only to be accepted but to be acknowledged and "seen" as "different"—and to be offered resources that sensitively dealt with that difference. These men appreciated their agencies' efforts to offer them support groups, trainings, and materials that were specifically geared toward their needs and experiences as gay male couples pursuing adoption. Several of them, for example, expressed their appreciation that their agencies provided gay prospective-parent support groups. These groups were seen as important in that they fostered the development of a gay parenting community. Additionally, several men described their gratitude for their agencies' efforts to share literature and anecdotes that clearly supported the claim that "same-sex couples raise healthy kids." Timothy, a 41-year-old White man who was pursuing a public adoption in a Northeastern suburb, recalled, "They told us up front that they had worked with gay couples previously and had very good experiences. They loved their gay families; they felt that they were some of the most successful adoptions that they ever had." Ryan, a 37-year-old White engineer who was pursuing a public adoption in a city on the West Coast, recounted this story:

> When we went to the orientation . . . it was kind of funny because there was a room full of maybe 20 people, there were about nine couples and a couple of single people, and at some point somebody came and passed out some extra material to us and a lesbian couple and just like a single guy and of course we never said we're a gay couple (*laughs*), but they sort of figured it out and gave us some extra information. The information was the results of a couple of studies talking about minority children and same-sex couples and you know, how in some cases same-sex couples may even be better for certain reasons for certain kids, so I thought that was pretty cool that they kind of went out of their way sort of to say, "You guys are not less than, actually we're glad you're applying."

By sharing gay-parent success stories and appropriate resources with gay prospective adopters, agencies clearly communicated their interest in and commitment to working with same-sex couples. Their straightforward efforts to explicitly recognize and encourage gay men as prospective adopters were gratefully acknowledged by these men, some of whom were surprised by the extent to which they were welcomed and supported. Further, these agencies' recognition of the unique aspects of gay-parent families can be viewed as a form of resistance to, and even disruption of, heteronormativity. Far from expecting gay men's experiences to be the same as those of heterosexual couples—and, in turn, merely extending a heteronormative framework to accommodate same-sex couples—these agencies acknowledged and embraced the unique needs and strengths of gay male-parent families.

Thirteen men (including two couples) noted their gratitude to be working with adoption agencies that had a history of helping same-sex couples, and whose clientele was peppered with—and in a few cases dominated by—same-sex couples. These men were relieved to be working with agencies that had positive track records regarding gay adoption, and they were appreciative of the fact that they were far from the only gay couple at agency trainings, classes, and support group meetings. Dennis, the 40-year-old White small business owner who was seeking a public adoption with his partner, Justin, observed:

> It's been interesting; the three classes we've been to there, the majority of the couples have been gay or lesbian. And we've—Justin and I, and then Justin and one of the other couples kind of remarked to each other about how it felt neat to be in a not-gay situation that was the gay majority. And the last class we went to . . . the whole, the front table was all gay and lesbian couples and then the back table was all straight people in various combinations.

For Dennis and others, the presence of other gay and lesbian prospective adopters had a notable impact on their sense of belonging and overall comfort with the adoption process. In particular, being in a "not-gay situation" where gay people just happened to be the majority was an unusual and pleasant experience that reinforced their enthusiasm for the adoption process and, specifically, their commitment to the agency.

In several cases, the men viewed their geographic location as a key factor underlying their positive agency experiences and interactions. These men, who lived in relatively progressive metropolitan areas such as San Francisco and Seattle, described the process of identifying a gay-friendly adoption agency to work with as relatively easy, which they attributed to the fact that they lived in an urban area with a large percentage of same-sex couples. In that gay parenting was relatively "institutionalized" and visible in their area, they had a number of gay-friendly agencies to choose from, and experienced

...nimal worry about the prospect of agency discrimination. Charlie, a 32-year-old Asian American man who worked as an operations manager, explained:

> We purposely went with an agency that focuses on same-sex couples. Fifty percent of their clientele is same-sex couples. And then we took our foster care licensing class with a same-sex couple that runs it. The class was geared toward same-sex couples. Being in Seattle, there's a lot of opportunity that way. It's a very active [gay] community.

When asked about how the adoption process was going for him and his partner, Trevor, Richard, a 37-year-old White urban planner, exclaimed:

> It has been really great. I can't imagine having gone through all of this with a different agency that wasn't open and comfortable working with same-sex parents. We haven't had problems—it's partly the agency and partly us, I suppose. I think a lot of it is where we are. If we were in a part of the country that was much more conservative it would be very different.

These men were aware that their positive experiences were in part a function of their liberal locale, and they sympathetically acknowledged that gay men pursuing adoption in rural or less progressive areas of the country likely would encounter far more barriers and fewer resources in general for same-sex couples (Oswald & Culton, 2003). The men's stories consistently highlighted the role of geographic context and urban locales they lived in shaping their feelings of comfort versus marginalization during the adoption process. Their stories also highlight the importance of attending to the intersections among gender, class, and sexuality in understanding men's experiences of pursuing adoption (Oswald, Blume, & Marks, 2005; Oswald, Kuvalanka, Blume, & Berkowitz, 2009). Gay men with geographic and class privilege may be better able to circumvent certain types of discrimination, whereas men with fewer resources in these regards may be exposed to additional vulnerability, such that their limited options may force them to endure heterosexism.

Birth Mothers

Gay men who pursue private domestic open adoption encounter an additional, unique challenge in the adoption process. Not only do they face the challenge of finding an adoption agency that will not discriminate against them as same-sex couples, they also confront the reality of discrimination by prospective birth mothers, as these women may be unwilling to consider a nonheterosexual couple. A 2003 study found that 24% of the adoption agencies surveyed reported that prospective birth parents had objected to placing their child with lesbians or gay men (Brodzinsky, 2003), and previous studies of gay adoptive fathers suggest that one of the most frustrating roadblocks that they encounter is resistance by some birth parents to placing their child with gay men (Downs & James, 2006). Echoing these findings, many of the men in this study who were pursuing open adoption noted that, according to their agencies, prospective birth mothers were simply more likely to choose heterosexual couples as the adoptive parents. Thus, at the same time that they appreciated the opportunity to be "out" in the open adoption process, these men also recognized that one potential liability associated with such openness was an extended wait period for a child. In this way, some men prioritized their values (i.e., the need to be open and honest about their sexuality) over pragmatics (i.e., a speedy adoption process).

Ten men in the study (including one couple) explicitly identified the fact that birth mothers were less likely to choose them as an additional challenge in the adoption process. These men had been warned by their agencies that they could expect to wait longer than heterosexual couples for a placement, given that "there are lots of other people out there that are going to probably look more appealing to most birth mothers because they're heterosexual." Such warnings were typically perceived as useful in helping the men to adjust their expectations and to develop a realistic timeline. Yet at the same time, they were frustrating and sometimes-painful reminders of the potentially long and uncertain road that lay ahead, and of the complex and multiple ways in which their sexuality and gender marked them as undesirable and "deviant" as potential parents. Russell, a 41-year-old White executive director who lived with his partner, David, in an urban area on the West Coast, recalled their initial encounter with one adoption agency:

And [the social worker] said, "You know, I have to tell you that our waiting period is twice as long for gay couples." She said the waiting period is on average twice as long for gay couples because mothers are just less likely to choose a gay couple. And she said, "If you're kind of on a schedule, then that is something you need to consider." And, you know, being 40-plus years old it's like, yeah, we kind of are on a schedule! So that was good advice and we didn't go with them. But it really, you know, I can understand a straight mother, you know, she understands the straight world, she's looking at this group of families, and she is going to idealize her family, and imagine her family for her child.

Russell described a sense of urgency associated with his age, such that, at "40-plus years old," he did not feel he could afford to spend years waiting for a child. He and David chose to go with a different agency, one that advertised a more optimistic timeline for gay couples. Yet notably, at the same time that he expressed impatience about a potentially longer wait time for a child, Russell also sympathetically acknowledged some of the factors that might lead a birth mother to choose a heterosexual couple over a gay couple as the parents of her child. His perspective is nuanced in that he did not assume that birth mothers' preference for heterosexual couples is necessarily rooted in homophobia. Rather, he considered the power of the simple fact that most birth mothers' preferences are shaped by their own family-of-origin experiences—most of which involve heterosexual parents—and by the broader heterosexual nuclear family ideal.

In several cases, men presumed that not only were they likely to wait longer than heterosexual couples, but they were also less likely to be placed with "healthy, Caucasian babies" compared to heterosexual couples. It was their sense that the "perfect babies" were simply more likely to go to the "perfect couples"—namely, heterosexual couples. They explained that babies who were non-White, were drug- or alcohol-exposed, or had known physical or mental handicaps were less likely to be accepted by heterosexual couples, and in turn, would be offered to them. This intuition mirrors previous research suggesting that agencies sometimes engage in a practice of trying to match the "least desirable" children (i.e., children with problems) with the "least desirable" applicants (i.e., lesbians and gay men) (Goldberg, Downing, & Sauck, 2007; Mallon, 2004; Matthews & Cramer, 2006; Ryan, Pearlmutter, & Groza, 2004). As the anthropologist Ellen Lewin (2009) observed, "In a system that ranks prospective parents according to a calculus of relative desirability, gay men tend to move to last place when children are allocated" (p. 32). In other words, as a microcosm of the larger society, adoption agencies operate within a heteronormative framework that marks gay men as deviant on multiple accounts, thereby making them acceptable parents only to the "least acceptable" children. Speaking to this notion, Thomas, the 36-year-old White real estate agent, asserted:

Most Caucasian babies will be adopted out, I believe, to straight couples. Unless—there is always that percentage [of birth mothers] that has a brother that is gay or an uncle that is gay; they have a connection with it.

They are more open. Other than that . . . there were 21 . . . birth mothers [working with our agency] and all of those birth mothers are having Caucasian babies and they are all going with straight couples.

Some men disclosed that because some birth mothers would perceive their sexuality as a liability, they felt pressure to "outdo" heterosexual couples on other fronts. For example, they hoped that by showcasing their educational attainment, their financial security, and their love of travel, they might attract the attention of some potential birth mothers. At the same time, some of these men expressed some reluctance about "showing off" their privileged lifestyle. For example, they observed that such purposeful displays of their relative wealth and resources further highlighted the social class inequities between adoptive parents and birth parents, a reality that made them uncomfortable. Others voiced a discomfort with such displays because they simply disliked the idea of "selling" themselves to prospective birth mothers—and yet they viewed such "showing off" as necessary in order to be competitive in the adoption process, as it served to offset the "liability" of their sexual orientation. Luis, a 45-year-old Latino man, worked as a surgeon, and his partner, Henry, was employed as a physical therapist. Luis described feeling a tension between wanting to stand out as prospective parents but also feeling uncomfortable with the idea of marketing themselves to prospective birth mothers:

We both feel that it's sort of—we feel that we have to do so much more than, you know, a straight couple would. When we were putting together our profile, we sort of figured, "God, you know, we really have to make this look so much better." You know, as if being the gay couple isn't going to make us stand out enough, we really felt that we needed to, not make excuses for it, but sell ourselves even more and that was just sort of, you know. . . . Again, the whole marketing point of it was a little bit distasteful to us but . . .

Thus, although Luis acknowledged that he did not feel entirely comfortable with the marketing aspect of open adoption, he nevertheless felt compelled to engage in it to get a child. In particular, he felt that he and Henry must "compensate" for their sexual orientation by "selling" their numerous strengths and assets. In this way, Luis and others illustrate how although gay men are marginalized for their sexual identities, those with class privilege can perhaps compensate for this. Financial resources may serve to offset other marginalized identities for any prospective adopter, such that a very affluent single adopter, for example, may be viewed as more desirable than a heterosexual married couple with few financial resources. Luis's and others' emphasis on their financial resources as a relative asset in the "competition" for a child highlights the complex configuration of privilege and marginality within and across families, and points to how certain types of families (e.g., gay male couples with few financial resources) may be doubly marginalized and disempowered in the adoption process.

Notably, 11 men (including one couple) actually framed their status as a gay male couple as a potential *advantage* with regard to being chosen by a birth mother. Intriguingly, these men all described having "heard"—primarily from their agencies and other gay adoptive parents—that some birth mothers purposefully opt for gay male couples because they wished to remain the only real or symbolic female in the child's life. That is, in contrast to heterosexual couples, in which there is one mother, and lesbian couples, in which there are two mothers, gay male couples represented a female-free parental unit. The birth mothers' perception as it was relayed to the men was that there was no female figure with whom to compete, no woman who would usurp the birth mother's maternal status, thereby rendering gay male couples the least threatening option. Russell, 41, explained, "We both heard that gay men would have the same luck or even better than a traditional couple, because a lot of birth mothers would want to be the only woman." Robbie, the 34-year-old White IT manager, similarly described a number of reasons why a birth mother might be more willing to choose a male couple over a heterosexual or lesbian couple, based on his recent conversation with a potential birth mother:

> In talking with the birth mom about why she was giving up her child for open adoption, she said that she did open adoption for a reason: she wants to somehow be connected or somehow be at least yearly or maybe every six months to be able to see the child and visit with the child. . . . So it was that safety net of, she is the only mother in the equation and that is real important to some of the birth moms. She likes that she is the only mom. Also, it seems like a couple [potential birth mothers] that we have spoken with, they have had issues in their past history where they didn't have good relationships with their fathers, so I think that they are looking for extra fathers in a way to be those type of roles. And as far as the same-sex [issue], what we were told by the birth mom was that she liked that it was a same-sex couple because with open adoption with a same-sex couple there is no hiding that the child is adopted, and with a straight couple that is not necessarily the case.

Here, in addition to highlighting some birth mothers' supposed preference for remaining the "only mom" in the child's life, Robbie also suggested that birth mothers' experiences and feelings about men, as well as their concerns about the possibility that heterosexual couples could be more likely to hide or minimize the adoption, might also play into their decision to place their child with a male same-sex couple. Although it is difficult to ascertain how commonly birth mothers express these sorts of considerations, their mention here does suggest that the agency party line—that gay couples are less likely to be chosen than heterosexual couples—is probably overly simplified (deBoer, 2009). Rather, *some* birth mothers, such as those with strong religious convictions and those who strongly value and adhere to a heterosexual, two-parent model for their child, are likely to prefer a heterosexual couple over a same-sex couple; whereas others, such as those who wish to cement their status as the only female in their child's life, those who wish to ensure that their child's adoptive status will be acknowledged, and those with gay family members or friends, may ultimately prefer a male same-sex couple. The possibility that some birth mothers may prefer gay men to heterosexual couples serves to complicate dominant stereotypes about birth mothers, such as the notion that birth mothers necessarily seek to place their child with a heterosexual married couple, thereby giving their child the family that they could not provide.

State Laws

State laws constituted a major systemic barrier for some of the couples. Couples who lived in states that did not allow same-sex couples to co-adopt were required to choose one partner to adopt as a single parent. Likewise, couples who adopted from abroad also had to choose one partner to adopt as a single parent, by virtue of the fact that none of the common sending countries (e.g., Russia, China) allows openly gay couples to adopt. As discussed, in such situations, the nonlegal partner can sometimes seek a second-parent adoption (which allows them to adopt their partner's child after the initial, official legal adoption) to ensure that their child will have two legal parents. In some states, however, same-sex couples have historically had little luck seeking second-parent adoptions (Goldberg, 2010a). Thus some same-sex couples are faced with making a decision about which partner will be the legal parent.

Choosing Who Will Be the Legal Parent

Thirteen of the couples in the study were required to choose one man to adopt as a single parent. These included eight couples who lived in states that did not permit co-parent adoptions by same-sex partners, three couples who matched with birth mothers who lived in states that did not permit co-parent adoptions by same-sex partners,[2] and two couples who were adopting internationally. These couples had to decide which partner would adopt as a single parent, and who, in turn, would be the sole legal adoptive parent, at least temporarily. Although the process of deciding who would be the primary adopter often highlighted differences in status and power between the partners, it was rarely described as causing any relational stress or tension. Rather, the decision of who should be the primary adopter was perceived by most of the men as relatively straightforward. In only one couple was it described as a decision that elicited conflict, such that it brought up concerns about equality in the relationship. This conflict, however, was easily resolved: the two men agreed to give their child the last name of the non-legal partner, who also intended to seek a second-parent adoption, as a means of "evening things out."

Most of these men discussed in their interviews how they had decided who would be the primary adopter. Four couples noted that they had been advised by their agencies to make the decision based on who made more money. Because they would be presenting themselves as single parents, only one of their incomes would be reflected, and thus they were encouraged to consider the fact that a lawyer's salary, for example, would likely be more attractive to a potential birth mother than a teacher's. In two cases, men's decisions were based in part on who had the higher job status (in both cases, one partner had a PhD or MD). Brendan, a 43-year-old White graduate student living in an urban area of the Midwest, acknowledged, "Kevin is more well established as far as the financial part of it. Plus, it doesn't hurt to be a psychologist." Four couples noted that their decision about who would be the one to pursue the initial adoption was based on which partner had better benefits, such as better health insurance or an adoption credit. One interracial (White and Latino) couple adopting internationally chose the Latino partner to pursue the initial adoption, since they felt that a single Latino man traveling with a Latin American child would raise fewer questions than a single White man traveling with a Latin American child. Finally, one couple chose the younger partner to be the primary adopter, out of concern that potential birth mothers might perceive the older partner's age (mid-40s) as a liability.

Although the process of deciding which partner would be the legal adoptive parent rarely caused interpersonal tension or conflict, it did elicit *intra*personal conflict in some of the men. Men who were unable to co-adopt experienced a range of emotions about being forced to formally closet their relationships and possibly risk having no legal relationship to their child. Three men expressed distress specifically about their invisibility and isolation during the adoption process. They felt "emotionally disenfranchised" and as though they "didn't exist" during the home-study process, in that their relationship—and their parental status—were not acknowledged. "I'm written up as a roommate; it has been horrible to have to be in the closet," shared Rett, 35. Four men experienced feelings of anger and worry specifically related to the possibility that they would not be legally related to their child. For example, Gregory, a 40-year-old White graduate student living in a suburb in the South, whose partner, Brian, was adopting from abroad, hoped to pursue a second-parent adoption when the primary adoption was complete. Brian, however, had suggested waiting to complete the second-parent adoption until they determined whether they would also seek to adopt a *second* child from abroad. By legally formalizing Gregory's relationship to their son, they were effectively declaring their status as a couple, thereby preventing a single-parent adoption in the future. But Gregory was uncomfortable with this suggestion:

> Brian said we could wait—and I thought, I'm not sure I like that, because it kind of reminded me that it's not just my rights, it's the child's rights. If I get killed in a car accident . . . the child has no rights to inherit anything from me. He has no rights to my Social Security, no one does actually. The adoption is also to give him rights to my assets and my government stuff.

Three men expressed mild negative emotions, noting that it was "irritating" and "a little demeaning" not to be able to adopt the child with their partner, but they also noted that "at least our agency treats us as a couple." In this way, they acknowledged feelings of annoyance with the systemic inequities they were forced to contend with, but they also expressed gratitude that on an informal, personal level, they were both being treated as the parents. Their agencies' support served to somewhat offset or mute the negative impact of being denied equal recognition at the state level (Goldberg, Downing, & Sauck, 2007).

Finally, three men expressed relatively neutral feelings about being unable to co-adopt, feeling resigned to having to "work the system," and noting that "the law is what it is and I can't change that in the near future, so if that is the way it has to be done then that's the route we are willing to go." When asked if the prospect of only his partner adopting had been stressful to contemplate, Brendan, the 43-year-old White graduate student, mused:

You know, it really hasn't been. Maybe it will be if it does have to happen that way, the reality of it might. Theoretically, I just think, whatever it takes to get the kid, within reason. Obviously, there are certain things you don't want to have to compromise on but if that's, like, the only thing I had to compromise on, I could live with that. It's not ideal but you have to work within the system. For lack of a better term, kind of play the game.

Brendan was aware that he might be unable to adopt his own child in his state of residence, but he accepted this as less important than his goal of actually becoming a parent. Recognizing his limited options, he had resigned himself to "play[ing] the game" to achieve his goal of becoming a parent. His behavior was framed in the language of accommodation rather than resistance; he viewed himself as working within the discriminatory legal system, rather than, say, tricking the system into allowing a gay couple to be parents.

Somewhat in contrast to Brendan's narrative is that of Barry, the 35-year-old White IT manager. Regarding the likelihood that his partner, Rett, would adopt as a single parent, Barry reflected:

It's a big part of my life to kind of negotiate my queerness in a straight world. So I guess I'm not a person who feels like he's beyond manipulating the system, even if that means having to suppress part of myself, or at least not publicly acknowledge it.

Barry viewed himself as "manipulating the system" by having one partner adopt as a single parent. At the same time, he referred to "suppress[ing]" parts of himself. In this way, he appeared somewhat conflicted or ambivalent regarding whether he perceived his behavior as radical and subversive (i.e., a strategy of resistance) versus assimilationist (i.e., a relatively passive response to the inequities in the legal system).

Minimizing Legal Inequities between Partners

At the post-adoptive placement interview, the majority of the nonlegal partners in these 13 couples noted their intention at least to *try* to seek a second-parent adoption. But not all men were confident that they would be successful. Six men lived in states with a solid track record of granting second-parent adoptions to same-sex couples and were very confident they would be able to adopt their child. Cooper, 39, whose partner, Frank, had completed the primary adoption in Texas, where their child's birth mother resided, asserted, "The second-parent adoption here in California is a piece of cake. We have our final court date for that in about a month and it is very simple to do." Five men were hopeful but somewhat uncertain about their ability to perform a second-parent adoption. These men noted that there was only one county or one judge in their state with a history of performing second-parent adoptions for same-sex couples, and unfortunately they did not live in that county or jurisdiction. These men intended to try to pursue a second-parent adoption but were not assured they would be able to do so, reflecting the unsteady legal landscape for gay couples in many parts of the United States (Goldberg, Downing, & Sauck, 2007; Human Rights Campaign, 2010). Joshua, the 40-year-old White administrative assistant whose story opened this chapter, explained:

> In North Carolina, basically, with a few exceptions, it's not feasible to do a two-party adoption. So once I've adopted, there's a possibility he can adopt, but we can't both petition for adoption at the same time because we're not really a couple. . . . So, it's conceivable that we could go for a [second]-parent adoption, but I know it's done in [county], but we don't live in [county], so I'm not sure what will happen in that regard. I don't know if we have to be a resident of that county.

Likewise, Carter, a 37-year-old White teacher who was living in a midwestern suburb, explained:

> There is one county that was well-known for doing second-parent adoptions and a high judge kind of took away all of the adoptions from that court and moved them to his own court. So there is one county in [our state] that will do them but you have to keep it kind of hush-hush and secret.

Carter described a subtle form of resistance whereby he and others were quietly working *within* the system, but also knowingly deceiving the system, in order to maintain the status quo (i.e., the limited legal rights to which they have access). Carter and others recognized that they were the less-powerful members in a system of power. They viewed this disadvantage as unfair, and they recognized, and grasped, opportunities to resist such power. In this way, they were part of a "common, albeit submerged stock of knowledge" (Ewick & Silbey, 2003, p. 1364).

Finally, two men were doubtful that they would be able to adopt successfully. One of these men noted that the judge in his county was new, and he was therefore unsure about whether she might rule favorably on second-parent adoption cases for same-sex couples. But he noted grimly, based on how the judges in neighboring counties had ruled on this issue, that there was no reason to be optimistic. The other man noted that the legal validity of all the second-parent adoptions that had been performed for same-sex couples in his county was currently being challenged, and therefore he was not optimistic about the prospect of being able to legally adopt his child.

Second-parent adoptions undoubtedly represent the most powerful legal means by which gay men who are unable to co-adopt can ultimately assert their parental status. They ensure that the rights of both parents are protected, and allow both parents to claim their child as a dependent for tax purposes, to provide health insurance to their child from their employers, to take their child to the hospital for emergency care, and to share child custody and support in the event that their relationship dissolves. Further, they provide a "seal of legitimacy" that may facilitate the previously nonlegal parent's sense of entitlement and parental confidence in relation to their child (Connolly, 2002b). But the men in this study recognized that second-parent adoptions are not the only means of asserting one's parental rights. Men who were uncertain about their ability to secure second-parent adoptions, as well as men who intended to pursue them but were unable to initiate the process until the primary adoption was finalized, employed other creative strategies aimed at minimizing both the legal and symbolic inequities to which they were exposed. Such strategies represented men's best attempts to create legal protections for the nonlegal parent (Bergen, Suter, & Daas, 2006). For example, seven men stated that they had updated their wills to reflect their new parental commitments—that is, their child was now reflected in their inheritance plans. Two couples mentioned that the legal adoptive partner had explicitly named the nonlegal partner as the child's guardian. Gregory, the 40-year-old White graduate student who lived in a suburb in the South, explained:

> We have to wait until he has been in the home for a year [to do the second-parent adoption] but we will have all of the paperwork ready to go. What we did do, for me, was draw up papers to declare me a legal guardian, which was great. The attorney we called . . . drew up special paperwork for the judge to sign saying that Brian is not relinquishing any of his parental rights. It just feels good because it feels like we covered something that we couldn't cover in a will or trust because we are both alive.

Arranging these alternative legal protections is expensive, and therefore is not really an option for lesbians and gay men with limited financial resources (Herek, 2006). This example highlights again the importance of class privilege in navigating and partially circumventing inequities in the adoption process.

Seven men stated that they had or were planning to hyphenate their child's last name as a means of communicating, without any doubt, that both men were equal and valid parents. For a few men, the importance of this gesture to the (currently nonlegal) partner was made clear during their first encounters with the outside world as parents. As Robbie, the 34-year-old White IT manager, learned, hyphenated names can function as particularly important communicators of parent-child relationships in the medical setting (Bergen, Suter, & Daas, 2006):

> It seemed like the natural thing to do [to hyphenate]. I know that when Finn went to his first visit at the doctor, they didn't have it as a hyphen, and legally, it makes him feel like less of a parent. It's just, it's just the situation and thinking back, he's more sensitive when it comes to that. If I would have known it was going to go this way . . . The reason we went this route to start with, with me as the primary, was because I get an adoption credit from work. If I would have known that it was going to be this, that it was going to turn out like this, I would have flipped it just because I wouldn't have, just because to me, it wouldn't have bothered me like it does him.

Hyphenating their child's last name was viewed by Robbie as one way to minimize Finn's sensitivity to the fact that he had not been the primary adopter, by clearly signaling his relationship to his child, and his relationship to Robbie, to the outside world. In this way, naming practices (such as hyphenating the child's name, or using one partner's last name as the "family" name) were used by some men to communicate family relationships (i.e., to "do family") in a way that was recognizable by their broader sociocultural context—a context that offered little in the way of structural support and recognition for same-sex relationships and families (Almack, 2005; Clarke, Burns, & Burgoyne, 2008). Men in the study resisted the power of heteronormative social structures to define (or fail to define) their family relationships, by actively employing the symbolic resources they had available to them. Their use of naming to assert their family status served as a symbolic form of resistance to heteronormative practices, such as marriage, that are employed to award certain symbolic privileges, such as shared names, to heterosexual couples only.

Perceptions of Legal and Symbolic Vulnerability:
Gay Men Consider Marriage

Regardless of whether they were able to adopt jointly, most of the men in the study felt that their families were legally vulnerable in relation to the outside world. Even when both men's relationships with their children were protected, they did not necessarily have access to marriage or civil unions, which rendered their relationships to *each other*, and their family unit as a whole, legally and symbolically vulnerable. Even among the few men who did have access to both co-parent adoptions and civil unions/marriage at the time of the interviews, some nevertheless recognized that while their family relationships were *legally* recognized, they were not necessary viewed as *symbolically* equivalent to those of heterosexual-parent families.[3] Many of the men in the study therefore experienced anxieties related to a number of situations (e.g., traveling, hospitalizations, registering their child for school) in which their rights vis-à-vis one another and their status as a family might be questioned. Daniel, a 38-year-old White graduate student who lived in the rural Northeast, recalled, "The head of our agency told us, whenever you're traveling around, two men and a baby, you have to have all the paperwork because depending on what state you're in, they're going to pull you over and not believe that this child is yours." Barry, the 35-year-old White IT manager who lived in a midwestern city, anticipated potential challenges in a variety of areas, including "dealing with the school system, hospitals, filling out forms. I guess I expect that frustration of having to explain our family situation. I guess I'm going into it expecting that I'll have to carry around a birth certificate, expecting that maybe traveling to a different country might cause problems."

For some men, becoming a parent had increased their awareness of their legal vulnerability, and, by extension, the importance of legal equality—particularly marriage equality—for same-sex couples. Charged by a sense of increased protectiveness for their children and families, 20 men (including two couples) expressed that they had become more concerned about the effect of not having certain legal protections like marriage, and they often espoused a more fervent interest in the possibility of securing marriage rights for same-sex partners. Some men's enhanced interest in achieving marriage equality was rooted in practical concerns: for example, they wanted access to their partner's health benefits, or they wanted to be able to file their taxes jointly. Trevor, a 38-year-old White man who worked as a technical support technician and who lived in a city on the West Coast with his partner, Richard, explained that although marriage had not seemed very important in the past, he now realized that if he and Richard were married, he would no longer have to work and could stay home with their child:

It has never [meant much] in the past but now that Chloe is here and I so badly wanted to just quit my job and stay home, it makes me a little bitter to think that if Richard and I could legally be married, I would be on his medical plan, dental plan, that kind of thing. If I wanted to . . . I *could* pay off the house we are living in and we would be [financially] comfortable, but I *can't* do that because I wouldn't have medical insurance, and that really makes me mad. It's just like, if we could legally be married then I could do that without a problem, but I can't because I need medical insurance because you never know what is going to happen.

Some of these men noted that they were more concerned about legal equality now that they were parents, because they felt it would add validation to their family unit and protect themselves and their children from discrimination. They emphasized that legal and social recognition of their partner unions was important because they did not want their *children*, in particular, to feel like second-class citizens. They wished that they could get married so that their children would recognize that their families were no less real or valid than heterosexual-parent families (i.e., they were not "pseudo-families"; see Oswald, Blume, & Marks, 2005). For example, when asked if his feelings about marriage had changed, Russell, 41, asserted emphatically, "Yes. It is weird that that changes but it does. I think with the addition of Christopher, it becomes more important. I don't want him as a child to feel second-class status about his family."

Interestingly, even among men who lived in socially progressive areas where they perceived little heterosexist discrimination, marriage seemed more important than it had pre-parenthood. Cooper, a 39-year-old multiracial physician assistant who lived in an urban area of California with his partner, Frank, asserted:

In California, the domestic partner benefits are pretty equivalent to marriage. It is pretty clearly spelled out in the law that you have adoption rights, medical and legal decisions—that stuff is pretty clear. I think it starts getting . . . there are a lot of inequities in the law like when it comes to things like taxes, eligibility for pension, there are still a lot of inequities. [Being able to get legally married] would make certain things easier. I think that in the eyes of probably society in general, it would probably add some validation to our family as a unit.

Likewise, Jake, a 30-year-old White graduate student living in a suburb of California with his partner, Sam, expressed that he had always felt strongly about marriage equality, believing that it was important on "a couple of levels," but emphasized that the "legal aspect" had become even more important when he became a parent. Further, he became increasingly bothered by the fact that although he could co-adopt his child with his partner, they could not get married, finding it "silly that we can be legally joined in parenthood but not in marriage."

This group of men desired marriage largely because they valued the symbolic and structural supports associated with it, and resisted the notion that they should be denied this symbolic and structural capital because of their sexuality. Their narratives reveal their conviction that lesbian and gay people should have the same right as the heterosexual majority. These men do not describe marriage equality, and their desire for it, as assimilationist; rather— perhaps in part due to the recent arrival of children—they appear to view the pursuit of relationship recognition rights as simply "rational," as one man said.

Many men, on the other hand, noted little change in their attitudes about and interest in marriage equality since becoming parents. Some of these men simply expressed that they had "always believed in marriage equality, and that hasn't changed with a kid," and indicated that they would most likely pursue marriage if it were available to them (26 men). Other men also described little change in their feelings about marriage, stating that they would likely pursue marriage if it was accessible to same-sex couples, but specifically noted that they felt relatively secure without it—a feeling that had not changed with parenthood (18 men). These men typically attributed their sense of security to their geographic location: their state had allowed them to adopt their child jointly or had passed registered domestic partner laws.[4] Indeed, nine men (including one couple) highlighted the fact that they had been able to co-adopt their child, and nine men (including two couples) emphasized their states' domestic partner laws (specifically, those of California, Washington, and Oregon), in explaining why they had few legal insecurities. Thus their access to state-level legal supports and recognition had helped to minimize their legal anxieties, such that they felt "almost on equal footing" with heterosexual couples with regard to legal protections. Richard, the 37-year-old White urban planner who lived in Oregon, emphasized that his sense of security was directly tied to the fact that he and his partner had been able to co-adopt their daughter. It is interesting to contrast his perspective, below, with the sentiments of his partner, Trevor, who described—in a previous passage—a strong desire for marriage equality so that he could obtain health insurance through his partner's employer and could therefore stop working. Richard stated:

> I feel pretty comfortable that we can do what we need to do legally with . . .
> I mean, she belongs to both of us, so if something happened to one or the

other of us as far as she is concerned—or I should say as far as the state is concerned—[in terms of] our parental status, on paper, we look like any other couple. So actually no, I am not worried about that at all.

Likewise, Carl, a 41-year-old White fund-raising director who lived in California with his partner, Jason, highlighted their access to both co-parent adoption and registered domestic partnership benefits as fundamental to his sense of security:

> I feel like in California we are pretty well protected with a lot of that as long as we register as domestic partners with the state. Yeah, it feels like, we've got it covered. She's got health insurance so if something is wrong with her, it's all covered. As long as our wills and powers of attorney and all that include her, which is our responsibility, then that's taken care of. I feel like once [the co-parent adoption] is finalized, like everything is finalized, then it's set. That's why I feel lucky to live in this state. We don't have to worry about the laws and stuff that are against everybody else.

Finally, six men were relatively indifferent to the prospect of marriage equality. They explained that whether they had access to marriage did not have any great impact on their day-to-day lives, and they were therefore indifferent to the future of marriage for same-sex couples. For example, Jim, a 36-year-old White cook who lived with his partner, Timothy, in a northeastern suburb, asserted, "It is not something I think about every day. I'm not an activist by any means. . . . I mean, just let me live my life and I'll let you live yours. I'm not out there, basically. I'm not an activist."

Two of these six men said that they did not "believe in" the institution of marriage. As Elliott, the 40-year-old White man who lived in an urban area of the Northeast with his partner, Nolan, explained:

> I'm not one of these people where I'm like, we need the right to get married because to me . . . I look at straight people and their whole marriage and their idea of marriage and I don't know, I just, I don't necessarily want to be like that.

Elliott was clear that his choice to adopt a child did not imply or require that he wanted access to the heterosexual institution of marriage. He clearly regarded marriage as something that "straight people" do, and something that he rejected for himself.

Thus, strikingly, for many of the men adopting a child was connected with a greater interest in getting married. Their feelings about and reasons for getting married shifted after they adopted, such that they became increasingly concerned with the ways that the absence of marriage rights might pose problems for their child and their family. This finding—that many participants desired marriage equality and couched this desire in their wish to ensure that their children did not experience symbolic or structural disadvantage—is particularly notable in light of some scholars' theorizing that the arrival of children may provide couples with additional impetus to seek legal and social recognition for their union (Oswald, Goldberg, Kuvalanka, & Clausell, 2008; Solomon, Rothblum, & Balsam, 2004).

 At the same time, not all the men wished to get married. Indeed, the men's attitudes about, and level of interest in, marriage were quite variable, mirroring the findings of prior surveys of sexual minorities, which suggest that they are far from unanimous in their feelings about marriage. One large-scale survey found that one-fifth of sexual minority respondents said that they would not want to get married if marriage to a same-sex partner were legal (Kaiser Family Foundation, 2001). Research suggests that sexual minorities who reject marriage for themselves may do so because they are resistant to the entire institution of marriage, or because they perceive efforts to secure same-sex marriage as conformist in nature (Peel & Harding, 2004). In contrast, sexual minorities who wish to marry may believe that marriage will make them closer and more secure, in part by creating structural barriers to relationship dissolution. They also may be attracted to the legal rights and benefits conferred by same-sex marriage, which they perceive as important in alleviating stress and hassle in their daily lives (Lannutti, 2005).

Conclusion

 Gay men may face a multitude of barriers in their efforts to adopt. Specifically, they may encounter heterosexism and sexism at various levels of the adoption process, including the legal system, adoption agencies, and birth parents. Heterosexism is institutionalized in the form of laws that deny same-sex partners the right to co-adopt, as well as adoption agency policies that either explicitly prohibit agencies from working with lesbian and gay couples, or the absence of formal policies that prohibit social workers from discriminating based on sexual orientation. Heterosexism is also embodied more informally, such as in the form of some birth parents' prejudice against sexual minorities and their resistance to placing one's child with gay or lesbian parents. The men's relative lack of power in the adoption process

forced them in many cases to work within the system in order to
example, they were aware that efforts to forcefully challenge the
ist and sexist language and assumptions embedded in their agen
ment of them might bias their social workers against them, and ultimately
extend their wait for a child. Fear of further discrimination paralyzed some
men from acting on their own behalf. Men who lacked geographic mobil-
ity and financial privilege were particularly likely to feel immobilized. The
men, however, occasionally used the limited power that they possessed to
resist systems of domination, for example, by crossing out heteronormative
language on required paperwork to accurately represent their families. These
men's experiences highlight how people in positions of lesser power are often
rendered immobile by intersecting systems of power—but they also show
how the less powerful may employ their limited resources as a form of (often
symbolic) resistance (Ewick & Silbey, 2003).

Many of the men whom I interviewed had found adoption agencies that
were respectful and supportive of them as gay prospective parents, and some
men had encountered birth mothers who selected them *because* they were
gay men. Thus adoption agencies and birth mothers, at times, served to challenge heteronormativity in that they resisted hegemonic discourses and supported gay men's efforts to build a family. In doing so, they arguably play a
role in facilitating the societal shift toward recognition of a broader range of
family forms. Nonetheless, all the men's family-building efforts were affected
to varying degrees by broader social discourses and institutions that uphold
heterosexual parenthood as the "ideal" (Goldberg, 2010a). Men who lived in
states that were more progressive or had more supportive laws pertaining to
gay adoption, as well as men who worked with gay-friendly adoption agencies, encountered fewer barriers and seemed to experience less stress. The
men's specific social locations thereby mediated the effects of institutionalized heterosexism, exposing men to varying levels of injustice and hardship.

The men expressed varying levels of frustration over legal discrimination.
Among those men who were not able to jointly adopt their children, some
men were fairly indifferent and apolitical, having resigned themselves to the
inequities inherent in the adoption system, whereas others expressed pro-
found feelings of anger and helplessness. In some cases, men used the limited
resources available to them to resist or lessen the inequities imposed on them
by the legal system. For example, by employing wills and powers of attorney,
men actively sought to protect themselves and their families amid broader
legal injustices. Likewise, upon becoming parents, some men described a
heightened awareness of legal insecurities and a corresponding increased
valuing of and desire for civil marriage. Others, however, regarded marriage

as relatively unimportant, often because they perceived themselves as having sufficient protections. Men living in states that offered domestic partnership benefits, for example, often did not see the necessity of marriage. To some extent, then, men's relative economic and geographic privilege appeared to shape their perspectives on marriage equality. In a few cases, the men's lack of interest in marriage seemed to stem from their perception of marriage as a problematic institution. Thus gay prospective fathers and adoptive fathers are a diverse group. Although they are arguably undertaking a public and even political act by seeking out fatherhood as gay men, many of them do not view themselves as particularly political—nor do they want to be. Rather, they simply want to become fathers.

This chapter reveals how the men's sexual orientation intersected with other social locations to shape their vulnerability and response to heteronormativity. Geographic privilege allowed the men to circumvent some forms of heteronormativity in the adoption process, such that, for example, men in gay-friendly, progressive areas were less likely to encounter agencies that treated them as deviant. Likewise, the men's geographic location influenced their access to various forms of legal protections for their families. Financial privilege further enabled some men to circumvent or minimize the negative effects of heteronormativity (e.g., by purchasing wills and powers of attorney). Thus the men's complex configuration of privilege and marginality influenced their exposure to both interpersonal and structural forms of heteronormativity and heterosexism.

3

Engaging Multiple Roles and Identities

Men's Experiences (Re)negotiating Work and Family

Sam, a 36-year-old White financial analyst, and Jake, a 30-year-old White doctoral student, were living in a suburb on the West Coast when they adopted their daughter, Hannah, via private domestic open adoption. Sam earned an income of more than $200,000 a year, while Jake made about $20,000 as a teaching assistant at the university where he was working on his doctorate. In explaining their decision to have Jake stay at home part-time while continuing to work on his degree, both men agreed that it "just made sense" from a financial stand-point. But they both also agreed that Jake could not be a full-time stay-at-home parent, because he did not want to halt progress on his doctoral degree.

When they adopted Hannah, both men felt somewhat torn about using a day care center. For example, Sam observed that Jake would "very much like not to have her be there. And I would also prefer that she's not there but I don't think that my feelings are as strong as his. . . . But of course right now there is no other option, especially when he's working on his degree and I need to work." Likewise, Jake expressed a sense of discomfort, even guilt, about the fact that his daughter was in day care part-time. He observed that he and Sam were financially stable and could probably afford to have one of them—or even both of them—stay home full-time with Hannah temporarily.

Both men loved parenthood but they both acknowledged challenges related to balancing work and family, and, specifically, to their part-time worker/full-time worker arrangement. Sam expressed empathy for Jake, observing that he had the "hardest job" in that he was trying to finish his dissertation while acting as the primary caregiver to Hannah. Sam, in turn, tried to do "as much as I can on the weekends" and also to "do the early-morning feedings and the middle of the night and stuff like that." Jake similarly noted that his biggest challenge was trying to "fit work in around everything else," but he gave Sam credit for helping out as much as possible. Sam's efforts to help—and Jake's willingness to let him—likely helped to account for the fact that neither partner felt particularly concerned that Hannah would become overly attached to Jake, a pattern present in some of the other primary caregiver/secondary caregiver families. As Jake pointed out:

> When I'm feeding her I feel completely bonded, and when he feeds her he feels the same way. I don't think there's an issue of jealousy, ever. We don't argue about who gets up at the middle of the night and we tend to stay respectful of each other in the sense that if I got up at night . . . then [the next day] he's happy to do [it]. Likewise . . . when I have the day off, the next day I'm more willing to give Sam a break. You know, it's good.

* * *

Becoming a parent is a major life transition, and one that requires individuals to shift their existing repertoire of roles and identities to make room for that of a parent. The division of paid and unpaid labor, for example, is often renegotiated when couples become parents (Deutsch, 1999). In heterosexual couples, this "renegotiation" process is often gendered, whereby women tend to reduce their hours in paid employment and take on more of the unpaid work (child care and housework; see Baxter, Hewitt, & Haynes, 2008; Kluwer, Heesink, & van de Vliert, 2002). Lesbian couples tend to share paid and unpaid work more equally than do heterosexual couples (Patterson, Sutfin, & Fulcher, 2004), although some lesbian couples choose a more specialized pattern, such that one mother spends more time in child care and the other mother retains greater responsibility for paid work (Goldberg & Perry-Jenkins, 2007; Reimann, 1997; Sullivan, 1996).

No research has explored division of labor patterns and processes among gay fathers in depth, although a few studies have dealt with this topic more cursorily (Bergman, Rubio, Green, & Padron, 2010; Gianino, 2008; Mallon, 2004). The study of how gay male couples negotiate the division of paid and unpaid labor is important, given that paid work has historically been associated with and viewed as a hallmark of masculinity, while housework and child care are deeply intertwined with notions of femininity (Coltrane, 2000; Kroska, 2003). As *gay men*, the individuals in the study are positioned to resist and disrupt such linkages, in that they pursue parenthood in a nonheterosexual relational context; but, at the same time, in that they are *men*, they are necessarily vulnerable to and may internalize (or at least wrestle with) such associations.

Deciding Who Will Reduce Their Time in Paid Employment

In heterosexual couples, the decision is typically not whether the mother *or* the father should stay at home, but whether the mother should continue to work or stay at home (Ericksen, Jurgens, Garrett, & Swedburg, 2008; Lupton & Schmied, 2002). In part, this is a function of the fact that historically, both men and women have tended to view the husband as the main economic provider, and the woman as the more appropriate parent to stay at home, at least temporarily (Lupton & Schmied, 2002). Stereotypes of women as more "suited" to stay-at-home caregiving, because of their presumed innate capacity for nurturance, may also play into decisions about the distribution of paid and unpaid work in early parenthood (Stoller, 2002). The reality that women often earn less than men may also lead couples to decide that it "just makes more sense" for the woman to stay home, at least part-time (Brandon, 1999). Gay male couples, in that they consist of two men, cannot rely on the gender structure to dictate the division of unpaid and paid labor. The question then becomes how couples in which both partners do not continue to work full-time explain their decision making about which partner will stay home or reduce their work hours.

In 14 of the 35 couples in the study, both partners continued to work full-time after becoming parents; in 16 couples, one partner continued to work full-time and one partner worked part-time; and in five couples, one partner continued to work full-time and one partner stayed at home full-time. Thus the following discussion refers to the 21 couples in which one partner reduced their work hours or stopped working altogether.

Income

Men in nine of the couples pointed to the difference in partners' income as the deciding factor in who would be the primary caregiver: the partner who made less money was described as the better choice for who should stay home, at least part-time. For example, Henry, a 45-year-old biracial physical therapist, maintained a small private practice, and his partner, Luis, was employed as a surgeon in the northeastern city where they lived. When asked how he and Luis decided who would cut down their work hours, Henry joked, "Well, salary. That surgeon thing really won over! But really, bottom-line, it was just money." Thus Henry suggested that had it not been for his partner's greater earning power, it might have just as easily been Luis who stayed home. Unspoken was the fact that Luis also had a higher-status career that had required more years of education to achieve, which Luis may have been more reluctant to give up. Indeed, Henry—as well as the other men in this category—focused on *income differences* within the partnership, as opposed to *status differences*, even though, in all nine couples, the partner with the higher income also had a higher level of education (in most cases, a doctorate) and a higher-status career.

Job Flexibility

Men in nine couples noted that the decision about who would reduce their hours in paid employment from full-time to part-time was in part influenced by one partner's greater job flexibility. Men defined "job flexibility" as having a fair degree of control over their hours and schedule, such that they were able to temporarily reduce their hours without penalty or job loss, work from home at least some days, or flex their hours. Men who were self-employed were particularly likely to describe their jobs as flexible, in that they often had the advantage of being able to dictate their own hours. For example, Frank, a 39-year-old White physician in private practice, had the ability to make his own hours—in contrast to his partner, Cooper, who worked as a physician assistant at a nearby county hospital. Frank shared, "I am half-time. And I am also working it out to come back only about three and a half days a week. So I will always be here [on] Fridays." In addition to being self-employed, being a student was described as a condition that promoted greater work flexibility, and served to influence the choice of who would stay home. Men who were enrolled in undergraduate or graduate programs had the flexibility of taking a reduced course load in order to stay at home at least part-time. Of note is that job flexibility (e.g., flexibility in terms of where and when work gets done) is more typical of white-collar as opposed to blue-collar jobs (Rosenfeld, 2001). Thus these men's social class and occupational standing affords them the privilege of considering job flexibility in determining who should stay home.

Job Dissatisfaction

Men in five couples noted that one partner's job dissatisfaction served as the "tipping point" in deciding who should stay home. These men—and their partners—emphasized that they were eager to "opt out" of what they viewed as unpleasant, unsatisfying, or menial jobs and to "opt in" to a parenting job that they viewed as inherently more worthwhile. Job dissatisfaction, coupled with a desire to be the primary caregiver, led these men to reduce or eliminate their time in paid employment. For example, James, a 41-year-old White man living in a city on the West Coast, who had previously worked as an urban planner, knew long before he quit his job that he intended to stay home with their child. He described how lack of fulfillment in the work sphere facilitated his process of "detaching" from his job, as he turned his energy toward parenting:

> Emotionally and practically, I was beginning the preparation of detaching [before I quit]. And I had been with the company for 10 years so a lot of my responsibilities, I needed to train up other people, I needed to pass that off to other people. Once we decided we were going to adopt, I told them, "Hey, ultimately, if we do have a child, I'll be leaving work." So I told them that there was a possibility that I might quit to stay home and we all collectively needed to be prepared for that to happen.

It is interesting to consider whether these men's positioning as *gay* men enabled them to feel freer to give up paid employment to stay home with their children. That is, they may have been more critical of and able to resist heteronormative discourses that equate paid employment with masculinity (Coltrane, 1996).

Better "Equipped"

Finally, men in four couples described one partner (i.e., themselves or their partner) as better "suited" to being the primary caregiver. Daniel, 38, explained, "When we would talk about it, [we said] that I would be the one that is a little bit more stable to stay at home, and he didn't think that he would be able to handle it so much (*laughs*)." Likewise, Henry, 45, explained, "I have 10 nieces and nephews, I've been around children for so long, it was more natural for me, actually, to be the one to do it." Thus emotional stability and patience, as well as prior experience with children, were identified as factors that made one partner a better candidate for the job of primary caregiver. These attributes are more often associated with the role and identity of "mother" than the stereotype of "father" (Johnston & Swanson, 2003). Yet the men did not identify these attributes as gendered, suggesting that in the context of two men, such characteristics may not be conceived of in terms of the heteronormative template.

Actively Negotiating Paid and Unpaid Labor Arrangements

As noted, in 14 couples, both partners were working full-time at the time of the follow-up interview (FT-FT); in 16 couples, one partner was working full-time and one partner was working part-time (FT-PT); and in five couples, one partner was working full-time and one partner was staying home full-time with the child (FT-SAH). Men in these three types of couples described both negative and positive aspects of their arrangements. Although there was overlap in the types of challenges and benefits described by men across groups (e.g., full-time employed fathers articulated challenges related to lack of time regardless of whom they were partnered with), there were also clear, although sometimes subtle, group differences. The men's perceptions of the negative and positive aspects of their arrangement were shaped not only by their own employment status (full-time, part-time, or nonemployed) but also by the employment status of their partner.

FT-FT Arrangements: Perceptions of Negative Aspects

The 28 men in the 14 couples in which both partners worked full-time in paid employment cited both negative and positive aspects of their arrangement. Namely, the time constraints associated with their arrangement (not enough time with their child; not enough time to keep the household running) were identified as drawbacks of their arrangement, and a greater sense of "balance" and the socialization benefits of day care for their child were identified as advantages.

"I WANT TO BE HOME MORE!"
Eleven men (including two couples) stated explicitly that the hardest thing about their current arrangement was that they were not at home with their child as much as they would like. These men strongly preferred to be working less and be at home more—and in some cases, vocalized their wish to quit their jobs to stay home full-time with their child. And yet, according to these men, their financial situation required that both partners be employed full-time. For example, Devon, a 47-year-old White man living in

a suburb in the South, described how he had recently returned to work out of financial necessity, after several months of leave from his job as an administrative assistant:

> It is still kind of rough because a lot of the time, when I get up in the morning—I am still getting used to the schedule, but I will sit there and feed her and change her and all of a sudden I just find myself not wanting to go anywhere. I just want to stay home with her. . . . But, I mean, it's just impossible to live on one income. Well, obviously people do it, but not us.

The tension between wanting to stay home but needing to work is one that is frequently voiced by some full-time employed heterosexual mothers but rarely by full-time employed heterosexual fathers (Johnston & Swanson, 2006; Rochlen, Suizzo, McKelley, & Scaringi, 2008). Working mothers also more frequently emphasize their desire to spend more time with their children as compared to working fathers (Roxburgh, 2006), although some studies of egalitarian men find that they describe similar sentiments (Coltrane, 1996; Henwood & Procter, 2003). These gay men's high investment in their parental role may in part be a reflection of their strong motivation to parent (Tyebjee, 2003) and their preference for egalitarianism (Carrington, 1999), as well as the fact that their relational context as two men does not allow them to "pin" the greater responsibility for child care on their partner, as might be the case in heterosexual couples (Goldberg, 2010b).

Most of these men were generally satisfied with their day care arrangements, which ranged from nannies to center-based care to family day care arrangements. But at the same time that they praised their child-care providers and acknowledged their good fortune in securing high-quality child care, they nevertheless expressed the wish that they could be the ones caring for their child. Corey, a 31-year-old White journalist living in an urban area of the South, confided:

> You know, there's a piece of me that I want to teach him, you know, that people have to work and, you know, if you want a nice life, you have to work. But the other side of me is like, I wish that we never had to send him to day care even though they are so nice and they take such good care of him. . . . But every morning, I feel like I have to put on a happy face in front of the women at the day care when I hand him over to them. You know, that's always kind of a thing at the top of my mind. Every time I hand him to them, I feel like I have this fake smile because I don't want to. I don't want to have to take him in there at all.

Men like Corey struggled to reconcile their yearning to spend more time with their child with the perceived need to work outside the home full-time. Contributing to their internal struggle may be the stigma associated with day care, which persists despite research showing that day care itself is not inherently bad for children, but rather that the quality of the day care is more consistently linked to child outcomes (Guendouzi, 2006; Holcomb, 1998; Howes, 1990). This stigma may contribute to a sense of guilt, where men feel ambivalent about their choice to place their child in day care and question whether it is the right thing to do.

THE TIME CRUNCH

Ten men described feeling that a major drawback of having both partners work full-time was that there were simply not enough hours in the day to do all the things they needed to do—much less enjoy time alone, either individually or as a couple. Finding the time to pay bills, do routine housework such as laundry and dishes, and return telephone calls was a daily challenge. Further, with both men were working, they could not pass off these duties to anyone else—although several men did mention that they had made the decision to employ a (typically female) housekeeper soon after they brought their child home. In this way, financial resources enabled some men to "buy out" of housework in order to spend more time with their children and partners, illustrating the role of economic privilege in offsetting potential stress in gay men's lives (Carrington, 1999).

Yet all of these men, even those who were able to buy out of certain forms of unpaid labor, described the daily challenge of trying to balance work, parenthood, their intimate relationships, and household management. Nathan, a 38-year-old White man who worked as the assistant director of a museum in a northeastern suburb, described:

> I do feel like I'm strapped for time. I get up in the morning—now mind you, Leah sleeps 10 hours a night, so again, we're going pretty good!— but from the moment I get up in the morning to the moment I lay down at night, every single minute of my time is accounted for, whether it is with Leah—and you want to spend quality time with her, you know? Or, you know, realizing "I have to do that laundry," or "Why didn't the housekeeper come today?," and figuring out, you know, "I've got to pay bills," to returning telephone calls, planning her baptism—there is always something. And the hardest thing for me is, I used to be able to carve out, I don't know, an hour a day for me to be reading or watching some idiotic

sitcom for an hour just to turn my brain off. . . . I don't have that anymore and that's been tough.

FT-FT Arrangements: Perceptions of Positive Aspects

BALANCE ("WE TREASURE OUR TIME WITH OUR CHILD")

Some men articulated advantages or positive aspects associated with their full-time/full-time arrangement. Echoing prior research with employed gay fathers (Schacher, Auerbach, & Silverstein, 2005) and employed hetero-sexual fathers (Haddock & Rattenborg, 2003), six men (including one cou-ple) emphasized that they enjoyed working and would not want to give up their jobs or careers to stay home. They were grateful to have jobs that they loved and derived satisfaction from, and felt that working outside the home afforded them greater balance and perspective than they would have if they were home all day with their child. Richard, a 37-year-old White urban plan-ner, felt that the fact that he and his partner, Trevor, were both working made them appreciate their time with their child more, as compared to when they were both on leave: "Now in the evening, instead of 'Will you take her for awhile?,' it's like, 'I get her next!' (*laughs*). Because we are both much more aware of the time we are spending with her and that's cool, I feel good about all of that." Likewise, Shane, a 32-year-old White sales representative, noted, "We did enroll him in day care, which has been great, because we can get so much done during the day and we find that we're just more attentive to him in the evenings." These men perceived their time away from their child—engaged in work that they enjoyed—as facilitating their ability to appreciate the time that they did spend with their child. They therefore demonstrated resistance to cultural discourses about the importance of a stay-at-home parent (Dillaway & Pare, 2008), apparently choosing to focus on the ways their involvement in enjoyable work might enhance their capacity to be good parents.

"OUR CHILD BENEFITS FROM DAY CARE"

At the same time that these working fathers often struggled to leave their children in the hands of non-parental caregivers, they also commented on the benefits they believed their children would enjoy as a function of being around other caregivers or children. Four men noted that they felt that being in day care afforded their child certain benefits that he or she might not enjoy if one parent was home with them full-time. They described increased opportunities for social interaction and increased independence as benefits of high-quality day care. Derek, a 32-year-old White software consultant living in an urban area of the Northeast, explained how he believed that his daughter, Lucia, would benefit from being cared for by a nanny in their home while he and his partner, Roger, worked:

> I think it's good for the kid to have different caretakers. Like, I want her to enroll in school really early so that will make her even more adaptive in social situations. . . . I'm a big proponent of socialization. I've seen children who have not been around anyone else other than their one or two parents until they're about three or four and it's hard. It's a hard transition to the worlds of other people.

Likewise, Drew, a 33-year-old White retail manager who lived in a West Coast suburb, remarked:

> I could not be a full-time stay at home parent. I just couldn't. And, she's, you know, I think she is doing fine [at day care]. I sort of justify it as, well, she is getting a great experience that she wouldn't get with me sitting at home with her, but it is sort of true. I mean, I think she doesn't need a lot of that but I think it just is kind of what it is. It would drive me insane to stay home all day. I don't think I could do it and I don't think it would be good for her.

It is interesting to consider whether, as Drew stated, these men in part sought to "justify" their children's full-time status in outside child care by emphasizing the benefits of child care on their social and emotional development. By framing their children's enrollment in organized child care as facilitating their adaptability and social development, they may neutralize potential feelings of guilt and conflict associated with their full-time employed status. Indeed, mothers who use day care for their children believe that children in day care are better adjusted than are children who are kept at home (Erwin & Kontos, 1998). Believing that one's child is benefiting from child care is therefore self-protective, in that it frees one from regret and indecision.

FT-PT Arrangements: Part-Timers' Perceptions of Negative Aspects

The 16 men who were working part-time while their partners worked full-time voiced a variety of perceived drawbacks and benefits of their particular labor arrangements. Perceived negative aspects centered on difficulty prioritizing work while caring for a child, and adjusting to the shift in role associated with their reduced work status, whereas a perceived benefit of their arrangement was the sense of balance that working part-time and caregiving afforded them.

DIFFICULTY PRIORITIZING WORK

Nine men voiced their perception that one challenging aspect of their work-family arrangement—and, specifically, their status as a part-time worker, part-time caregiver—was simply making time for work. Their difficulty in this regard was directly linked to the nature of these men's work: they either were students or worked from home, making the separation of family and work especially difficult. Most of these men counted on their children's nap times and the evening hours to get work done, including writing papers and making telephone calls to clients and colleagues. By extension, they often found it challenging to fit work in around their children's unpredictable schedules, a situation that ultimately led them to feel "stressed." For example, when asked about how his partner, Chris—who was staying at home with their child and also working part-time—was handling the adjustment to parenthood, Eric, a 40-year-old Latino marketing executive living in a metropolitan area on the West Coast, observed:

> He's handling it very well. He enjoys it. He says it's not hard. The hard part is trying to juggle, when he's got to juggle a conference call and the baby needs a bottle. That's the stressful part. It's not really doing either one. It's just like having to juggle schedules and when things don't go as expected. Like usually, we're on the schedule and it works. But, you know, on those rare occasions when something changes, it can be difficult.

Similarly, when asked when he worked on schoolwork toward his master's degree, the 38-year-old Daniel, who lived in the rural Northeast, explained: "Evenings or on the weekends . . . on the weekends Vaughn will usually take her. A lot of the time during the day when she's sleeping, I can actually do my research, and then I'll write my papers and do that at night. But it's, you know, I'm trying to figure her [schedule] out."

Daniel was not alone in highlighting his reliance on his partner to get work done. Justin was a 42-year-old White man who was employed as a computer programmer for a small company in an urban area on the West Coast, but he had cut back his hours significantly when he and his partner, Dennis, adopted their toddler-aged son, Judah. Justin felt that he had to "battle" for time to get his own work done, now that Dennis's work seemed to take priority:

ıere's a certain amount of battling between Dennis and I because, of
ıurse, he's got a start-up company and could easily work 80 hours a week
if, you know, he had the time. So it's a bit of a battle between us for me to
get enough time to get some work in.

Here, Justin suggests that he perceives Dennis as somewhat unfairly prioritizing his own work over Justin's, an issue that had apparently caused some
tension. Although theoretically released from heteronormative scripts that
prioritize men's work over women's work, gay men in couples in which one
partner was working part-time sometimes encountered challenging power
dynamics such that the part-time worker was regarded as the "default" person for child care, and was therefore in a less-powerful position to advocate
for his own work needs and interests. In this way, structural arrangements,

as opposed to gender, contributed to differing expectations for men's "roles,"
and, in some cases, to differing levels of power within the couple, thereby
mirroring heteronorms where men's work lives take priority over women's.

SHIFT IN ROLE

For some men, cutting back their work hours to stay at home with their
child part-time created shifts in their daily schedules—and an accompanying
sense of isolation. Namely, for six men, spending half of their time caring for
a young child was perceived as difficult in that they felt somewhat deprived
of social stimulation and contact. Henry, the 45-year-old biracial physical
therapist, exclaimed, "Oh, it's definitely more isolating, definitely. And not
having other gay parents nearby—it is definitely different." Such feelings of
isolation and confinement were perhaps accentuated by these men's continued involvement in the paid employment sphere: juxtaposed with their jobs
as students, consultants, and therapists, their work as infant caregivers could
seem even more isolating.

For three men, going from full-time to part-time meant a shift in income
that ultimately challenged them to revise their perception of their provider
or breadwinner status. Rufus, 37, the White self-employed computer programmer, revealed:

You know, I struggled with it more than I thought I would. I'm in a little
playgroup with another guy who adopted a girl. And he was never the primary breadwinner in his relationship with his partner and so he's more
naturally taken to that role. And I used to be the primary breadwinner, so
it's been sort of weird for me . . . it just feels weird for me to always be relying on him for money.

Rufus suggests that he identified more with an image or identity of himself as the primary breadwinner than he had realized, such that relinquishing that role caused a "weird" shift in his identity. Consistent with prior research on gay fathers (Schacher, Auerbach, & Silverstein, 2005) and heterosexual stay-at-home fathers (Doucet & Merla, 2007), Rufus indicated that he continues to be influenced by dominant notions of traditional masculinity, which emphasize breadwinning and climbing the corporate ladder (Coltrane, 1996; Maurer, Pleck, & Rane, 2001). Thus, at the same time that he was actively constructing an identity for himself that deviated from dominant constructions of masculinity (e.g., he is a gay, primary caregiver father), he maintained an awareness of the broader sociocultural norms that govern family, gender, and relationships. His narrative speaks to an undeniable tension faced by some gay fathers: even as they enact roles that appear to challenge dominant notions of masculinity, they cannot fully escape hegemonic masculine norms, such as those that assign greater value to breadwinning than to caregiving (Sanchez, Greenberg, Liu, & Vilain, 2009).

FT-PT Arrangements: Part-Timers' Perceptions of Positive Aspects

Echoing some previous research on part-time employed heterosexual mothers (Johnston & Swanson, 2006), five men emphasized that a chief benefit of their part-time worker/part-time caregiver status was the sense of balance it afforded them. These men felt that they were better workers and better caregivers by virtue of the fact that they were not "burned out" in either domain; rather, their time in each served to (re)invigorate and (re)fuel them, facilitating their focus and commitment in both spheres. Being at home with their child was "wonderful," but maintaining their involvement in work was also important in that it allowed them time to have "an adult conversation" and enabled them to "continue to do something I love." Frank, the 39-year-old White physician in private practice, exclaimed:

> It is interesting. I actually find that being able to go to work is helpful for me. It's really very demanding and exhausting being home alone with the baby all day. I mean there are a lot of really neat, wonderful things about it . . . and it's really neat. But you have no other adult contact and you're not as good at it as you are at your regular job. I think for me, a balance of going to work—and if anything I get a little bit rejuvenated from some of that and then I can really give more of myself to Benny. I think it actually has been good, having that 50 percent time. It is working out really well.

All five of these men emphasized that they simply "could not" be full-time, stay-at-home parents, feeling that they derived too much pleasure and meaning from their jobs and academic pursuits to give up on them completely. These men were rather matter-of-fact in vocalizing their desire and "need" to maintain at least part-time involvement in work; yet at the same time, running through their narratives was a discourse of guilt: they felt that perhaps they *should* stay at home full-time. Finn, a 44-year-old White hospital administrator living in an urban area of the South, reflected:

> As much as I would like to say, "Yes I would like to not work and just completely raise him," I'm not the type of person. . . . You know, it's not that I need to work, I enjoy working. I enjoy what I do. You know, I went to school and I worked hard to get where I am and I really love what I do and it's a challenge, and I like to think that I'm good at what I do. And I don't know, I like to work, and I need to work and you know, make money to retire. I think it'd be good, it's good to work. Of course I would like to spend more time with him but . . .

Likewise, Jake, the 30-year-old graduate student whose story was described in the opening to this chapter, revealed:

> It's really upsetting to have to drop her off at day care. I hate the idea of day care for an infant, but you know, we have some pretty good providers. That's really the only hard part, I think that we've had to deal with, and everyone says, "Well, you know when you're a working mom you have no choice!" But you *do* have a choice, you can quit. But we decided not to quit and that makes me feel kind of guilty, but we keep saying, "Well, it is expensive, we need the income," but we really don't, we could probably both not work for a couple of years and be just fine in our current house and make the mortgage; we're pretty pampered. But because we have this goal of me working and Sam not, we have to keep working so I can write my dissertation so I can get a job so he can quit. But we promise her, as soon as I get a tenure-track job she's got one full-time stay-at-home daddy.

Finn, Jake, and others alluded to perceived pressures that they "should" stay home if they were financially capable of doing so. They struggled with the societal discourse that working for enjoyment's sake was not a sufficient reason to choose to *not* stay at home (Lupton & Schmied, 2002). In this way, at the same time that they emphasized the sense of balance they enjoyed as a function of retaining their involvement in paid work, they grappled with feelings of guilt regarding their decision to do so. Such sentiments are reminiscent of the guilt that is so associated with heterosexual *female* parents that it is called "mommy guilt" (Guendouzi, 2006; Tan, 2008). Indeed, traditional heteronormative motherhood ideologies define a "good mother" as full-time, at-home, middle-class, and entirely fulfilled through domestic aspirations (Dillaway & Pare, 2008; Johnston & Swanson, 2006). Gay men are not women, but in that they are purportedly fulfilling the (socially constructed) roles of both father and mother, they may be sensitive to the ways they are providing their child with adequate "mothering." Gay fathers who work part-time and stay home part-time may be particularly likely to experience internal conflict about whether they are living up to intensive mothering expectations, in that they may feel that, as the child's primary caregiver, *they* are the ones leaving their child when they go to work. They are more frequently forced to justify their working to themselves, in that they are constantly reminded of their dual roles. Thus, unlike their partners (who, as the primary income earners in the family, do not need to justify the necessity of their employment), gay men who work part-time may question whether they "need" to work, and whether their child would be better off at home with them full-time.

FT-PT Arrangements: Full-Timers' Perceptions of Negative Aspects

The 16 men who were working full-time, while their partners worked part-time, articulated a number of different perceived drawbacks and benefits of their particular arrangements. The desire to spend more time with their child and the perception that their partners were overwhelmed were identified as drawbacks; whereas personal fulfillment through work and minimal reliance on non-parental care were identified as benefits of their arrangement.

"I WANNA BE HOME MORE!" (I FEEL LIKE I'M MISSING OUT)

Like men in full-time/full-time arrangements, the men whose partners worked part-time sometimes lamented that they wished they worked fewer hours and could spend more time at home. But in contrast to full-time workers partnered with full-time workers, these men emphasized that they felt that they were "missing out." They implicitly or explicitly contrasted their own time with their child with their partner's, a comparison that left them feeling somewhat deprived. Five men voiced that they felt they were missing out. As Carl, a 41-year-old White fund-raising director living in a West Coast suburb, mused:

Ideally, I think Jason and I would both be home at the same time for half the week, then work for half the week. I definitely, it's just way more fun when we're both here with her, like, "Look at her! Did you see what she did?," rather than coming home and having him say, "Oh she smiled today." . . . It's tough to feel like a family when someone is always gone. If I had my ideal, I would still, I need to be out and with adults and all that kind of stuff, too, so I wouldn't want to just give up my job and stay at home full-time, but I definitely would like more time together as a family.

Carl and others expressed an explicit wish to have both partners work part-time, but they simply could not afford it. Kevin, a 40-year-old White psychologist in private practice in an urban area in the Midwest, elaborated:

You know, if we could afford it, I'd work less. . . . At some point I would like to work a little bit less. I don't know if it is feasible from a maintaining-my-office standpoint, but I think I would like to have more time to be a parent and not sort of squeeze it in. So I think that's why I am more likely to just leave things at work now; I'd rather be at home.

These men's narratives illustrate how some men longed for more family-friendly arrangements that would enable both partners to significantly reduce their hours and work part-time. Given that this type of arrangement was typically regarded as impossible on practical grounds, they tried to cut down their work commitments as much as possible in order to spend more time at home.

PARTNER IS OVERWHELMED

Another negative aspect of their current arrangement, named by full-timers specifically, was their perception that their partners were overwhelmed. Five men acknowledged the challenging predicament that their partners were in, trying to maintain jobs or complete degrees while acting as the primary caregiver for their child. These five full-timers empathized with their partners' struggle to meet all of their responsibilities, noting in particular the difficulty of getting work done while caring for a young child. These men asserted that they took over childcare duties during evenings and weekends so that their partners could catch up on work. Sam, the 36-year-old financial analyst whose story was outlined in this chapter's opening, remarked:

It's been difficult in that I want to be here and it's been very difficult on Jake because he is trying to finish his dissertation and he has been the one to stay home most of the time so he's more behind than he would like to be. He's been, obviously, dealing with stuff in the week and I try to do as much as I can on the weekends. It's difficult to leave and be gone all day, especially when—sometimes she's asleep by the time I get home. So that's really depressing so I always make sure I'm the one to do the early-morning feedings and the middle of the night and stuff like that.

Several men struggled with the tension of wanting to give their partner a break at the end of the day but also feeling exhausted themselves. Trey, the 32-year-old White dermatologist, asserted his concern for his partner, Rufus, whom he described as overwhelmed and exhausted. At the same time, he admitted that he was also burned out:

It's hard in that, for him, he's with her all day, he's exhausted and I come home and of course I'm exhausted because I've been trying to cram my entire work day into a nice nine-to-five schedule. And then there becomes that stress when you come home where he would like a break and I would like to give him a break, but I'm also feeling like I need a little bit of time to, you know, not all of a sudden be "on" taking care of Daria. And things are much better now because she's older, she's taking naps, she actually can sort of play on her own a little bit. And I think we've reached a better groove with how this works. But I think it was a little trickier than I thought it was going be in the beginning. You know, just sort of feeling like I would be able to work all day and then play with Daria all night and that's hard, that's being "on" as well.

For Trey and others, the lived reality of the "second shift" was much more challenging than they thought it would be. As Trey observed, home was no longer viewed as a haven of relaxation and leisure, but was now experienced as a place of work as well. Yet he also voiced optimism that life would get easier as his infant daughter became more self-sufficient.

FT-PT Arrangements: Full-Timers' Perceptions of Positive Aspects

"I'M GLAD I'M WORKING"

Six of the men who were working full-time while their partners worked part-time emphasized how grateful they were to be employed full-time because they enjoyed their jobs and felt that having a career facilitated their self-worth and well-being (Haddock & Rattenborg, 2003). As Eric, the 40-year-old Latino marketing executive, asserted, "I'm so happy that I'm working. I don't think I could stay home all day. . . . I don't know if Chris's schedule will continue to allow him to stay at home as much as he's been staying at home, but that's the goal." Thus these men expressed gratitude for the fact that they could afford to have one parent at home part-time, but they also asserted that they were glad to be the ones working full-time, often alluding to their high job satisfaction and strong work ethic. In this way, they explicitly voiced their awareness of the ways they were benefiting from their partners' willingness to stay home: they did not have to give up their jobs, and their child had a part-time, stay-at-home parent. Implicitly, they also acknowledged that staying at home (i.e., their partner's job) was, in some ways, the harder job.

MINIMAL RELIANCE ON OUTSIDE CHILD CARE

According to three men, one benefit of having one partner stay home part-time was that it minimized the couples' reliance on outside child care. Having one partner stay home at least part-time was perceived as desirable for financial reasons (it cut the cost of day care) and for more value-based reasons (the men believed that parent care was best). These explanations are consistent with the reasons offered by heterosexual couples for having one parent, typically the mother, work part-time or stay at home (Doucet & Merla, 2007; Stone & Lovejoy, 2004). Kevin, the 40-year-old White psychologist, observed:

> It is a pretty crucial time for having a baby and we were able to do it finan-
> cially, and it would be very stressful if he went back to work and we had
> to find a sitter or day care and kind of juggle that with jobs. So I think in
> some ways it kind of minimizes some of that. And I think Brendan just
> felt it was more important that—this is a time that we're not going to have
> again, this is a time when he is a little tiny baby, so we would rather spend
> the time with Brody rather than bring him to day care.

Kevin's statement that "Brendan just felt it was more important" reveals how partners' individual parenting values may ultimately plan into work-family arrangements. Brendan, at least according to Kevin, apparently felt more strongly about having one parent stay at home, at least part-time. His stronger feelings regarding the importance of a stay-at-home parent—as well as his greater flexibility, and lower income, as a graduate student—ultimately contributed to the fact that it was he, and not Kevin, who ended up staying at home part-time.

FT-SAH Arrangements: SAH Parents' Perceptions of Negative Aspects

In five couples, one partner was staying home full-time while one partner was working full-time. Stay-at-home fathers voiced both negative and positive aspects of their particular arrangement. On the one hand, staying at home with their child full-time was sometimes experienced as isolating and exhausting. On the other hand, the men appreciated the sense of meaning and fun that accompanied their new role, and several also felt that staying at home with their child was the most logical care arrangement for their family.

All five men who were staying home acknowledged that at least some aspects of going from full-time employee or student to full-time caregiver were challenging. Echoing previous studies of stay-at-home mothers (Barclay et al., 1997; Johnston & Swanson, 2006; Stone & Lovejoy, 2004) and stay-at-home fathers (Doucet & Merla, 2007; Merla, 2008), isolation, boredom, and a sense of never getting anything accomplished emerged as salient themes from their narratives. All these men had traded paid employment for staying home with a young child. They sometimes missed both the social aspect of their jobs, including the sense of camaraderie and fun that came with working around other people, and the daily sense of accomplishment and productivity they had enjoyed. Further, the work of caring for a young child was described as "exhausting," and by the end of the day, some men "couldn't wait" for their partners to come home from work to relieve them of some of the responsibilities of child care. Darius, a 41 year-old White graduate student, explained, "By the end of some days, I'm really tired, I'm really, really tired. . . . Sometimes I get a little stir crazy, where it's like, 'Okay, I need to talk to an adult!'" Nick, a 38-year-old White man living in a metropolitan area on the West Coast, who had taken an extensive leave from his job as a public relations manager, described his adjustment to staying home:

> I did have this grandiose idea that in addition to, you know, being a stay-at-home dad and taking care of Emmett, that this was going to afford me all this time to do all the things that I've been wanting to do forever and ever. And within days I was like, okay, that ain't going to happen. And, you know, I had maybe a short period where I was kind of disappointed about all of that. But, you know, then I was like, well, that's really not why I'm doing this, so I'll just go with the flow. So it's been really good. So we have a little bit of a routine. It's amazing how the days fly by. And I am

kind of a doer, or I think of myself as a doer, and so every once in a while I have a day where it's a bit frustrating where it's like, wow, that day went by where I accomplished nothing. Maybe it's because I was raised Catholic, but I feel this need to feel like I've accomplished something. And of course we have accomplished something—I've had another phenomenal day with my son—but in terms of like crossing things off a list, no.

Nick was not alone in expressing his surprise at the all-consuming nature of stay-at-home parenthood. Several stay-at-home fathers described, with some humor, how they had gradually relinquished fantasies of picking up old (or new) hobbies, finishing various home repair projects, and cooking "gourmet meals," as the reality of their new lives as stay-at-home parents set in. As Nick articulated, these men were forced to adjust their expectations of what they could "accomplish" while staying at home with their child—and, even further, they were pushed to redefine what "accomplishment" meant, in the context of their new role as parents. It is possible that these men's discomfort with not "accomplishing" things in the work-related sense was facilitated by their male socialization, and their sensitivity to dominant discourses that equate breadwinning with masculinity. At the same time, their narratives reveal how they were slowly adjusting to a new definition of accomplishment—one that was not predicated on turning out "product" in the employment sphere. In this way, the men's evolving definitions of accomplishment can be viewed as contributing to alternative meanings of masculinity—and, therefore, as functionally challenging traditional notions of masculinity.

FT-SAH Arrangements: SAH Parents' Perceptions of Positive Aspects

"MY NEW JOB IS MEANINGFUL AND FUN"
At the same time that all five men identified feelings of boredom and exhaustion as challenges in their daily lives as stay-at-home parents, they also emphasized that staying at home with their children was both meaningful and fun. They treasured their children's "firsts" and took pleasure in their role as the primary caregiver. They were unanimous in describing their role as the stay-at-home caregiver as special and as an opportunity they were grateful to have. David, a 33-year-old White former massage therapist living in a West Coast city, exclaimed:

I love it. It's really, it took adjusting to. It took a while to get over, "Okay, the things that I want to do really have to wait." That was an adjustment process. But the past few weeks have just been really great. I feel like I'm in a groove. I just love being home with home and seeing how he changes every day and the things that interest him. He was able to clap his hands in front of him for the first time, basically, yesterday. I mean, that's huge. That's the first he's done that. I love being here for that.

"IT'S THE MOST EFFICIENT WAY TO BE A FAMILY"

Two men emphasized their belief that staying at home was simply the best decision for their family. They articulated the belief that it would be much harder, perhaps even impossible, to manage a household and raise a child if both parents were working. They felt that an arrangement where one partner specialized in child care and one partner worked outside the home was the most efficient and logical way of managing their new lives as parents. As Doug, a 37-year-old White former bank manager living in an urban area on the West Coast, asserted, "I don't know honestly how we would have done this with both of us working. I don't think it would have worked out very well with the housework and focusing on him. I don't think it would have been as good of situation for us. Other parents can do it but I don't think that we could have done it."

FT-SAH Arrangements: Full-Timers' Perceptions of Negative Aspects

The full-time employed partners of the men who were staying at home with their children voiced a different set of perceived drawbacks and advantages to their arrangements. Namely, the major drawback they voiced was a lack of time with their child, whereas the major advantage they described was their exclusive reliance on parental care.

"I WANNA BE HOME MORE" (ENVY)

The five men who were working full-time while their partners stayed at home with their children were acutely aware of their drastically different roles. Similar to full-time employed men partnered with part-timers, these men tended to focus on the ways they were missing out on experiences and milestones that their partners had the opportunity to enjoy. But their descriptions of "missing out" were more intense, such that they tended to describe feelings of *envy* in relation their partner's role with their child. For example, Brett, a 42-year-old White lawyer, mused, "I have jealousy at times because I have to leave and go to work and he's becoming the primarily identified parent." These men also emphasized concerns about the potential implications of their strongly differentiated roles: they worried that over time, one

ould become more identified as the "mother" and one parent would
more identified as the "father."

e men expressed feelings of envy related to not being their child's
pr... y caregiver. Heterosexual fathers often tend to presume, and accept,
that the mother will be the primary caregiver, and by extension rarely voice
feelings of intense regret or disappointment about being the secondary parent (Ehrensaft, 1990; Hiller & Philliber, 1986). In that gay men who become
fathers are typically highly committed to fatherhood (Goldberg, 2010a) and
also compare their parental role to that of another man, not a woman (Goldberg, 2010b), they may have higher expectations for their own involvement.
The marked difference in time spent with their children as compared to their
partners therefore evoked feelings of discomfort and loss for some of the
full-time-employed gay men in this study.

FT-SAH Arrangements: Full-Timers' Perceptions of Positive Aspects

"OUR CHILD GETS A FULL-TIME PARENT"
Three men emphasized that the most positive aspect of their arrangement
was simply the fact that their child was being cared for by one parent, as
opposed to "a stranger." These men expressed varying degrees of resistance
to the notion of outside child care, but they were unanimous in believing
that the optimal arrangement was having one parent stay home with the
child, at least for the first year or two. This sentiment is commonly voiced
by heterosexual couples in explaining why they chose one parent—usually,
but not always, the mother—to stay at home (Doucet & Merla, 2007; Merla,
2008; Stone & Lovejoy, 2004). For example, Russell, a 41-year-old White man
employed as an executive director in a city on the West Coast, stated, "We
just always thought that it was important for one of us to stay home with
him. I think that the first five years is a precious gift, and economically we
can sacrifice for a few years."

Changed Identities, Refocused Priorities:
The Relative Salience of Work and Family

Becoming a parent prompted many of the men in the study to adjust their
commitment to paid work. The men described several different types of
shifts in their identification with and investment in paid work. Namely, some
men described becoming less committed to work, whereas others described
becoming increasingly committed.

Reduced Emphasis on Work: "I'm Less Committed to My Job"

Almost half the employed men whom I interviewed expressed that they had experienced a substantial shift in their identities upon becoming a parent, whereby they felt a diminished identification with and commitment to their work role and identity. Many said they were proudly identified with their work roles prior to parenthood, but described at least a modest diminishment in their identification with work, as their parent identity came to supersede all other roles. As they described it, becoming a parent had "added clarity about the things that are important." These men's reduced focus on work occurred at both a psychological level (they cared less about work, they thought less about work) and a practical level (they did less work). For example, these men found themselves turning down opportunities for promotion, to travel, to take on new projects at work, and to attend work-related events.

They also described various specific and practical changes they had made in relation to how they approached their jobs, which clearly reflected their reduced prioritization of work. For example, 16 men described doing the bare minimum at work—a change that involved both a shift in expectations, as well as a reduction in effort (Voydanoff, 2005). These men described routinely leaving work undone at their jobs—something that would not have occurred to them pre-parenthood, but which they now viewed as necessary, given their commitment to spend as much time as possible at home. Thirteen men stated that they had made or were considering making changes in their schedules or jobs to spend more time at home. For example, several men had retained jobs with the same company but reduced their hours to part-time status, and others had convinced their bosses to allow them to work from home at least one day a week. Men whose bosses had denied their requests to work fewer hours, flex their hours, work at home, or relinquish certain work responsibilities were currently considering job changes. Finally, 11 men had made an explicit effort to be more efficient at work to free up their time at home for child care and family time. Better time use often meant "working faster" and "multitasking," as well as curtailing "social time" at work.

This greater focus on family—and a willingness to reduce one's commitment to work—following the transition to parenthood is more typical of mothers than fathers (Cooper, 2000; Stone & Lovejoy, 2004), although prior research on egalitarian heterosexual fathers (Henwood & Procter, 2003) and gay fathers (Bergman, Rubio, Green, & Padron, 2010; Mallon, 2004) has also found evidence of a reduced commitment to work. The men's narratives deviated from—and perhaps represented a form of resistance to—dominant masculinity ideologies that emphasize breadwinning and career success as central to masculinity in general and "good fathers" in particular (Cooper, 2000; Lupton & Schmied, 2002). Eric, the 40-year-old Latino marketing executive who was working full-time while his partner, Chris, worked part-time, stated:

> I think that [being a parent] is like the most important thing I do now. Before, it was my profession. It's all about him now. And it's good, it's more important, it's more fun. Normally I would be putting more of everything that I have into this new job. And I'm working, but I definitely . . . when I'm not here I'm not working or thinking about it the way I used to. I try to be in the moment, and when I'm with him, I'm with him.

Likewise, Patrick, a 41-year-old White college professor who resided in a midwestern suburb, mused about the shift in both his and his partner Carter's prioritization of work (both men were employed full-time):

> Both Carter and I used to go in early and stay late at work. Now it's like, whatever. Our work attitudes have really changed. You know, we are still doing the work. We're not slacking or going to be fired or anything like that. You know, you suddenly realize that there is more to life than spending every day focusing on work. It's broadening your focus. We don't watch TV anymore. We watch her on the floor playing on her little play mat or in her bouncy chair doing her thing. It's just amazing to watch.

In some cases, the desire to shift their attention away from work and toward family surprised men, in that they had expected to feel more torn between work and family and to perceive any reduction in time and energy at work as a sacrifice. About becoming a parent, Lars, a 36-year-old White human resources assistant who was now working part-time while his partner, Joshua, worked full-time, mused:

> It has surprised me in that I thought (*laughs*), going back to my being totally selfish and self-involved, I thought my main priorities would stay where they were. I would just have to make all these, all these big sacrifices. And suddenly it's not really, they're not really sacrifices as much as I thought they would be. I mean, suddenly I'm making these choices to move things around, but it's what I'm *wanting* to do.

In most cases, then, men experienced little to no tension surrounding reduced work investment. They did not perceive themselves as *sacrificing* work for family, but rather as easily and appropriately choosing family over work, given that their "priorities [had] shifted more toward being a parent." In some cases, however, men experienced tension around this reduction in focus. Of the men who described themselves as de-prioritizing work, about one-third articulated tensions surrounding their changed priorities. They expressed feelings of guilt or concern about how their reduced work focus might be viewed or how it might affect them in the long term. Such feelings may reflect men's awareness of traditional sociocultural scripts of fatherhood and masculinity (Coltrane, 1996), as well as their previously strong identification with the work role. Brian, a 52-year-old White sales manager living in a northeastern suburb, said simply, "I am struggling with [the fact that] I may not be everything I used to want to be in my job because I'm a parent." Dean, a 30-year-old Asian American man who worked as the assistant director of a small nonprofit organization in an urban area on the West Coast, observed:

> I was definitely the person that would work weekends. Work, you know, do things to get the job done. But now I'm like, I really can't. I travel less. I used to travel a lot for work and now I'm kind of going, "No, I don't really want to do that, no, I'm not really willing to go there." So there is some, in the back of my head, some worry of like, really, how effective will I be? And I think I used to be, and people would say that I was definitely an overachiever and outperformer, and that I would get stuff done usually quicker than most people would I think, and so now that I've flaked out a bit—I guess I'm still performing the norm, but it feels like it's stepped down.

Dean expressed some ambivalence and tension in resolving the kind of worker that he "used to be" with his increased prioritization of family. He seemed firm that he was not willing to "go there" in terms of exerting as much effort as he used to, but at the same time he worried about how effective he would be now that he was a parent, and, in turn, how his colleagues and supervisor might regard him. He was currently struggling to adjust to his "stepped down" performance and his reduced (perhaps more realistic) expectations of what he could accomplish.

In a similar vein, in discussing his decision to take on a new role at his company, Ray, the 37-year-old White pharmaceutical representative who lived in a northeastern suburb, remarked:

> There is a little bit of anxiety about, "Oh, where is my career going?," and everything. I think, ultimately, I'm just coming to terms with that that's not

where my priorities are right now, and that that's okay, and it's much more important to me and more valuable to me to have quality time and the ability to parent my daughter at this very important stage of her life than it is to propel my career in any sort of way. So if at some point when she gets into school or whatever it may be, I feel that there are opportunities for me to do something different and put more into work, I can do that. But it's just a work-life balance [issue] and I decided that I need to balance it this way for right now.

Likewise, Gerard, a 48-year-old White architect living in a metropolitan area in the Northeast, revealed:

You know, I am really kind of shifting my work right now. I am in the midst of . . . I have been holding two positions for the last year and a half in our organization. And I'm working at shedding most of the responsibilities of one of them. I have two titles, two different entities that I work for and have been running two different sets of operations. So it has been very stressful in that way. And I'm actually kind of choosing the less-prestigious position to focus on because it allows me a more sane life. Whether or not that is the best choice, career-wise, I don't know and some would say probably not. But for me it is really the only choice I can make right now.

Gerard acknowledged that some people might say that he is not making the "best choice, career-wise," but maintained that for him, "it is really the only choice" he could make. His narrative reveals how his newfound commitments as a parent had altered his perspective of and commitment to work, whereby he felt compelled to make certain "sacrifices" in the work domain to better accommodate his new family responsibilities.

The men's tensions surrounding the potential long-term implications of and outsider reactions to their career "sacrifices" may in part reflect their status as men, and their vulnerability to masculinity ideologies that prioritize breadwinning as central to identity construction (Coltrane, 1996; Connell, 1995). But such tensions may also reflect these men's general tendency to be engaged in relatively high-status occupations that emphasize advancement and competition (Schieman, Glavin, & Milkie, 2009). Gay men employed in middle-status occupations who work in noncompetitive work environments might express less conflict surrounding the future implications of their diminished commitment to work.

Increased Emphasis on Work: "I'm More Committed to My Job"

For six men, parenthood was experienced as having *increased* their commitment to their jobs. Upon becoming a parent, work had taken on a new significance in men's lives, because they were aware that they needed the income to provide for their children's present and future needs. Their narratives echo and converge with those of heterosexual employed fathers, who often emphasize that working hard to provide income for their families is a fundamental, and valued, way of expressing love and care for their children and spouse (Riggs, 1997; Townsend, 2002). It is notable that all six of these men were employed in high-status, high-paying, fairly "masculine" occupations (e.g., doctor, engineer) and were the primary financial earners in the family (i.e., they made at least half as much more than their partners). Their high earning power, coupled with their employment in high-status careers, may have facilitated their identification as the "breadwinners" and thus their increased commitment to paid work: "There is a sense that I am working for my family in addition to just for myself, [which] adds a certain degree of meaning to work." Donovan, a 42 year-old Latino engineer living in a northeastern suburb, observed about parenthood:

> Oddly enough, in some respects, it makes you *more* focused on what you're doing at work. I'm committed to my job more so than before. I'm planning the rest of my life. We have college funds budgeted. You really think about the future. I'm much more goal-oriented, much more into long-term planning.

Similarly, Michael, a 33-year-old White psychiatrist living in a metropolitan area on the West Coast, remarked:

> You know, it's very interesting. For most of the time Damian's been here, Carlos has been off and I've been at work. Carlos has been pretty much his primary caretaker. And so, I haven't really had as much of a drive in that perspective, but it's more of a drive to, you know, make sure that financially we're more in a sound place, so we have money for his education and some other things down the road. So, that's kind of an orientation I've never had. That's very important to me. Paying the bills, yes, but this is more like we need to be actively saving money so that he's got enough money for what he needs when he gets older.

When All Is Not Equal: Managing Differences in "Roles" within PT/FT and SAH/FT Couples

Employed men's adaptation to the role of "working parent" was necessarily affected by the employment status of their partners. Men who were partnered with men who were staying home part-time or full-time encountered the added challenge of adjusting to a reality in which their own roles and responsibilities diverged significantly from those of their partners. Whereas they were at work all day, their partners were spending time with and bonding with their children for at least some of that time. Men who were the part-time or full-time caregivers of their children also had to adjust to this new reality.

Different Roles, Different Attachments

Men in 10 couples (four FT/SAH couples, six FT/PT couples) acknowledged that their children seemed to be somewhat more attached to the parent who was at home more often. In some cases this differential attachment was described as a source of concern and stress—typically by the full-time-employed, non-preferred parents, who longed for a greater connection to their child. For example, Dennis, a 40-year-old White small business owner who worked full-time while his partner, Justin, worked part-time, explained:

> I think [his attachment to me] has been a little bit slower because, in part because of our schedules. Justin is with Judah more hours of the week, more days of the week. And we've done some adjusting and it's a little more even now, but still, he has Judah more time. So I think that, that changes it a bit. I do think I tend to be more anxious about things [like this] and Justin tends to be more focused on making do with the current situation.

Dennis suggested that he tended to be more "anxious" about the differential attachment that appeared to be developing because he was the non-preferred parent. Justin, on the other hand, was perceived as passively accepting the situation—possibly because he was the preferred parent and therefore did not see a "problem."

Several preferred parents, however, did also describe some level of discomfort surrounding their children's unequal attachments. They vocalized feelings of guilt related to their children's greater attachment to them, and sometimes articulated their preference for a more balanced set of attachments. As Finn, the 44-year-old White hospital administrator who was staying home part-time, mused:

> I think, I'd say probably [he's more attached to me] because I have stayed with him so much. I think when he looks—you know, we'll stand side by side, he'll probably look at me first. And I kind of feel guilty for that but really, I can't, it's just the way it is. And I think Robbie accepts that because he'll always say, "He always looks at you." So he'll get in between me and him, so that he has to look at him, and you know, usually, when that happens, I actually will walk away so that he can have dad time with Travis and Travis will look at him. You know, I'm real mindful of that because I do know, and most anybody will say, you know, if there are five people in the room, the baby is going to just stare at me, the most familiar face and his playmate, and I try to be very mindful about that. I don't want Robbie to feel any less of the parent, you know. So, yeah, I think he probably has bonded more with me.

Men like Finn tried to maximize both partners' opportunity to bond by "backing off" when their partners arrived home from work, to allow their child and partner solo bonding time. Likewise, couples often described their efforts to split the care of their child care as evenly as possible as a means of promoting more equal attachments and avoiding highly differentiated roles. Thus, when the working parent was home, he was often the one to take over diapering, feeding, and soothing. In this way, these men strove to create as much balance as possible, despite the structural differences in their roles. As James, the 41-year-old White urban planner turned stay-at-home father, explained:

> He's not with her as much. And so some of the way we run it is, when he is home, he is the primary parent. Brett leaves the house about quarter of eight in the morning and is gone until about 7:30 at night. So when he comes home at 7:30, I pass her off to him, and you know, he can work with her. He does the last feeding of the night, and then puts her to bed. He gets up in the morning, that's his primary handling. You know, yeah, I like the break. I welcome that, a chance for a little down time. And that's when he wants to care for her, so he can, any opportunity he can spend more time with her.

Likewise, although the 37-year-old Rufus, who was the primary caregiver, observed that their daughter was probably somewhat more attached to him, he also made a point of emphasizing that his partner, Trey, had "been get-ting up with her in the morning and putting her to bed sometimes if I've had sleep deprivation doing it. I think he just wants to be such a part of it that we haven't sort of fallen into that sort of dad/mom stereotype of one really engaged and one a little less."

The narratives of these primary-caregiver fathers contrast with research on heterosexual couples, which often finds that both employed and stay-at-home mothers desire more help from their husbands (Edwards, 2007; Stone & Lovejoy, 2004; Wiesman, Boeije, van Doorne-Huiskes, & den Dulk, 2008). Consistent with prior research on lesbian parenting (Goldberg & Perry-Jen-kins, 2007; Goldberg, Downing, & Sauck, 2008; Patterson, Sutfin, & Fulcher, 2004), these men appeared invested in minimizing inequities between them, and described actively strategizing to ensure that both partners enjoyed close and meaningful relationships with their children. Such efforts to ensure that the full-time-employed parent spent as much time as possible engaged in child care not only may reflect concerns about attachment and equity, but also may have been implicitly aimed at minimizing the overall degree of spe-cialization in their roles.

Three men, all of whom had adopted older children (i.e., toddlers and school-aged children), voiced their concern that their children would come to view the partner who worked more as the "daddy" and the partner who worked less, and who engaged in more child care and housework, as the "mommy." In this way, they further revealed their concern that their *chil-dren* might view them as enacting or imitating heteronormative roles and identities. The 37-year-old Ryan, for example, who was working full-time as an engineer while his partner, Harvey, continued to work part-time in sales, mused:

> I think it's been different. . . . I don't know if it's been better or worse for him but as much as we've tried to avoid it, we've kind of gotten in this situation where Harvey is more like mom sometimes, or "mom," and I've been the "dad" in some ways. For Solomon, or his perception, is that Harvey does the cooking and more domestic stuff and he works a little less, about three-quarters of the time, so he is home earlier—and it's not deliberate, it just kind of works out that way. He's home more, he doesn't take his work home with him, his responsibilities pretty much stay with him at work so he tends to run the errands and cooking. . . . So anyway, I think in Solomon's mind we've sort of fallen in these mom and dad roles, which is not what we wanted so we're working to sort of undo that.

Different Roles, Different Household Responsibilities

Men in couples in which one partner stayed at home part-time or full-time sometimes described shifts in their division of labor that went beyond the division of child care and paid work. Specifically, men who stayed home were often performing most of the regular household duties, in addition to caring for the child. Most of the men described this shift matter-of-factly. But in eight cases, men experienced some distress regarding the current division of labor. In five of these eight cases, it was full-timers who felt guilty about their partners doing household chores for which they had previously been responsible. As Carl, the 41-year-old White fund-raising director living in a suburb on the West Coast, stated:

> I feel like the only dynamic that has changed is that Jason staying home and I think that sort of changes our dynamic and the fact that he's home during the day now, so he's got, he gets stuff done more around the house. He's more chore-oriented. So like, I leave in the morning and the laundry needs to be folded and I say, "I'll do it when I get home." And then when I come home he's done it. And it's not like, he doesn't resent it, I don't think . . . it's just, you know, like our balance of power has sort of shifted around a little bit, I think.

Carl's discomfort with the new status quo is interesting, given that he was the one who is theoretically benefiting. That is, Jason was performing more housework and therefore Carl was relieved from performing certain routine chores, allowing him more time for other things (such as spending time with his child). Yet Carl indicates that he was discomfited by this new arrangement, in that "our balance of power has sort of shifted around." This discomfort reflects his preference for maintaining the relative equality that characterized their division of labor pre-parenthood. Carl may be reluctant to enact, or to be viewed as enacting, a division of labor that clearly disadvantages his partner, insomuch as domestic labor is generally regarded, by much of society, as "unworthy and of little value" (Carrington, 1999, p. 70).

Bill, a 38-year-old White director of programs in a city on the West Coast, similarly described a shift in the division of labor, which he perceived as overly burdensome to his partner, Darius:

> What somewhat typically happens is that, I'll get home and get cleaned up and then I'll take Joey and then Darius will either have already started dinner, or he'll throw something together. And if he's not in the mood for

cooking, he'll continue to hold Joey and I'll get dinner ready. But the roles have shifted a little bit because I was the cook [before], and now he does a lot more of the cooking and prep—or at least prep work, for meals. I feel like he's getting the brunt of the work. I mean, because, even in one day a week I realize how much work it is, and it's exhausting, and so I'm very empathetic, how difficult every day it is for him to do that, and so I try to call during the day and see how things are going and kind of lend whatever moral support I can, but I do feel like he's really taking the brunt of it. He's got the hardest job.

Full-timers like Bill typically expressed feelings of empathy and guilt regarding their partners' heavy load. Their acknowledgment that their partners both needed and were entitled to "personal time" reflects their capacity to empathize with them and to recognize the actual work involved in caring for a child. Further, their egalitarian philosophy is evident through their desire to share as equally as possible in the caretaking of their children. These men expressed discomfort with sharply segregated roles, preferring to maintain more equal arrangements.

Several partners of full-timers—that is, the primary caregivers—also highlighted concerns related to their heavy domestic load. Interestingly, their concerns mainly centered on the implications of their disproportionate involvement in domestic duties for their gender identities. Namely, three men expressed feeling somewhat "emasculated" and "domesticated" by their new roles. They felt that their gender identities were being challenged by their new roles as domestic caretakers, echoing hegemonic masculine discourses that privilege masculine gender presentations over feminine ones, even within gay male communities (Connell, 1995; Taywaditep, 2001). For example, Henry, 45, observed, about the transition from full-time worker to being both the "domestic goddess" and child-care provider:

It was weird, because it was very—if I'm speaking to you honestly, it was a very weird change in the relationship for me and Luis. Luis was always more the one who did things in the home. You know, looking at us, you know, I'm 6'2" and 200 pounds and he's, you know, 5'9" and a hundred and whatever. You know, I'm more aggressive in personality. It's just weird for me to be the one now pushing a stroller. Not that it doesn't look right, but I don't think people would've thought that I'd be the one doing that.

Henry suggests that his greater responsibility for child care and housework did not fit with his self-image as the more "masculine" of the two. His quote indicates that he perceived himself as more traditionally masculine than Luis, in terms of his physical build, his personality, and his previous contributions to domestic labor. Previous research with heterosexual stay-at-home fathers suggests that when faced with gender-role discrepancy, men have the option of maintaining or changing their perception of gender-role norms (i.e., changing one's idea of what it means to be "masculine" so that caring for one's child is considered an important way of providing for one's family), or actively disengaging from or rejecting masculine ideals (Rochlen et al., 2008). In that Henry's current role as the primary caretaker of their child served to challenge his gender identity, it may ultimately lead him to alter how he thinks of masculinity; or it might lead him to alter how he thinks of his own gender identity (e.g., as more feminine), and in turn to distance himself from traditional masculine ideals.

Different Roles but . . . "We Are Not Like Heterosexual Couples!"

Fourteen men in seven couples (two FT/SAH, five FT/PT) explicitly emphasized that despite the fact that they and their partner performed different amounts of paid and unpaid labor, their work-family roles could not be understood in terms of the heteronormative template of stay-at-home (or part-time-employed) mother and full-time-employed father. They seemingly offered up these assertions to deflect any misassumptions about how their relationships and parenting arrangements were "like" those of heterosexual couples. In other words, they seemed to anticipate, and reject, the notion that their paid/unpaid work arrangements mirrored those of heterosexual couples. For example, Jake, the 30-year-old White graduate student who was staying at home part-time with his child, explained:

> We obviously don't fit into traditional sex roles, and I think that anyone could say, "Oh, no, we don't follow traditional sex roles," but if you are a male/female couple, it's going to hang over you like a shadow. There will be a time, whether or not you're a stay-at-home mom, someone looks at you and thinks you're a stay-at-home mom. But with us, we really are free from that. Like, if I were to be a stay-at-home mom, I still wouldn't feel like I fell into any traditional sex roles.

Jake articulated a belief that conformity to traditional gender roles was simply impossible for a same-sex couple, by virtue of their positioning outside the heterosexual nuclear family ideal. Behaviors, activities, and roles that would be considered "traditional" in a male-female union cannot be considered as such in a male-male union, he argued. He asserted that whereas heterosexual couples are inevitably governed by the template of traditional gender roles, gay men's behavior was not measured against the same template. This allowed him the freedom to choose to be a "stay-at-home mom" if he wanted to, without feeling that he was conforming—or failing to conform—to traditional gender roles. Jake does not appear to view his hypothetical embodiment of the stay-at-home-parent role as imitative or derivative of heterosexual couples, such that he would be taking on more of the "mother" role (and his partner, who presumably would be working, would be taking on more of the "father" role). Rather, he seems to view this hypothetical arrangement as fundamentally different from the parallel arrangement enacted in the heterosexual context, by virtue of the fact that two men would be enacting it.

Four of these 14 men further noted that their status as two gay men—and therefore their lack of scripts for how parenting/work roles should be enacted—made them more intentional and thoughtful as parents. Speaking to this, Russell, the 41-year-old White executive director whose partner, David, was staying at home full-time, asserted, "There are already clear social roles for [heterosexual couples]. They can challenge them or change them, but there is a default handbook. So, there is no handbook for us and we have to re-create everything from making bottles to buying stuff. I think it makes us more thoughtful really." Likewise, James, the 41-year-old White urban planner turned stay-at-home father, stated:

> We're really good about sort of, talking things out. We talk it out. I think partly because it's two guys raising a kid. It's not like one of us socially or culturally is dictated to act in a certain way. I'm the mom and you have that role, or I'm the dad, and I have that role. It's very equal. We parent our child not as mom and as dad.

Conclusion

As we have seen, the men in this study were highly committed to parenthood, as demonstrated by the fact that they endured the often lengthy and grueling process of adoption in order to become parents. Their high level of intentionality regarding parenthood necessarily had implications for their experiences of balancing work and family. For example, many men reduced their work hours to care for their child, and many men who were working full-time—and part-time, for that matter—experienced tensions related to wanting to be home more often. Men who wish to be highly involved parents (as opposed to being minimally invested in the parental role) who also have challenging and time-intensive jobs will almost inevitably experience some level of work-family conflict. Many men dealt with this conflict by reducing their time or energy in paid work in order to devote more time to family: indeed, almost half the men described a reduced commitment to work once they became parents. They did this in the context of broader societal ideologies that strongly emphasize breadwinning as a fundamental component of male (and paternal) identity. In turn, some of the men did mention anxieties related to the future implications of their career sacrifices. In general, however, even those men who identified a tension between their own reduced work investment and broader masculinity ideologies tended to espouse little ambivalence related to their choice to prioritize family. As gay men, they are released somewhat from heteronormative pressures related to breadwinning and from the associated guilt that comes with prioritizing family. But at the same time, as men who are highly committed to parenting, they are not released from the tension and guilt that may arise as a function of trying to balance working with parenthood. Indeed, in the context of heterosexual couples, this guilt is often referred to as "mommy guilt" (Guendouzi, 2006); we rarely hear of fathers who experience similar feelings to warrant the term "daddy guilt." Although akin to mommy guilt, the nature and meaning of the guilt these men experience is inevitably different, in that it is shaped by their male gender socialization, their gay male sexual identification, and the context of sharing parenting with another man.

Couples who established fairly segregated roles (i.e., couples in which one partner stayed home full-time or part-time) found themselves navigating a new set of challenges. Specifically, the fact that one partner was at home more often with the child meant that the men's experiences in both the home and the work sphere were different. Although it might be tempting to view these couples as imitating a heteronormative model (in which the mother reduces her time in paid employment, assuming greater career sacrifices, and the father continues to work full-time), the men's descriptions of these arrangements—and their associated feelings and perceptions—suggest that such a conclusion would be overly simplistic and inaccurate. The men in these couples appeared highly committed to shared child rearing, in general, and they described strategies aimed at maximizing equality. Also of note is that the partners of full-time and part-time stay-at-home caregivers often described concern and empathy for them (e.g., they worried that their partners were overwhelmed or burned out, or they expressed feeling that the division of labor was unfair to the primary caregiver). This suggests a heightened level of awareness of equality that carried over into the parenting sphere.

The gay men in the study, then, regardless of their work arrangement, appeared to be aware of and to some extent influenced by dominant masculinity ideologies surrounding work. These ideologies are fundamentally interconnected with and foundational to heteronormativity, in that that they position "real men" as those who are career-focused and financially successful, and "pseudo-men" as those who are unproductive in the breadwinning sphere. The men, however, largely resisted such imperatives, constructing their identities as men and as parents in ways that defied such stale representations of what real men are. Their ability and willingness to push back on dominant ideologies about family, gender, and work highlight the creative potential of all families who are "parenting against the grain" to define and enact their own unique parenting roles. Of course, certain personal and social conditions may have facilitated their ability to resist dominant discourses. For example, their status as *gay* men may have encouraged such resistance, in that they did not conform to other standards of "true" masculinity. It is also likely that their generally high levels of education and their high levels of motivation to become parents also affected their willingness and ability to challenge dominant notions of masculinity, parenthood, and the division of labor.

4

Kinship Ties across the Transition to Parenthood

Gay Men's Relationships with Family and Friends

Henry and Luis, both aged 45, had been together for just about two years when they began the process of adopting a child. Henry, who identified as half-Spanish, was self-employed as a physical therapist, and Luis, who identified as Cuban American, worked as a surgeon at a local hospital in the Northeast metro area where the couple lived. At the pre-adoption interview, they both described themselves as "fairly close" to Henry's family, including his mother, father, and sisters. As Luis noted, "His family, his sisters, and nieces and nephews are all . . . as supportive as anyone can possibly be." Both men were not particularly surprised when Henry's family responded positively to their news that they were pursuing adoption. And yet, although his entire family had reportedly expressed excitement about their efforts to adopt, Henry noted that his mother "had had her struggles in the past" with his sexuality, and he wondered whether these might resurface when he was actually a *gay parent*. Both men described less support from Luis's parents, which they attributed to their first-generation immigrant status and their more "traditional" attitudes surrounding marriage and family. Luis, however, expected his mother to "accept the child" despite the fact that she "obviously wouldn't have wanted it this way," whereas he expected very little support from his father, for whom his sexuality had been a "bigger issue" (e.g., his father had not come to his and Henry's wedding).

Concerning friends, at the pre-parenthood interview both men described a fairly large support network made up of friends both gay and straight, coupled and single. But as Henry noted, "We have plenty of straight friends who have kids but no gay couples that have kids." In turn, Henry felt prepared for changes in their friendship networks, including not seeing their nonparent friends as frequently: "Every book you read, they talk about it."

When Henry and Luis became parents to their daughter, Madison, a biracial infant whom they adopted via a private domestic open adoption, both men observed that Henry's family, as expected, was highly supportive and involved. Henry recounted that the night they arrived home with Madison, his parents and siblings were "all there, waiting for us." He noted that his mother "really surprised me because of the whole gay issue. . . . She's like, 'Oh, you're going to come by [with Madison] on Halloween, aren't you, so I can show my friends?' She's been great. Yeah, I mean, they're really great."

In contrast, Luis's family offered limited support. "My parents are [still] completely against my lifestyle," Luis stated. And yet, at the same time, both men viewed Luis's family as ultimately "accepting" the child, despite their personal difficulties with homosexuality. Luis explained:

> My mom came and visited for her christening and was just, you know, they're very, very, happy beyond . . . this is their first grandchild. So, they're responding to her in that way. . . . My dad hasn't met her yet; he's ill, so he can't travel. But they're very much, she's no less their grandchild because she's adopted or because she's the product of my and Henry's relationship.

Both Henry and Luis agreed that their friends had been supportive, but they qualified this by stating that, as Henry put it, "no one is rushing to come spend the day with me." In this way, friends were viewed as being congratulatory but not particularly involved, especially with the practical aspects of parenting. Henry further qualified his response by emphasizing that his gay male friends were less supportive than were his heterosexual friends: "My gay male friends will call and, you know, they'll be like, 'How is she?' every once in a while, but you know, on the other hand they'll be like, 'When are you ready for a boys' night out?' My straight friends will buy her little gifts and come over." Henry acknowledged feeling somewhat sad about the ways his social life was clearly diverging from that of his gay male friends—but noted that these changes had already begun to unfold prior to his becoming a parent, when he moved in with Luis and began to "settle down."

* * *

When heterosexual couples announce that they are going to become parents, this news tends to be met with joy and anticipation by both family and friends. The arrival of a child is typically met with excitement and interest, as well as offers of practical assistance. Family members such as parents and siblings may be especially likely to provide both emotional and practical support, thereby helping to temper the responsibility of parenting (Fischer, 1988; Gattai & Musatti, 1999). The arrival of a child may also help to solidify family relationships, bringing family members closer to one another as they bond over the new child (Bost, Cox, Burchinal, & Payne, 2002; Fischer, 1988). Heterosexual parents often report greater closeness to their own parents following the birth of a child (Levitt, Weber, & Clark, 1986). In contrast, contact with friends tends to diminish following the transition to parenthood (Bost, Cox, Burchinal, & Payne, 2002; Carberry & Buhrmester, 1998; Gameiro et al., 2010). Couples may also restructure their friendship networks once they become parents, such that they spend less time with nonparents and become closer to individuals with young children (Brown, 2010; Cronenwett, 1985; Drentea & Moren-Cross, 2005; Lewin, 1993).

This is not necessarily the scenario that plays out for gay male couples when they become parents. Studies indicate that the family members of sexual minorities demonstrate a range of reactions to their coming out, with responses ranging from outright rejection to grudging tolerance to acceptance and pride (Weeks, Heaphy, & Donovan, 2001; Weston, 1991). When children enter the picture, some individuals experience an intensification of rejection by family members or a withdrawal of acceptance and support. Politically conservative and religious family members in particular may hold the belief that children do best when raised by a mother and father, and may disapprove of gay men's parenting intentions (Goldberg, 2010a). On the other hand, some experience a reversal of rejection such that family members become more involved with and accepting of their gay family member once he or she announces the intention to parent (Goldberg, 2006; Sullivan, 2004). Family members who once experienced discomfort about men's sexual orientation may find that this sentiment is overridden by excitement about the reality of a new family member (Ben-Ari & Livni, 2006; Sullivan, 2004). Further, gay men's expression and enactment of stereotypically heteronormative interests and life goals may in some cases have the effect of "erasing" (or at least diminishing) their sexuality such that they are accepted, even embraced, in a way that was unimaginable pre-parenthood.

Sexual minorities who become parents may encounter a different set of reactions by friends. Mallon (2004), who studied gay men who had become parents in the 1980s, noted that some of the men in his study described negative reactions from gay men in particular, who challenged them for trying to "be [like] straight people" (p. 89). Similarly, in her study of gay fathers, Lewin (2009) noted that some men described having lost friendships once they became parents, in part because their old friends could not get used to the constraints that parenting imposed on their social life. In some cases, gay fathers described hostility from gay male friends in particular, who viewed them as selling out to the "straight world." In other cases, though, men reported that their friendships with their gay friends were maintained, despite the divergent nature of their social worlds.

The narratives of the gay men in this book provide rich evidence of the complex ways that parenthood significantly altered the quality and nature of their social networks. As we will see, there are dramatic and sometimes unpredictable shifts in gay men's family and friend relationships, which may have long-term implications for the kind of social lives the men lead, the kinds of resources they bring to parenthood, and so on.

Men's Pre-parenthood Perceptions of Support from Families of Origin

As in Luis and Henry's case, I asked the men pre-adoption how supportive their families and their partner's families were of their plans to adopt. In general, the men described feeling fairly well supported by their families of origin with respect to their adoption plans during the pre-adoption period. They attributed their family members' support or nonsupport to a variety of factors.

Supportive Families

Two-thirds of the men (46 men, including 18 couples) described a supportive response to their adoption intentions by one partner's family of origin, and one-third of the men (22 men, including eight couples) described both partners' families of origin as responding to their parental aspirations in a positive and supportive manner. Carter, a 37-year-old White teacher living in a midwestern suburb, recalled his own and his partner Patrick's families' response to their announcement that they were pursuing adoption:

> We actually got to tell all four parents on the same evening. They had all come over. We live about two hours from each of our parents and we had them all over for dinner. Right before dinner, we were all making a toast. Patrick led right into the conversation. He made the toast to family and he said, "And to expanding ours!" You could have heard a pin drop. Tears were shed and joys were expressed.

Many family members expressed their support by inquiring regularly about the adoption process (e.g., asking, among those couples who were pursuing open adoption, whether they had gotten any calls from prospective birth mothers) and buying items (e.g., toys, clothes, and furniture) for their future family member. These actions functioned to acknowledge the reality of the men's impending parenthood ("You are going to be parents") and to communicate acceptance of this reality ("And we are happy for you"). In this way, their families' support represented an indirect rejection of the heteronormative nuclear family model, whereby heterosexual-parent families are viewed as "real" families (Oswald, Blume, & Marks, 2005). Robbie, a 34-year-old White IT manager living in a metropolitan area in the South, described his partner Finn's family like this:

> Everyone is supportive, even his extended family. Cousins and aunts and uncles, they are all real supportive and there're all real excited and his parents even moved here in hopes that they would be grandparents. So they can't wait. Every day they are asking, "So how did it go today?" We call and stop by and give them the scoop on everything.

As Robbie's quote indicates, family members' excitement was often directly related to their longing for grandchildren. In a few cases, the men were actually viewed as their parents' "only hope" for grandchildren (e.g., because they were only children or because their siblings were not planning to have children). The men's announcement of possible parenthood was met with surprise, relief, and excitement, especially because many of their parents had assumed they would never become grandparents because their sons were gay. As Vaughn, a 39-year-old White man asserted, "My sister is going for her PhD, and she's declared that she's not going to have any children. And so my father says, 'You're my only hope for grandchildren.' I'm like, I love it!" Likewise, Patrick, a 41-year-old White man, revealed, "My brother and sister in-law are having fertility issues. I think my parents are eager to be grandparents." Thus, somewhat ironically, some gay men were viewed by their parents as more likely to provide them with grandchildren than were their heterosexual siblings, at least in the immediate future.

For many of these men, their families' support came as no surprise. They described their families as having always been accepting of their sexuality and current relationship, and they did not expect anything less than excitement and enthusiasm when they shared their parenthood plans. In a few cases, however, the men described their families as more supportive of their adoption plans than they had anticipated. These men were sensitive to the fact that tolerance of homosexuality does not necessarily extend to tolerance of homosexual parenting (Gallup, 2010), and they were aware that even family members who were relatively accepting of their sexuality might not support them in their parenthood aspirations in general or their choice to adopt in particular. Thus they recalled having been anxious about whether their family members would accept their child—concerns that fortunately did not come to pass. As Finn, a 44-year-old White hospital administrator in an urban area of the South, recalled:

> It was really funny because I never told anybody that I wanted to be a parent. Robbie and I definitely decided this was what we were going to do before we [told them]. I went home for the holidays and I was going to tell Mom and Dad about it and it was like fifty-fifty—either they are not going to like this or they are going to like this. I really did not know what to expect. I was waiting for the right moment and it came. So we sat down for about two hours, and I did my little spiel about open adoption and talked about it. I covered every base that I could possibly cover. They were sitting there, just nodding. I was like, "Do you have any questions?" My dad gets up and he does this little happy dance and he grabs his belt loop and says, "Finally, my boy's grown up!" He was so happy, he was just beside himself.

Unsupportive Families

Not all men were met with unconditional support when they announced their intentions to adopt. Two-thirds of the men (i.e., 46 men) described one partner's family of origin as supportive of their parenthood aspirations; thus two-thirds of the men described at least some members of one partner's family of origin as unsupportive. According to these men, their family members' lack of support was rooted in several different beliefs and concerns. Not surprisingly, there were overlaps among them, and some participants described their family members as having multiple reasons for resisting men's parenthood aspirations.

HOMOPHOBIA-RELATED REASONS FOR NONSUPPORT

Many of the men described their families' lack of support as stemming from homophobia. Specifically, 18 of these men (including three couples) described their families' lack of support of their parenthood aspirations as a natural offshoot of their long-standing disapproval of homosexuality. Certain members of their family had been explicitly unsupportive of their sexuality or their partner relationships, and proved unsupportive of the men's decision to become parents. Luis, whose story was profiled in the opening of this chapter, revealed:

> It's a difficult situation. My father is not accepting at all. . . . My father didn't come to our wedding. He is not supportive of my relationship and my life-style. So, you know, as much as I think he would love to have a grandchild, he thinks that it'll be made somewhat hard by my life, so to speak.

Thomas, a 36 year-old real White estate agent living in a southern suburb, recalled his partner Devon's mother's stunned and upset response to their announcement that they were adopting:

> She was like, "Why are you doing this?" I know that she has told family members that she is concerned that babies cost a lot and blah blah blah. But she doesn't know how much we have in our savings and she doesn't know how much we make. I think it boils down to the gay issue. I truly do. I think she has given every family member every excuse except what the true matter is, which is the gay issue.

Consistent with previous research that suggests that lesbians and gay men often attribute their family members' accepting or rejecting behaviors to their religious views (Oswald, 2002; Rostosky, Riggle, Brodnicki, & Olson, 2008), nine of the men (including three couples) explained their families' lack of support for their parental aspirations in terms of their families' religious or politically conservative values and communities, which condemned non-heterosexuality and regarded "homosexuality" and "family" as incompatible entities. These men often emphasized that their families lived in rural or conservative areas of the country and were heavily involved in their churches; they blamed these influences on their families' negative attitudes regarding gay parenting. Brian, a 52-year-old White sales manager in a northeastern suburb, described his partner Gregory's mother's negative response to their adoption plans as firmly rooted in her staunch religious convictions:

His mother is still fairly against the idea of us having a child. She actually thinks that we're both going to hell. She's Baptist. She's pretty hardcore. So, even though she treats me with a lot of respect and has treated us as a couple with more respect recently, at the core she still believes that this is wrong and that we're going to hell as a result of it. So the idea of us having a child doesn't sit right with her, and no matter how much we try to give her the rational explanation of why we'll be such good parents and why this is a good thing, it doesn't matter. It's interesting, because I bet that she would probably say that we would be good parents, it's just still that because homosexuality isn't right, then it's not right to raise a child in that environment either.

Thus, because of their close adherence to conservative religious or social values that condemned homosexuality, their family members apparently felt compelled to denounce gay men's parenting intentions. Their refusal to support the men's parenting aspirations had both practical and symbolic consequences. On a practical level, their lack of support effectively denied these men—and themselves—the pleasure of collectively anticipating the arrival of a new family member. On a symbolic level, their unwillingness or inability to support these men's parenting aspirations functioned to uphold and reify heteronormativity (Oswald, Blume, & Marks, 2005).

Eight men (including two couples) perceived their family members' lack of support as rooted in concerns regarding the well-being of children raised by gay parents. According to these men, their family members generally tended to express two primary concerns: all children need a mother, and children raised by gay parents will be teased or harassed about their family structure. In essence, family members believed that it was "unfair" to bring a child into a situation in which he or she might be disadvantaged because of the lack of a maternal presence, or stigmatized because of his or her parents' sexual orientation. Such concerns reflect and are rooted in broader heteronormative ideologies that depict heterosexual, two-parent families as the norm (Clarke, 2001; Oswald, Blume, & Marks, 2005; Stacey, 1996). For example, Harvey, a 41-year-old Asian American sales representative who was living in an urban area on the West Coast, described his mother as "apprehensive" of his plans to adopt, because she "still thinks that a mom and a dad is the better situation." Scott, a 47-year-old Latino physician living in a Northeast metro area, said that his sister's first reaction to his plan to adopt was to admonish him, saying, "You know, that kid will need some kind of maternal figure, or, you know, a female figure in her life or his life." Joshua, a 40-year-old White administrative assistant who resided in a suburb in the

South, recalled his father's concerns related to the potential for stigmatization and teasing:

> Dad's the one who was more vocal about being opposed to it. His only comment was, "I kind of have the same feeling I have with mixed-race couples having kids. I mean, if you want to get married and you're mixed race, that's fine, and if you're gay and want to live together, that's fine. But when you bring a child into it, it stigmatizes them and they have all these things to deal with." And, okay, I can understand my dad's perspective on that. However, the reality is that these kids have had so much that they've dealt with, that if you have a stable home, that would be a great plus for them. So, the fact that they're having to deal with "Heather has two mommies" or "Daddy's roommate," eh . . . I don't think that he is looking at all the data, I don't think he's processing all the data. I think he's looking at it from a limited perspective.

Timothy, a 41-year-old White sales manager in the suburban Northeast, described similar concerns from his parents, but, like Joshua, he rejected the notion that the possibility that a child might be teased because of his parents' sexual orientation meant that he should not adopt:

> I think they're a little worried that we're, you know, taking it a little casually. We keep saying, "We understand, we're going to talk to him, we'll help him understand, and yeah, some kids might make fun, but we'll deal with that." They're a little worried about, are we taking it as seriously as we need to? And they see it as being a huge, huge obstacle and we see it as being a bump. So, I don't want to dismiss it, but I don't want to dwell on it either, otherwise, no child would ever get adopted, if people dwell on it too much.

Both Joshua and Timothy acknowledged that their parents' concerns about teasing were not unwarranted—perhaps in part because of fear of the social repercussions of dismissing such concerns. Indeed, gay men may worry that were they to resist the common assumption that children of gay parents will be taunted—or, even further, the notion that an elevated risk of teasing is justification for denying gay couples the right to adopt—they will be attacked as selfishly dismissing what is so obviously in "the best interest of the child" (Clarke, 2001). At the same time, these two men—as well as several others—asserted their conviction that the benefits of being adopted into a loving home far outweighed the potential "costs" of being a member of a socially stigmatized family structure. In this way, at the same time that gay men may pay "lip service" to societal concerns about gay parenthood, they actively assert their *right* to adopt, thereby rejecting the assumption that gay parents are less legitimate or capable than are heterosexual parents (Clarke, 2001; Goldberg, 2010a).

Finally, nine men (including one couple) observed that their families' lack of support for their parenting intentions in part derived from the family's fear of being outed. According to these men, their family members were concerned about how they would explain the "situation" to neighbors, church members, colleagues, and other extended family members, and how such individuals might react to the news that they had a gay son/sibling. These family members had previously been successful in concealing the men's sexual orientation. They were concerned about how men's decision to become parents would affect *their* lives and privacy, because their new status as grandparents would inevitably raise questions about the men's relational status, means of becoming a parent, and so on (Sullivan, 2004). And yet all the men asserted that, although they loved their family members, they would not support or participate in their parents' closeting. For example, Nolan, a 36-year-old White man, responded to his parents' anxieties about being "outed" to their extended family and neighbors—and, specifically, their panicked question, "What are we going to tell people?"—by saying, "I don't know, but you're going to have to tell them something because I'm not going to hide my life. If you're going to be involved in my life and [my family's] life, you're going to have to figure something out." Likewise, Drew, a 33-year-old White retail manager living in a suburb on the West Coast, asserted:

> They're getting there. Have you ever heard of the expression "keeping up appearances"? That's kind of my mom. It's about keeping up appearances and what would the neighbors say and so on. So there's definitely a sense of, they really weren't quite sure what to make of it or what to think or say or do. And I think part of it is, "How do I explain to the neighbors when your 'friend'"—as they sometimes refer to him—"and you have a baby?" I think that was the initial sense around that. [So] we've basically told them that once we get a child, the child will come first, above anybody and everybody else. I think they're starting to realize that.

As Drew's quote illustrates, the men typically responded to their extended family members' concerns by emphasizing their commitment to their child, above all else, and by firmly refusing to compromise their own families' integrity to make their extended families more "comfortable." In this way, they clearly communicated that their family members would need to move beyond their comfort zone in order to have a relationship with their grand-child, niece, or nephew—and not the other way around. The men's refusal to participate silently in their family members' closeting represents a powerful act of resistance. Although they strongly desired their family members' support and involvement, these men were unwilling to compromise their own families' integrity to achieve it.

ADOPTION-RELATED REASONS FOR NONSUPPORT

Some of the men perceived their families' nonsupport as stemming in part from concerns or biases regarding adoption. Six men (including one couple) noted that at least some family members had concerns about the "unpredictable genetics" involved in adoption, and would have preferred that men have their own biological children (e.g., by pursuing surrogacy). Family members appeared to hold the belief that their own genes were invariably superior to those of potential birth mothers, who were often stereotyped as more likely than not to be drug addicted and mentally ill (Dorow, 2006; Wegar, 1997). These beliefs reflect the dominance of genetic discourses to cultural understandings and definitions of "family," which, as the psychologists Shona Crabb and Martha Augoustinos (2008) argue, "can function to mark out 'real' families from others, and to reproduce and construct as 'natural' socially conservative notions of the family" (p. 305). Frank, a 39-year-old White physician in an urban area of the West Coast, shared:

> I think that my dad falls a bit in the narcissistic spectrum, and he sort of feels that it would be much better to have our genetics in this kid, and you definitely don't want some stupid woman, to get their kid, or somebody who's all drugged out, to get their kid. I think from his standpoint, he just thought that surrogacy was a much safer way to go, even to the point where he was like, "You know, if you do surrogacy I'll help pay for it, but if you do adoption, I won't."

Five men (including one couple) noted that their family members had expressed worries related to the possibly transracial nature of the adoption, whereby they were resistant to the notion that they would be expected to bond with a child of a different race, or were concerned that adopting a child of a different race would make the men's families "too visible." Such expressions of concern may also reflect family members' worries about how *their* lives might be affected, as well as their preference for a less "noticeable" family—that is, one that conforms (at least on the surface) to dominant notions of what a family "should" look like (Goldberg, 2009b; Goldberg, Kinkler, &

Hines, 2011). In explaining why his mother would have preferred that he and his partner adopt a White child, Derek, a 32-year-old software consultant, who was Italian, explained:

> My mother is married to a man who is very bigoted. Not like full-fledged Nazi, but like Archie Bunker. He's like a buffoon, he's like a racist buffoon. But in the same sentence that he insults somebody, he says that he loves everyone. So it's just strange. And I think because my mother is in such an insular Italian community where, you know, to be different is such a, it stands out so much, I think that's what she is reacting to—the possibility of being different and the possibility of how that could be awkward. Like being a gay parent makes you even more visible as a gay person than you've ever been before, and so I think having a Black child, for my mother, it's like, too visible. Like obviously they're going to be like, "Oh, where's the mother of the baby?"

Several of these men, including Derek, acknowledged that they came to appreciate their family members' concerns about the ways that adopting transracially might expose their families to a particularly high level of scrutiny. Further, they noted that because they desired their families' support, they felt somewhat compelled to pursue a same-race placement. Joshua, a 40-year-old White man, affirmed, "Lars and I are both open to a child of any race or ethnicity; however, we want the support of my parents and they're not supportive." Desiring their family's support, and unwilling to risk losing it because they adopted a child of the "wrong race," these men yielded to their parents' racial values and preferences. It is notable that all the men who described accommodating to their families' racial preferences resided in rural or small metropolitan areas, relatively near their families of origin, and described their families as their primary support network. They were therefore in a less powerful position than other men in the study to advocate for their racial preferences because, had they dismissed their families' racial attitudes, they risked losing their primary support resources.

OTHER REASONS FOR NONSUPPORT

The men described several other worries that their families had expressed upon learning of their parenthood intentions. Three men (one couple) noted that their family members had questioned their decision to significantly alter what they perceived as a fun and independent lifestyle, and wondered whether they were prepared to make the changes in lifestyle that parenthood required. Gerard, a 48-year-old White architect in the urban Northeast, described how his brother and sister-in-law had repeatedly asked him, "Do you really know what you are getting yourself into?" Gerard recounted, "They look at us, we are a gay couple, we have a very nice lifestyle, we travel, we do a lot of great things and they're thinking, this does not mesh with the lifestyle we have right now. Why would they want to choose this?" According to Gerard, then, his family members were not resistant to the notion of him parenting because they believed that gay couples could not be good parents; rather, they seemed to question why he and his partner would *want* to become parents, as well as whether they were truly prepared for the commitment that parenthood entailed. In this way, although their apparent concerns are not ostensibly homophobic, they do hint at stereotypes of gay men as pleasure seeking and consumerist (Stossel & Binkley, 2006).

Two men noted that their sisters were currently dealing with fertility issues and were therefore upset by the possibility that their gay brothers might become parents before they did. Their inability to conceive in the context of heterosexual marriages created feelings of resentment concerning their brothers' family-building efforts, which they did not attempt to hide. While their own "normative" parenthood strivings were being frustrated, their gay brothers were actively seeking to fulfill their own "nonnormative" desires.

Men's Post-parenthood Perceptions of Support from Families of Origin

The arrival of a child marks a dramatic shift in individuals' lives, as they reconfigure their roles and identities to reflect and accommodate the newest addition to their families. For extended family and friends of the new parents, the arrival of a child may also initiate changes in roles and identities. For example, family members may lay claim to their new roles as grandparents and aunts and uncles—and, accordingly, offer emotional and instrumental support to the new parents. Some family members, however, may fail to respond to the arrival of a child as a cause for celebration—indeed, their own values, beliefs, and concerns regarding gay parenting and adoption may preclude an affirmative response. As we will see, the families of the men in this study were described as responding in diverse ways to their transition to parenthood. In some cases, the men's families' level of support—or nonsupport—was expected, therefore provoking little surprise or adjustment on the part of the men. But in some cases, the men observed dramatic and surprising shifts in their families of origin's endorsement of, and engagement with, their families of creation.

Families Consistently Supportive: No Change

Many of the men noted that those family members who had been supportive of their parenthood aspirations before the adoption continued to be supportive once they actually became parents. For example, Finn, the 44-year-old White hospital administrator, who had described his family as very supportive pre-adoption, exclaimed, "Everybody, our friends our families, they just fell in love with him immediately. They've been really just wonderful and supportive." In many cases, although their families' support was anticipated, the men were surprised by just how much practical support in particular they received from family. They expressed gratitude for the gifts, child-care assistance, meals, parenting books, and hand-me-downs that family members gave them in the few short months since they had brought their children home. As Russell, a 41-year-old executive director, exclaimed, "Visits, home-cooked meals, offers for babysitting . . . people were always incredibly supportive but I didn't realize there would be so much practical support and how valuable that would be. It is more the actual actions." Similarly, Carl, a 41-year-old White fund-raising director living in a suburb on the West Coast, expressed gratitude for the practical assistance that he and his partner, Jason, had received from their families, particularly the free babysitting they provided:

> I feel like we're just lucky that we have that added in. I almost feel like, you know, we definitely could not be doing our work schedule at all if our families weren't helping out, that's for sure. Jason definitely needs to go in a day or two a week and I still need to be at my job full-time so it's, not having family around, there's no way we would have been able to make that work. We would have had to hire a nanny or put her in day care early or something like that.

Carl recognized that in the absence of such immediate and extensive family support, he and Jason would have had to rely on a more complicated and expensive child-care arrangement. Implicitly, he suggests that free babysitting is the type of help that family members—but not necessarily friends—voluntarily provide, and he is therefore grateful to have "family around." This sentiment, although only implied, supports the notion that for many new parents—heterosexual and gay—family members occupy a unique role in that they can be counted on to provide the kind of regular "free" care that would be difficult, and perhaps impossible, to ask of friends (Gattai & Musatti, 1999; Lewin, 1993). It also highlights the potential significance of social and instrumental resources—familial or not—in shaping couples' adjustment to parenthood.

Families Increasingly Supportive: Positive Change in Support

Some of the men described dramatic shifts in the support they received from family, whereby at least some family members were perceived as becoming more supportive once the men became parents. Indeed, 23 men (including five couples) noted that members of their own or their partner's families had expressed concern, discomfort, or ambivalence regarding their parenthood aspirations prior to the adoption—but they emphasized that these individuals were now "completely on board." Thus half the men who had described previous nonsupport from their families perceived them as becoming more supportive. These findings are consistent with those of the sociologist Maureen Sullivan (2004), who interviewed 34 lesbian-mother families in the San Francisco Bay Area and found that many women recounted what Sullivan referred to as "conversion narratives" in connection with their parents' (and other family members') responses to their children's arrival. These women asserted that their families' bigotry or indifference to their parenting efforts had "melted away under the charm of a baby and the symbolic weight of . . . kinship" (p. 131). Similarly, many of the men whom I interviewed attributed their families' change in sentiment to the fact that "everybody loves babies." They observed that their families could not help but fall in love with the newest, adorable addition to their families, and now expressed a strong desire to be involved in the child's life—despite a previous lack of acceptance of men's sexuality and parenthood aspirations. As Frank, the 39-year-old White physician, who had previously worried about his parents' level of support given their difficulty accepting his homosexuality, revealed:

> They've been very supportive. My mom came out here and stayed with us for a week. My brother stayed for a little while. Cooper's dad came out and stayed with us for a week. And then my parents are throwing us a little party to welcome Benny into the family. So everybody has been incredibly supportive. It is actually kind of a surprise for me because my parents, they had a lot of trouble with my being gay. It was years and years and years before we could even really have a visit where the issue didn't come up in some negative way. And I distinctly remember, probably about 10 or 15 years ago, when I first mentioned to my mom that I might adopt someday, she just, she flipped. And she was like, "How could you do this to yourself? How could you even think of doing that to a poor innocent little child?"

And those are things that sort of stick with you as a gay person. But she has been amazing. She is just so thrilled and I think really, just in many ways, this has finally contradicted all of her fears that she has had—that I wasn't going to be happy, that I would never have a family, that I would never fit into society. And Benny is just so adorable; she just fell absolutely in love with him.

According to Frank, although his mother was previously worried that her son would never lead a "normal" life, yet was also vehemently against the idea of him adopting a "poor, innocent" little child, she ultimately "fell absolutely in love" with Benny. The experience of becoming a grandmother presumably helped to minimize or overshadow her objections about gay parenthood. In this way, gay male parenthood has the potential to engender greater affirmation from family members, in that their family status may make them more "intelligible" (Lewin, 2009). The gay men in this study tended to respond to increased acceptance from family members with pleasure, perhaps reflecting their preference to maintain relationships with families of origin, even those that may be fractured in some way. Their desire to be accepted by their families of origin may reflect, as the anthropologist Ellen Lewin (1993) has argued, their desire to be "connect[ed] . . . to a larger kinship grouping, making it more durable and resilient and offering continuity over time," as well as their yearning to be "legitimated," given that the broader society often refuses to accept or validate their families of creation (p. 94).

Although most family members' initial lack of support was viewed as originating in their religious beliefs or general disapproval of homosexuality, in a few cases it appeared to be related to concerns about adoption that had, over time, dissipated. The "adopted child" that they had once envisioned was now simply their grandchild (or niece or nephew). Stan, a 32-year-old White professor living in an urban area on the West Coast, described his partner Dean's family's evolution in support like this:

I think we had some anxiety about Dean's side of the family because traditionally, in Chinese culture, adoption is something that only happens within families. You would simply not adopt someone else's baby unless that baby was your kin, in which case then you raised that baby as yours. . . . You may raise your sister's kid as your daughter but that's not considered adoption in the same way as raising a stranger's kid as your daughter. And so we had some anxiety about that. Dean's mom had made a couple comments about how she would never love the baby because it wouldn't be hers. And it would never be her grandchild and other stuff.

And then when we got to their house with Caitlyn and they met, she went completely out of her mind. She's so in love. She was so excited. She had gone out and got all this stuff and she had told all these people that her new grandbaby was coming and she was just nuts about her. His mom . . . usually, she just needs time . . . to kind of work through stuff on her own and she doesn't communicate that's what she's doing but then she gets to a point of being pretty resolved to whatever it is that she was trying to work through. It was encouraging and a pleasant surprise but it was definitely a bit of a surprise *(laughs)*.

Of note is that three men of color (two African American, one Latino) viewed their families as becoming more supportive because they had adopted children of their same race. These family members—who were originally described as unsupportive due to their religious beliefs or negative ideas about adoption—were ultimately more embracing of the child than the men expected, which the men attributed to their "relief" that the child was non White—and, more specifically, was of their same race. Todd, a 46-year-old African American man who adopted an African American male infant named Emmett with his partner, Nick, who was White, stated:

It's been kind of weird for people to say like, "Oh, you know, he kind of has your nose. He kind of has your eyes." But, you know, it's been fine. . . . I mean, it's kind of nice and I think that my family looks it as you know, it's the first child that Todd has, and, you know, it kind of looks like him, or you know, he has his color. Because I think that—I don't think they would have abandoned me if we had a child that was White, but I think it would have been [rough]. . . . Because, you know, there aren't any White children in my family.

Todd's adoption of a child that "kind of look[ed]" like him presumably facilitated his family's ability to more easily connect to their new family member. As Todd suggests, his family may have struggled to relate to a White child because "there aren't any White children in my family." Indeed, his family members may have felt ill prepared to deal with the racialized dynamics of being the African American grandparents to a White child, for example.

In addition to the 23 men who noted dramatic positive changes in their families' level of support, seven men (including one couple) observed "slight movement toward the positive" in their families' level of support, but emphasized that their families far from embraced their new status as parents.

Donovan, a 42-year-old Latino engineer living in a northeastern suburb, asserted about his brother, "John was very uncomfortable with it, but I think he is a little more comfortable now [that the child is home]. Hopefully what it is, is that he is seeing that we are just parents, parents of a normal child."

IMPROVED RELATIONSHIPS

Importantly, nine of the men who perceived their family members as becoming more supportive over time emphasized their perception that the adoption had actually functioned to improve their relationships with family members. They felt that becoming parents themselves had brought them closer to their families of origin. Indeed, the birth or adoption of a child often helps to reestablish links between family members (such as between parents and their grown children) that had become distant over time (Gattai & Musatti, 1999). For example, James, a 41-year-old White urban planner turned stay-at-home father, asserted about his sister, "I think it has strengthened our relationship. . . . I mean, I don't want to be unrealistic and make it seem like we're the best of friends because we're not terribly close, but it has definitely, it has improved our relationship." Several of these men noted that their family members' increased support appeared to extend beyond encouraging them as new parents, such that they now seemed more accepting of the men's relationships with their partners. Cooper, a 39-year-old multiracial physician assistant living in an urban area on the West Coast, shared:

> When his parents first met me, they weren't really happy about it. Frank had never brought anyone home before me. They knew that Frank was gay or that Frank had told them, but it wasn't really talked about. But I think that they were sort of able to kind of ignore it as an issue or as a part of his life because there wasn't any real, concrete reminders of it. . . . It was kind of tough in the beginning but they opened up over the next few years. After we adopted Benny, in the last few months, we just get a lot of calls from them. The family—I think it has really helped our relationships with our families. In some ways, maybe in my dad's mind, it sort of puts me on par with my brother who has got kids and it sort of validates my relationship with him.

As Cooper highlights, some family members—particularly parents— were perceived as becoming more accepting of men's sexuality and partnerships during their transition to parenthood. Perhaps because these men had recently become parents, their parents were prompted to accept their intimate-partner relationships as more or less permanent. Also, Cooper suggests that to his father, his becoming a parent "puts [him] on par with [his] brother who has kids." Becoming a parent made his own family more valid, real, and "intelligible" in his father's eyes (Lewin, 2009); that is, he was viewed as having the same kind of conventional desires and lifestyle as his brother—and also his father. In this way, some of the men's involvement in parenthood had the effect of (hetero)normalizing them in some family members' eyes. Of course, the very fact that becoming parents rendered these gay men more acceptable to some family members serves to expose the power and ubiquity of heteronormativity (Oswald, Kuvalanka, Blume, & Berkowitz, 2009). Gay men who become parents may be viewed as more normative (less deviant) than gay men whose desires and kinship structures do not match the heterosexual nuclear family ideal, thereby reinforcing bifurcated notions of the "good gay" (i.e., the gay that acts/looks straight) and the "bad gay" (i.e., the deviant, non-family-oriented gay) (Landau, 2009).

For several men, adopting a child required them to come "out" finally to certain family members, an event that, although sometimes scary, ultimately fostered greater honesty and closeness in their relationships. Miles, a 40-year-old White consultant living in a northeastern suburb, described how parenthood had brought him closer to family members from whom he had previously felt relatively distant:

> I have extended cousins and aunts and uncles, none of whom I have ever told I was gay, and it sort of weighed on my mind and I'd say to my dad and my sisters who would run into these people, "You know, just tell them for me," because I don't see them unless it is a funeral or something. . . . So anyways, I did tell the family and actually my sister told my aunt, who now watches him one day a week and they were all completely fine with it. And you know, I was talking to my aunt this morning when I dropped him off and I realized that this is the longest conversation I have had with her in my entire life. . . . So it's funny because it is like he is bringing everybody together. She was saying that my uncle comes down and holds Dylan and laughs when Dylan is at their house. The other day he yelled to my sister when she was leaving, "Tell Miles that he has got one beautiful baby here! I just love this guy!" So you know, they are all just totally accepting.

For Miles, the simultaneous events of coming out and adopting actually seemed to bring him closer to family members with whom he had had previously had very little contact. Far from rejecting him for his sexuality, some of his extended family members actually became regular child-care providers. The issue of Miles' sexuality was perhaps rendered less salient by, or more acceptable in the context of, his newly acquired parental status—and, in turn, the delight that his family members experienced when interacting with Dylan. In this way, Dylan's arrival functioned as a relational bridge in that family members of different generations were brought together to celebrate his existence.

FAMILY MEMBERS ARE MORE OUT

Five men described their families as not only more supportive, but also more "out" in their own lives as a result of becoming grandparents. As Maureen Sullivan (2004) described, gay parenthood can prompt a phenomenon where "straight becomes gay": heterosexual family members become progressively more open about being "gay by association" in their interactions and relationships with neighbors, colleagues, friends, and community members. By publicly acknowledging and embracing the reality of men's homosexuality, heterosexual family members actively resist heteronormativity (Oswald, Blume, & Marks, 2005; Oswald, Kuvalanka, Blume, & Berkowitz, 2009). For example, the 35-year-old Barry, a White IT manager in an urban area in the Midwest, similarly recounted how his partner Rett's mother threw them a "baby shower," to which she invited many members of her extended family:

Rett's got kind of a big extended family. They're all pretty conservative, and they live in a rural area. So we weren't quite sure what to expect. But his mom told us that she was having all the aunts over. And she never called it a shower, but it was just all of the aunts and the female cousins and us, and they all brought gifts for the baby, so it was essentially a baby shower that she had organized, but nobody had called it a baby shower. And it was just so—so heartwarming to see everybody get together and celebrate Christopher.

Similarly, Theo, a 40-year-old White chef living in a West Coast suburb, described how his father had sent out holiday cards with his daughter's picture on them—an act that represents a bold, and proud, symbolic assertion of who is considered "family" (Almack, 2008):

My father sent out Christmas cards with Emma's picture on them this year. Now, that was a huge issue for him, because all of his brothers and sisters are Evangelical Christians and he is not. He never mentioned anything about me being gay or anything like that. I mean, when my sister had her wedding, Dashaun came with me but we just did, "This is Dashaun, he is a friend of mine." Basically we didn't want to bring it up. Well, he sent out these Christmas cards and it was sort of his coming out. . . . It was rough and you never know when you come out how people are going to react. He actually got quite a bit of support. They were like, "We have known he was gay for years." . . . Yeah, I mean, and we had all figured that they had figured it out, but being Evangelical we didn't know how they were. So my dad just went through that and that was pretty tough for him, I think.

Both Theo and Barry described ways in which their family members had unequivocally affirmed them by announcing their growing families—and, in doing so, risked possible rejection from (conservative) extended family members. Such public acts of resistance to heteronormativity are particularly notable in that they came from heterosexual family members, who had "something to lose" (heterosexual privilege) by publicly legitimating these gay men's family identities. Of interest is *why* family members would out themselves and risk possible rejection. In her book on lesbian motherhood, Sullivan (2004) offers a suggestion as to why the arrival of a new family member, such as a grandchild, inspires family members to reveal what they once kept hidden within the privacy of their own family. She observes that "the addition of a human link to the family who would experience homophobic hostility at some point in her or his life seems to expose the injustice [of heterosexism] in a way that the same hostility experienced by the lesbian daughter could not" (p. 150). In other words, she argues, a child's arrival enables nongay family members to "see that the only 'problem of homosexuality' is the problem of societal heterosexist organization—that simply by virtue of their connection with their lesbian parents, children would be exposed to vicarious discrimination and hostility" (p. 150). It is possible that for family members who were previously unable to move beyond the feelings of shame about the men's sexual orientation, the arrival of an "innocent" child prompted them to engage in a more emotionally complex confrontation with the realities of heterosexism, and to acknowledge the "queerness" in their own families with greater confidence and even pride. In this way, the arrival of a child stimulated not only increased support of their gay family members but possibly shifts in their own identity as the parent (or sister, or brother) of a gay person.

Ambivalent: Supportive Yet Concerned

In four cases, men described their family members as supportive and involved but observed that they continued to grapple with issues related to their homosexuality. According to the men, these family members believed that homosexuality was wrong and that gay persons should not adopt, yet their lived experience with gay parenting significantly clashed with these views. They were faced with the challenge of reconciling the disparity between their religious conviction and the reality of their own lives (Lease & Shulman, 2003). For example, the 37-year-old Ryan, a White engineer in a metropolitan area on the West Coast, remarked:

> I think [Harvey's] parents and my parents are sort of in the same place, which is that they're pretty religious and conservative, and I think that they have mixed feelings. They think it's great on one hand, but they're not sure where that squares with this larger political thing about same-sex marriage and what they think about gay rights and stuff like that. It's like they support us, but they're not sure where that jibes with the political stuff, and [they are] trying to make sense of all that. . . . It reminds me of, at some point I realized that what I was taught in Sunday school didn't really work with what I was being taught about [science]. . . . So I think that's the closest I can come to understanding their struggle of fitting this together with their kids that they love and their grandkids who they love. They think it's great on a personal basis but they can't quite fit it together with their beliefs and what they're told and what they hear.

Family members such as Ryan's parents were depicted as enthusiastic about the new addition to their families at the same time that they continued to maintain certain religious and political beliefs that denigrated homosexuality. Perhaps fearful of censure or attack (from community members, other family members, or God), they avoided challenging or even confronting heteronormativity, choosing instead to maintain their current system of beliefs while offering ambivalent support to their gay family members.

Families Consistently Unsupportive: No Change

Eight men (including two couples) noted that certain family members had been resistant to their parenthood plans pre-adoption and showed no change in their attitudes after they had adopted. The arrival of their child, then, had not had any effect on their families' disapproval. It is notable that all these individuals described their family members' nonsupport as stemming from their disapproval of homosexuality coupled with religious or socially conservative belief systems. As Chuck, a 38-year-old White web developer in a northeastern suburb, stated, "There was always some division in my family in that my father and my brother are very conservative and my mother and my sister are more liberal. That existed before and the same amount of contact exists now as before. So it hasn't really changed much in relation to my family. It just sort of is." Similarly, Drew, the 36-year-old White retail manager, in referring to his partner Allan's brother, asserted:

> He never called. We sent out announcements, we sent out e-mails, there wasn't a thing said, and we were getting ready to go back and visit, and Allan is like, "I don't want to see him if he's going to be an asshole." So eventually Allan called him and said, "Is there a problem? You haven't acknowledged the fact that you have a new nephew and that I've had my first-born son." . . . And he quoted something about, "Some people say it's wrong for gay people to have children, but that's not really for me to decide." And we're like, "Well, no, it is up to you to decide whether it's right or not. And if you think it's right, then that's great, and if you don't, then we respect that but we'll take action accordingly. But don't detach yourself from it all."

Thus, although all these men acknowledged that their family members' lack of support, often evident in the form of silence or non-acknowledgement of the new arrival, did not generally come as any huge surprise, they expressed varying levels of disappointment regarding this nonsupport. Some men, like Chuck, simply resigned themselves to their families' non-involvement. But others, like Drew and Allan, were more confrontational, demanding clarity on exactly where their families stood so that they could "take action accordingly."

Families Less Supportive: Negative Change in Support

Two men reported that their families had actually become *less* supportive of the adoption across the transition to parenthood. These men's families were described as highly religious and thus minimally supportive of the men prior to becoming parents, and as withdrawing this minimal level of support once they became parents: "My father launched into this whole tirade about how he could not accept this and that it was against the Bible and all that good stuff." Thus, to these family members, gay parenthood represented a fundamental challenge to heteronormativity—and the gender, sexuality, and family binaries that they clearly valued (Oswald, Blume, & Marks, 2005).

Men's Pre-parenthood Perceptions of Support from Friends

Of course, family members were not the men's only source of support. The men in this study described rich and complex relationships with their friends, whose support was similarly variable in both the pre- and post-adoptive stages of parenthood.

Supportive Friends

Pre-parenthood, three-quarters of the men whom I interviewed (52 men, including 14 couples) described their friends as largely supportive and excited about their parenthood intentions. As the 38-year-old Nathan asserted, "Our friends have been, without exception, amazingly supportive of the entire process." Like family, one way that friends demonstrated their support was by inquiring about the adoption process. They asked questions, requested updates regarding the men's progress, and were open to learning about the intricacies of adoption. They also offered practical support in the form of hand-me-down clothes and furniture, as well as babysitting promises.

Select friends were designated as "godparents" and "aunts and uncles," suggesting that some friends were expected to play a special familial role in their child's life. As Doug, a 37-year-old White bank manager turned stay-at-home father on the West Coast, exclaimed, "They are all really excited. We have a lot of aunts and uncles all lined up. Everyone has said—well, they say it now whether or not it is true—they said they are going to be great babysitters (*laughs*), doing respite care and all that kind of stuff." By using the terms "aunts" and "uncles," which are typically terms designated for families of origin (and specifically for sisters and brothers), Doug implied a definition of family that was inclusive of very close friends. Some scholars (Allan, 2008; Spencer & Pahl, 2006) suggest that some friends may be "incorporated into the domain of family, usually because they have demonstrated a strong commitment and solidarity across time that is above that normally expected of friendship ties based on personal liking and sociability" (Allan, 2008, p. 7). Gay men and lesbians may be particularly likely to consider friends as family, in that rejection from families of origin may lead them to establish families of choice that are defined by the mutual exchange of social and instrumental support (Carrington, 1999; Weston, 1991). In this way, the boundaries of family membership are blurred and expanded to include non-biological, non–family of origin relationships (Oswald, Blume, & Marks, 2005).

Importantly, approximately half of the men who described their larger community of friends as largely supportive tended to also note explicitly that their friends were heterosexual and/or were biological parents. As Thomas, the 36-year-old White real estate agent, stated, "Most of our friends, probably 95% of our friends, are straight couples that we have known for years. Our best friends are a straight couple that we have known for 15 years and we live 10 minutes away from each other. They have been completely on board." Men's emphasis on these features of their friendship may function to illustrate how accepted they were by their straight friends, and how "unimportant" the issue of sexual orientation was in their larger friendship networks. Indeed, Stan, the 32-year-old White college professor, exclaimed:

> I think we're really lucky in that we have a community of friends that are just spectacular. Our Jewish community is extremely, extremely supportive. We have a group of, there's about eight young couples who are all in our late 20s, early 30s, and everyone in that group—a few couples have already had their first kids, but right now someone just had their baby a week ago and another one's due next month, and another one's due in March. And so it's sort of our pregnancy is being considered by that group of folks exactly the same as their pregnancies. You know, they're like, "Oh great, and depending on when you get chosen, have all of our hand-me-downs." It's like we're sequencing as a community of friends in the arrival, however it happens, of all of our kids.

Despite the fact that Stan and his partner, Dean, were unique in their circle of friends in that they were adopting a child, Stan observed that their adoption journey—which he actually refers to as their "pregnancy"—was not treated as any less meaningful or significant than their friends' pregnancies. Far from focusing on the ways the men's journey to parenthood differed from their own, his friends were depicted as excitedly sharing in the commonalities of their experience and looking forward to a shared future of playdates and birthday parties.

Not "Parent People" but Relatively Supportive

Twelve men (including one couple) described their friends as "not 'parent people' but relatively supportive." That is, their friends were described as being "in a very different place than we are" and as not having or wanting children, but offering a reasonable amount of affirmation in relation to the men's parenting aspirations. In contrast to the men described above, these men tended to characterize their social circles as largely comprising nonparent friends or gay friends. As Eric, a 40-year-old Latino marketing executive living in a metropolitan area on the West Coast, shared:

> Our friends have been pretty supportive. They're very curious about the whole process. It's actually kind of interesting because we don't really have

friends who are parents . . . so we get a lot of interesting looks from our friends. They don't really understand what we're doing or what we're thinking. They're in a different place in their lives. It's hard when we make different decisions and it's going to be a lot of sacrifices that we have to make in our lifestyle. They do know that and it kind of makes them nervous.

Thus, although friends offered their support for the men's decision to adopt, they also acknowledged that they were personally "in a different place in their lives," which limited the extent to which they could relate or be helpful. By extension, these friends reasonably anticipated that parenthood would mark a point of further divergence in their lives, interests, and activities. For example, Gerard, the 48-year-old White architect, expressed his sense that his friends "see this as something that potentially distances us from them because our lives are heading on a different path. . . . They somewhat joking said as soon as I told them, 'Okay, write you off the social list, we'll never see you again,' which I hate because I don't want that to happen."

According to the men's descriptions, some friends seemed somewhat ambivalent in their support. They responded to the men's announcement of their parenting intentions with muted enthusiasm, focusing mainly on how the men's becoming parents would affect *them*. Of primary concern was the likelihood that they would lose valued (child-free) time with their friends. Finn, 44, recounted his best friend John's response to his announcement: "He was like, 'Are you out of your mind?' It was because he was thinking of himself. He was thinking we would never be able to go to the gym again, we would never be able to do this or that again." John's shocked reaction (at least as recounted by Finn) suggests that in his eyes, Finn's decision to embark on parenthood signaled the eventual displacement of their eight-year friendship.

Gay Friends Less Supportive Than Straight Friends

Consistent with research showing that sexual minorities sometimes encounter a surprising lack of support and, in some cases, explicitly "negative feedback" from the gay community when they become parents (Lassiter et al., 2006; Ross, Steele, & Sapiro, 2005), seven men (including two couples) explicitly noted that their gay friends had been less supportive of and enthusiastic about their parenting intentions than were their heterosexual friends. They recounted that their gay friends had tended to respond to their news of parenthood with reactions that ranged from shock ("Are you insane?") to indifference, whereas their heterosexual friends were generally supportive, pumping them for information and offering them hand-me-down clothes and baby furniture. As Scott, a 47-year-old Latino physician living in a Northeast metro area, explained, "My closest friends were the most resistant to it. They were saying, 'How are you going do it? Are you crazy? Why are you doing it?' And the people who have known me the longest who are gay are the ones who are a little bit more questioning." Likewise, Drew, a 33-year-old White retail manager who resided in a suburb on the West Coast, asserted:

> Friends are generally supportive. It's interesting; I think some of our gay friends are not. It seems our gay friends are possibly having a harder time with it than our straight friends. Because our straight friends are like, "Great!," if they like babies. Then there are some people who are just like, "You want kids?!" But above all they're all very supportive and wonderful. Half of our gay friends have had a bit of a hard time with it, and see it from the perspective of "Why would you want to do that?" Not necessarily "Why do you want to imitate straight people?," but I don't know, just—I think some people come out as gay and feel like, "Okay, this isn't where I am," and then they don't do the family wedding and the children thing or the family thing. So it's like, "Why are you going there? That does not make sense."

To some of their gay friends, the men's plans to become parents did not seem to fit into their preconceived template of the "gay life cycle." To these gay friends (at least according to the participants), being gay meant not participating in weddings, children, and family, as these were artifacts of the heterosexual "way of life" they had renounced when they came out. In turn, they could not directly relate to the men's parenthood aspirations. To some extent, the men may have been viewed as violating gay normativity, or homonorms (Kurdek, 2005); that is, their pursuit of parenthood represented a transgression of norms associated with the gay community.

In contrast, the men's desire to parent was seen as more culturally accessible and acceptable to their heterosexual friends, for whom parenthood represented an expected stage of the life cycle (Letherby, 1999). Further, in that most of their heterosexual friends were already parents, the men's pursuit of parenthood represented an additional domain of shared interests and experiences. Elliott, a 40-year-old White executive director from a metropolitan area of the Northeast, stated, "It's just funny how a lot of my old friends that are straight and are married and have had kids have been so interested in the process, so excited about it. . . . So it's almost like a bonding thing."

Men's Post-parenthood Perceptions of Support from Friends

As with family, the arrival of a child may initiate positive and excited responses from friends. In particular, friends who are already parents may respond positively, because their own social lives easily intersect with those of the new parents. In contrast, friends who are not parents, or friends who resent, disapprove of, or are jealous of the gay men's decision to become parents, may respond poorly. As we will see, the gay men in this study described their friends as responding in both predictable and unpredictable ways to their transition to parenthood.

Consistently Supportive

Many of the men perceived their friends as consistently and uniformly supportive across the transition to parenthood. Approximately half of the men described their friends as expressing unwavering enthusiasm for their parenting efforts throughout the adoption process and beyond. For example, Barry, the 35-year-old White IT manager, recalled the first few months of parenthood as a time when "people were coming over nonstop, holding the baby. It was sort of this whirlwind of community and friends and celebration." Although their friends' support was not unexpected, some men described feeling genuinely moved by the remarkable outpouring of warmth and support that they received from friends once they actually became parents. Thomas, the 36-year-old White real estate agent, exclaimed, "We didn't realize how blessed we were with friends until this adoption. We are kind of homebodies and kind of loners and we have some close friends, but I didn't realize how many people really truly cared about us. It has really made us appreciate them more and become more involved in our friendship." Thus, for some men, parenthood had served to solidify and even enhance some friendships.

Many of the men reported being particularly appreciative of the practical support that they received from friends. Such support came in the form of house-sitting and pet care (e.g., while men traveled to get their child), prepared meals, baby clothes, baby furniture, and babysitting. As Trey, a 32-year-old White dermatologist, remarked, "Our friends are our babysitters (*laughs*). Everyone's been so good across the board; it's really been a wonderful thing that way." Likewise, Darius, a 41-year-old White graduate student, noted, "We've gotten so many hand-me-downs [from friends] that we haven't had to buy anything and probably won't for the first couple of years." Such offerings of practical support were appreciated in that they enabled men to

focus on learning the ropes of parenthood, bonding with their ne
and getting as much rest as they could.

In several cases, the men emphasized that even though their frie___
not "parent people" themselves, they had nevertheless been relatively supportive. As Gregory, a 40-year-old White graduate student, reflected, "We
have not had any friends that have not been totally supportive. We had
friends that said, 'We would never have children ourselves, but we think it's
great that you're doing it.'" Thus a lack of personal interest in parenthood did
not necessarily translate into lesser support for men's parenting pursuits.

Loss of Friendships: "We're Leaving the Gay Scene Behind and Becoming Part of the Parenthood Culture"

Strikingly, more than one-third of the men (27 men, including five couples)
described growing distance between themselves and their nonparent and
single friends, many of whom were gay. They described this distance as
encompassing both emotional and physical dimensions, such that they felt
less close to certain friends and also saw them less frequently. As Vaughn, 39,
observed, "We somehow don't fit into their dinner party kind of crowd anymore." These findings are consistent with previous research on lesbian mothers (Gartrell et al., 1999) and gay fathers (Bergman, Rubio, Green, & Padron, 2010; Lewin, 2009), which found that some participants reported losing
some close friends when they became parents—often friends who were gay
or not parents themselves.

Some men observed that the divergence in their lifestyles had actually
begun pre-parenthood, as they became more "conventional and domestic"
while their friends continued to enjoy a more "urban lifestyle." Adopting a
child had merely deepened the growing gulf between them. In attempting to
explain why he had not seen many of his friends since he became a parent,
Nathan, a 38-year-old White man who worked as the assistant director of a
museum in a northeastern suburb, mused, "There's a certain number of our
single gay friends who, the whole thing is just kind of a little too much for
them: 'Oh, they live in the suburbs and they have a kid . . . ' I think it's all a
bit too much for them. It's not even like we live in the city, you know what I
mean?" Likewise, Todd, a 46-year-old African American man who worked in
marketing and lived in a metropolitan area on the West Coast, observed that
over time, his single friends had come to see him differently, stating, "They
really look at it as, 'You're not really that single person anymore. You're really
married and you're really a parent,'" which ultimately translated into fewer
party invitations and, in turn, less social time with single and nonparent

friends. Finally, David, a 33-year-old White massage therapist turned stay-at-home-parent, revealed:

> There are some friends that have dropped off the radar. I think that they are just at different points in their lives. There is actually a little mourning going on with losing some friendships that were valued. They don't have kids. Their lives are moving in different directions. I mean one friend in particular, I don't think he really knows how to communicate with me because our realm of experiences is different. I don't know if it's a friendship that will last.

David observed, with some sadness, that becoming a parent had created an undeniable distance between himself and some of his friends, such that they could no longer easily relate to one another. In turn, David expected that some of these friendships would probably dissolve, as their "realm[s] of experience" became further differentiated. For these gay men, friendships with other sexual minorities may have played a crucial role during an earlier stage in their life (e.g., during the early years of establishing a gay identity) but were less central during their current, family-building stage of life. Gay men, like heterosexual men and women, may restructure their friendship networks once they become parents, such that they spend less time with nonparents and become closer to individuals with young children (Brown, 2010; Drentea & Moren-Cross, 2005)—and yet for gay men, this shift is further qualified by the reality that their friendships with gay nonparents are not easily replaced by friendships with gay parents.

INCREASED CLOSENESS TO HETEROSEXUAL-PARENT FRIENDS

Of note is that 19 of the 27 men who described increasing distance between themselves and their gay nonparent friends also observed that since becoming a parent, they had become closer to and were spending more time with friends who were parents—many of whom were straight. These findings are consistent with the limited research on gay fathers, which indicates that gay men who become parents often describe themselves as having more contact with, and becoming closer to, heterosexual parents (Lewin, 2009; Mallon, 2004). Gay men may increasingly find themselves interacting with heterosexual parents via day care, school, and family-oriented community events; they may also, upon becoming parents, simply become closer to existing friends and acquaintances who have children. Consistent with this notion, many of the men in the study described how, when faced with the reality that many of their old (mostly gay) friends could not fully understand or relate to their experiences as parents, they increasingly looked to their (mostly het-erosexual) parent friends and colleagues for support and community. Allan, the 36-year-old public relations manager, explained:

> It's been kind of interesting. Probably the biggest shift is in terms of our friends. We certainly have a lot of really good friends that are still incred-ibly supportive and are part of our lives and stuff, but I would say that I have become closer to my friends that are parents and coworkers that are parents. And Drew, I think, would say the same thing. And most of our friends that are parents are straight and some of our gay friends—I mean, it ranges from outright hostility to indifference to not quite getting it. And then of course we do have some gay friends that are, like, supportive, but kind of in a way that they're like, "We don't know quite how or what to say to you but we're happy if you're happy."

Thus, although many of Allan's gay friends were relatively supportive, they could not relate to his experiences as a new parent. In turn, he found himself drawing more on the support of (mostly straight) friends and coworkers who were parents, with whom he felt he could more easily share the challenges and joys of parenthood. Becoming parents, then, may prompt changes in lifestyle and community that are somewhat bittersweet, as gay men restruc-ture their kinship networks in ways that reflect their changing families.

Notably, seven of these 19 men emphasized that becoming a parent had not only facilitated increased closeness to heterosexual-parent friends and colleagues, but had actually served to connect them to the larger commu-nity of parents as a whole. In this way, they viewed parenthood as a unifying experience and identity, and one that dwarfed the significance of sexual ori entation in their everyday relationships. As Jake, a 30-year-old White gradu-ate student living in a West Coast suburb, mused, "We don't think of our-selves as really gay; first we're parents. . . . Gay or straight parenting is very similar, really. We see somebody out and their kid is throwing a fit, and you know what they are going through." Similarly, Frank, the 39-year-old White physician, exclaimed:

> What I'm surprised about is just how the fact that we're a gay couple, you know, two men, has so little to do with anything about raising a child. We have spoken to so many other couples who are gay, straight, single parents, and the experience is just the same. It's just amazing. Everything that we are experiencing is what they experience. When I said I feel very mainstream, I mean it is sort of like, you know, it's down to the kinds of shopping that we

do, the kind of things we talk about. I talk about poop and how many diapers. . . . It is not about clubs and raves and things like that.

For Frank and others, being a parent was experienced as representing a far
more salient aspect of their everyday lives than their sexual orientation, and
was viewed as an immediate bridge to other parents in their communities.
This finding echoes prior research by the anthropologist Ellen Lewin (1993),
who found that lesbian women also tended to describe changes in their identities upon becoming parents, in that their sexuality became a less-significant
aspect of their sense of self than their parental status. Insomuch as being a
parent represents an all-encompassing identity, replete with boundless obli-
gations and responsibilities—as well as indescribable rewards and joys—the
men often regarded their identity as *gay* men as less central to their overall
sense of self, post-parenthood. Frank's assertion that "it is not about clubs and
raves and things like that" represents perhaps a direct assertion of the type of
gay man he believes he is *not*—that is, single, pleasure-seeking, and enter-
tainment-oriented. Further, he positions this stereotypical image against his
description of himself as "mainstream," suggesting that not only does he seek
to establish an image of himself as "first a parent, then gay," but also that he
desires to assert how legitimate and normal he is. His narrative can be best
understood in the context of the larger societal discourses surrounding gay
fatherhood. Gay fathers may feel that they must defensively assume the "we
are so normal" stance to deflect the attacks of antigay opponents, who argue
that "gay life" is incompatible with parenthood (Clarke, 2001; Lewin, 2009).
In this way, men like Frank can be viewed as unconsciously reifying the nor-
mative/nonnormative distinction (Oswald, Kuvalanka, Blume, & Berkowitz,
2009), in that their assertions of being "mainstream" seem to lay claim to a
type of (hetero)normativity that contrasts sharply with, and is distinct from,
the gay "lifestyle."

DESIRE FOR MORE GAY-PARENT FRIENDS

Becoming a parent prompted some men to identify gaps in their social
support networks. Specifically, 12 men (including one couple) observed that
they longed for more gay-parent friends. Some of these men were among
those who had recently experienced some distancing from their gay nonparent friends or who were forming closer ties to their heterosexual parent
friends. Such men often expressed appreciation for their (mostly heterosexual) parent friends, whom they could relate to and confide in regarding
the joys and challenges of new parenthood, but they observed that these

relationships lacked a certain element of connectedness. Eric, the 40-year-old Latino research scientist, observed:

> It's been interesting because there's definitely a shift where we're a little isolated now. We have our gay friends who we would go out with, have dinner with, go to movies with, and do things with. And we don't see them hardly ever anymore. And then we are transitioning to this new gay dads group, but we haven't really bonded with anyone yet. So we're kind of an island, we feel. We're trying to figure it out. Mainly our friends are straight couples who have children. Which is fine, but it lacks one level of, you know, things to talk about, because their experiences are different.

Eric's description of himself and his partner as an "island" perfectly captures the predicament of some gay parents: they share certain elements of connection with their gay friends and certain elements of connection with their straight-parent friends, but they lack a community of gay parents who fully "get it." As the sociologist Christopher Carrington (1999) has pointed out, although lesbians and gay men are increasingly becoming parents, there are still relatively few lesbian and gay parents. Gay parents "may find it quite difficult to establish social links," which "further encourages [them] to establish stronger relationships with biolegal kin" (p. 133). One reason for gay parents' increasing closeness to family—as well as to heterosexual parents—may be the paucity of other lesbian and gay parents in their immediate communities.

Some of these men were engaged in active efforts to meet more gay parents. For example, several men mentioned starting or joining groups for gay parents as a means of creating community for themselves and their children. As Rufus, a 37-year-old White computer programmer, explained, "We've now made friends with other gay couples who also have girls. In fact . . . there are three gay couples with girls and we want to have a little club called 'Guys with Girls.'" Likewise, Chuck, the 38-year-old White web developer, asserted, "We are getting involved with the Rainbow Families group to meet more couples and couples with kids and stuff." Attending gay parenting groups is important in that it enables both parents and children to see and interact with other similar types of families, which has the potential to increase feelings of pride and to affirm one's sense of family (Suter, Daas, & Bergen, 2008). Perhaps reflecting their awareness of the unique benefits of creating gay-family community, these men were intentional and resourceful in seeking out other families like themselves.

Friends Increasingly Supportive: Positive Changes in Support

Two men noted that their gay friends had initially been resistant to the idea of them parenting, but had gradually become more supportive as the adoption process unfolded and the men were ultimately placed with a child. These men described their friends as initially "jealous"—since they were concerned about being "replaced" by a child—but as ultimately "coming around" to the point where they actually enjoyed spending time with the men and their newly adopted children.

Conclusion

All new parents may experience changes in their social networks. For gay men who become parents, this transition is complicated by the fact that gay parenthood is still being debated and contested at the societal level and within the gay community (Mallon, 2004). As we saw in this chapter, the arrival of a child initiated a range of reactions from the men's family members and friends. Consistent with prior research on lesbian mothers and gay fathers, the men in this study often perceived their families of origin as more supportive and involved once the men became parents. The men's narratives suggest that for many family members, feelings of excitement and joy—and the desire to play an active role in a child's life—overrode concerns related to societal heterosexism and its potential effects on a child, the potential "inferior genetics" of an adopted child, and so on. The high level of support that the men perceived, on average, from their families of origin is notable, particularly given the fact that the children they were welcoming into their lives were adopted. Prior research with lesbian-mother families created via alternative insemination suggests that extended family members tend to be more involved when they are biologically related to the child (i.e., the biological mother's parents tend to be more involved than the nonbiological mother's parents; see Patterson, Hurt, & Mason, 1998). Biological parenthood for gay men, of course, is more complicated and expensive to achieve. Hence, adoptive parenthood may be embraced by gay men's families because it may be more than most of their families had ever imagined or hoped for.

It is notable that the men described their family's support as extending, in many cases, beyond excitement about their new child. In some cases, they perceived their families as increasingly supportive of their sexuality and intimate relationships. In others, they observed greater closeness between themselves and their family members. In still others, they noted that their families had become more "out" in their own lives. Thus the men's transition to

parenthood seemed to stimulate changes in their family members' a
and beliefs as well as their own identity (e.g., as the mother/father/si
a gay man). Much in the same way that a stone tossed in the water generates
an expanding series of concentric circles, gay parenthood has the potential to
cause reverberations in the men's social networks that may ultimately stretch
far beyond their extended families.

In addition to describing changes in family support, the men also
described various changes related to their friendship networks. Many of the
men described a growing sense of alienation from gay nonparent friends
and increasing closeness to heterosexual-parent friends. The transition to
parenthood therefore resulted in sometimes surprising shifts in their social
networks—shifts that were initiated before parenthood, as the men's lives
became increasingly domestic, suburban, and "settled." One could read the
shift in the men's social networks as evidence of their growing conformity to a
"heteronormative" lifestyle; that is, upon becoming parents, one could argue
that they are indistinguishable from heterosexual parent couples except for
the fact that they are two men. Yet such a conclusion would be shortsighted.
As previous chapters have demonstrated, gay men do not necessarily "do"
parenthood in ways identical to heterosexual parents. In fact, they may challenge the heteronormative nature of parenthood (Oswald, Blume, & Marks,
2005) in multiple ways. Gay men may expand traditional notions of parenthood and family by choosing to adopt their children (despite familial pressures to pursue surrogacy), counting friends as family, and seeking out other
gay-parent friends, to name just a few examples.

And yet the men did appear to become increasingly incorporated into,
and often accepted by, the "straight world" once they become parents—
which is ironic, given the highly politicized and debated nature of gay parenthood. Despite the controversy surrounding gay parenthood in general and
gay adoption in particular, gay men who become parents may be regarded
as more "relatable" by both their own families and the larger community of
(mostly heterosexual) parents. Parenthood ironically desexualizes gay men
such that they are seen as "a parent first, gay second." Further, as we saw,
gay men may engage in discursive strategies to perpetuate this notion. The
men's use of language such as "we are just parents," for example, may serve a
number of purposes. First, the men may use this type of language in an effort
to emphasize that "parent" now supersedes all other identifiers (including
"gay"). Second, the men may also aim to assert how "normal" they are in part
to deflect attention from their sexuality. Third, such language may also serve
a relational purpose, in that the men are asserting their interest in, and connection to, other parents in general (e.g., those in their families, friendship

networks, and communities). Such positioning strategies, although understandable in light of the men's marginalized status in society and their desire to shield their families from shame and isolation, may arguably help to strengthen heteronormativity and the normative/nonnormative distinction. Likewise, family members' and friends' increased acceptance of these men further reinstates the dominant heteronorms. These men are rendered more acceptable by virtue of their "laying claim" to traditional family values—and, in turn, gay men who do not wish to parent (or to embrace various aspects of domesticity; see Carrington, 1999; Seidman, 2002) are marginalized as deviant.

5

Public Representations of Gay Parenthood

*Men's Experiences Stepping "Out" as Parents
and Families in Their Communities*

The 38-year-old Daniel and 39-year-old Vaughn, both White, were living in a rural area in the Northeast when they adopted Miri, an African American baby girl, via private domestic adoption. Out in public, both men noted that they felt somewhat more "out" as parents, in that Miri's presence served to clearly identify them as a family   and, in turn, to bring attention to Daniel and Vaughn's status as a *couple.* They were both pushing her stroller, feeding her bottles, and wiping her nose, and this made it obvious that they were both her parents, and, by extension, that they were a couple. Vaughn, who described himself as "liking [his] privacy," struggled with this new visibility more so than did Daniel, who viewed himself as the more "flamboyant" one. They both agreed that the fact that Miri was racially dissimilar from them also served to draw attention to the *adoptive* nature of their family. Vaughn described his particular concern about how African American adults might react to the fact that two White men had adopted an African American girl: "I'm a little bit more concerned about that than I am about anybody else's reaction." Importantly, though, Vaughn had not actually encountered any negative reactions from African American individuals at the time of the post-placement interview.

Both men described their immediate community as very liberal and progressive, but also as "very White" and lacking in racial diversity. They sometimes encountered racial stereotypes and generalizations that they typically viewed as reflecting the speakers' ignorance, rather than as evidence of hostility. As Daniel mused, soon after adopting Miri, "One of our friends here, she keeps on mentioning, 'Black kids this, and Black kids that, and Black kids this,' and my mother does the same thing." Both men struggled with such generalized statements, but at the same time minimized them, noting that "most people are not really directly confrontational."

Both Daniel and Vaughn further noted that although they had not encountered negative remarks about their being gay parents or about the biracial nature of their family, they believed that such experiences would be more likely to occur in the future, as their daughter grew older, and also when they traveled outside their immediate community. Vaughn explained:

> We're more or less staying in [state] until everything's finalized because everybody's told us, have the paperwork with you no matter where you go. You know, because two men driving around with an African American baby just doesn't seem right, you know, to most people. It's not saying that anybody's going to pull you over purposefully, but if something happens, and somebody pulls you over, then . . . well, you go through that whole thing.

As Daniel and Vaughn's story illustrates, gay male couples may encounter increased visibility as they interact with their communities as parents. Although they were previously able to pass as good friends, roommates, or brothers, the presence of a child now rendered men's relationship status more visible, a reality to which the men responded in different ways. Some of the men balked at the loss of their privacy, whereas others used their heightened visibility as an opportunity to educate others. Men who adopted racially dissimilar children were further "outed" not just as gay parents, but also as gay *adoptive* parents. This chapter explores the men's experiences of visibility and invisibility as they step out as partnered parents for the first time.

* * *

When partnered gay men become parents, they may encounter shifts in how they are perceived by their communities. Specifically, a gay couple pushing a stroller may be seen differently from a gay couple walking down the street alone. They may be more readily recognized as a family and their sexuality may seem to be more on "display" than before, when they could possibly be mistaken as buddies and therefore garner little attention from outsiders. Simply put, some gay men may experience a heightened visibility upon becoming parents, in that the presence of a male partner and a child renders their homosexuality visible, and their families deviate in multiple ways from the idealized notion of the standard nuclear unit (e.g., as a function of their homosexuality, their adoptive status, and, in some cases, the multiracial nature of their families; see Ryan & Berkowitz, 2009). Importantly, however, the degree to which men feel more visible may be shaped by their social context (Brickell, 2000; Steinbugler, 2005). For example, men living in urban, progressive communities may perceive less of a change in their communities' reaction to them than men living in rural, conservative areas, in that they may be one of many gay-parent-headed families in their communities, and may therefore feel no less out than before. Men's feelings of visibility may also be shaped by other factors, such as how out they were in their communities pre-parenthood.

Alternatively, some gay men may in fact feel that parenthood makes their sexuality *less* visible, and may therefore feel less out as gay men. They may feel—particularly when out with their child alone, without their partner—that man plus baby automatically marks them as "probable heterosexual." Gay men may experience a confusing shift in the way they are "read" by their communities, whereby they are suddenly seen as more heterosexual than before. Being so misread may be experienced and responded to in a variety of ways. The literature on sexual minorities and "passing," for example, suggests that some gay men and women experience minimal discomfort associated with unintentional passing. Some individuals may actually appreciate the opportunity to pass as heterosexual, which enables them to avoid intrusions on their privacy (Anderson & Holliday, 2004; DeJordy, 2008; Fuller, Chang, & Rubin, 2009). Other sexual minorities, however, feel that passing as heterosexual violates their sense of personal integrity, and they may seek to correct presumptions of heterosexuality (Anderson & Holliday, 2004; DeJordy, 2008; Fuller, Chang, & Rubin, 2009). Such corrections function to disrupt others' heteronormative assumptions, and to complicate—and perhaps even expand—dominant notions of family and sexuality (Oswald, Kuvalanka, Blume, & Berkowitz, 2009).

The gay men in this study often reflected on their public identities as gay fathers—and, specifically, the degree to which they felt more or less out as gay *parents*—as well as their affective and behavioral reactions to perceived shifts in their public identities.

"I Feel More Out Because We Are So Obviously a
Family": Stepping Out and Sticking Out

Twenty-four men (including three couples) articulated that they felt much
more out as gay men as a function of becoming parents. These men observed
that before becoming parents, they could perhaps have been "read" as two
friends having dinner together, or two brothers shopping. Now, as two men
having dinner with a baby or buying diapers together at the store, "it just
puts it out there that yes, we are a family. . . . It solidifies the fact that we are
a family," as David, a 33-year-old White father to an infant Latino boy, put it.
They specifically felt more conspicuous as *gay* men, whereby the combined
presence of a child and a male companion seemed to shine a spotlight on
their sexuality—which was rendered visible and "different" against the backdrop of mainly heterosexual-parent families in society in general and their
communities in particular. As the gender scholar Chris Brickell (2000) has
argued concerning heterosexual sexualities, "Heterosexuality is naturalised
and universalised such that it is invisible in public space, despite heterosexual practices in fact being dominant and omnipresent" (p. 165). By extension,
homosexuality—and, in turn, homosexual-parent families—is "marked out
as specific and visible" (p. 173). In that their family relationships were recognized as deviating from heteronormative family configurations (Chambers,
2000), the men were sometimes the recipients of inquisitive looks, curious
stares, and, occasionally, expressions of disgust. Scott, a 47-year-old Latino
physician who lived in a metropolitan area in the Northeast, remarked:

> I think I've become aware that when we are out in public and we have Tara
> with us, we have more people who look at us, and our own paranoia. . . .
> Gerard said, "They are looking at two males with a baby." A friend of ours,
> when she heard that, said, "I think they keep looking at you because peo-
> ple always look at babies and they always look up at the adults or parents.
> It is not a big thing; it is just what people do. It has nothing to do with the
> fact that you are two men." And like, oh, okay, that could be true. But I do
> think that we as two men walking down the street, we wouldn't necessarily
> feel like, undercover, but I think it is a little bit more out there . . . like *really*
> out there, like, people notice the fact that we are a couple more and I can
> sense that. At least I think that.

Scott observed that although before becoming parents, he and Gerard
were not necessarily trying to hide their sexual orientation (i.e., they were
not "intentionally passing"; see DeJordy, 2008; Goffman, 1963), parenthood

had made them more recognizable and identifiable as a gay couple, eliminating the degree to which he and Gerard could blend in while walking down the street. Parenthood had reduced the control they had over their own outness, such that what was once private was now rendered public (Steinbugler, 2005).

Many of the men highlighted this sense of feeling exposed in a new way. Bill, a 38-year-old White director of programs who lived in an urban area on the West Coast, similarly observed:

> Having a child is, like, there is no more closet door anywhere. Like, you can't even appear straight in public anymore. I mean, I just feel so exposed, and I don't mean that in a negative connotation, it's just like, I feel extremely visible. With two guys and a baby, because people figure it out pretty quick, you know. I'm carrying the baby and Darius is pushing the stroller, and, you know, people can put two and two together.

Bill described how, at least when out with his family, he could no longer blend into the background as a "probable heterosexual." Whereas before, he was able to manage his visibility as a gay man (e.g., to choose whether to be affectionate with his partner in public spaces), he now possessed very little control over this information because his family structure by itself represented a visible marker of his sexuality. Becoming a parent was experienced as exposing his sexual orientation to the world and making it impossible to "pass." As we saw in the prior chapter, at the same time that becoming parents may render coupled gay men as more assimilable (i.e., less gay) among kin or in private circles, it may also have the effect of making them less assimilable (i.e., more obviously gay) in public/community settings.

Indeed, many men emphasized that there was a distinct difference between how they seemed to be perceived now— and, correspondingly, how much attention they received—and how they were perceived when they were a childless couple. For example, Nathan, a 38-year-old White man employed as the assistant director of a museum in a northeastern suburb, observed that his interactions with his partner, Ray, and his daughter, Leah, likely cued outsiders to recognize that they were, in fact, a family:

> Being a gay dad forces you to come out constantly. You can walk down the street with your partner and people just think you're friends. If you're in a restaurant or whatever with Ray and the baby and we're constantly passing the baby back and forth . . . you know, and we do take Leah everywhere. So if we're constantly passing the baby back and forth, you know, we're

obviously both the father. We are constantly coming out. Like, we joined a church and . . . there's this whole membership thing where you stand in front of the church and the congregation welcomes you. So it was, "Nathan and Ray and their daughter, Leah!" We stood in front of the congregation and I thought, "Oh my God, I've never felt so exposed," you know? But you know, "Yep, I'm gay! Hello!"

In some of the cases described above, men acknowledged feeling more exposed as a function of "stepping out" as a family, but expressed a minimal level of discomfort associated with their increased visibility. Other men, though, acknowledged more overt discomfort with their new visibility. They strongly preferred to blend in, or to "pass" (Goffman, 1963), and were uncomfortable with a lot of attention, particularly attention that was, at least in their eyes, related to or directed at their sexuality. They preferred to maintain their privacy, but recognized—somewhat resentfully—that "people are going to be nosy, and we have to deal with it because within the context of society, you can't avoid it." For example, Vaughn, who lived in a rural area in the Northeast and whose story opened this chapter, explained what happened when he and his partner, Daniel, took their daughter to the mall for the first time:

We walk in . . . and it was like I was on stilts with spotlights on me. It was the weirdest thing. I don't know if it was me being sensitive to it or what, but I swear everybody was just staring at me. I felt *so* uncomfortable. I was like, oh, this is weird. It was like I was onstage. I'm not the kind of person who stands out. At least I try not to be. To be in that position was very weird.

Gregory, a 40-year-old White graduate student living in a northeastern suburb with his partner, Brian, and their son, Aiden, was similarly uncomfortable with the increased attention he perceived as a gay-parent family. But he had resolved to be "honest" and to deal with people directly, even if he felt uncomfortable:

That's been interesting. Not that that ever has been an issue for Brian; it's probably been a bit more of an issue for me. Brian tends not to worry what people think, and I still have that part of me that's there. I'm better than I was but I still have that stereotype—that whole Catholic upbringing and worried about what people think. I probably notice glances more than Brian does. . . . But you really do have to be much more honest with people. This happened before we even got him, when we were looking at day cares. Even when I called people to say, "I have a partner. I don't have a wife. I want to make sure that's not going to be an issue and please be comfortable to say that it is so that we aren't wasting each other's time." That was a real leap for me, but it was really necessary. I did not want to have to deal with that in a school setting, at all.

As Gregory observed, such up-front pronouncements of his family structure, although somewhat uncomfortable, felt necessary. These announcements represented an effective, though scary, means of "weeding out" unsupportive individuals and institutions, and were indirectly aimed at reducing or circumventing heterosexism and homophobia.

Living in gay-friendly and progressive areas of the country did not necessarily negate the experience of feeling more out. In a few cases, the men noted that they were surrounded by lots of gay couples and gay-parent families, but nevertheless felt that their sexuality was rendered more visible—and vulnerable to commentary—upon becoming a parent. Stan, a 32-year-old White college professor who lived in a city on the West Coast, explained:

We live and work in extremely queer-friendly environments and [city] is really queer-friendly. So I would say it's really been mostly a nonissue. This thing that is still kind of hitting me every day a little bit differently is that any time we go anywhere as a family, we are a walking political statement. We're not just a family, we're that family on display everywhere we go all the time. So that sometimes gets a little exhausting. When it's Thursday afternoon after work and what I really want to do is just go, you know, get a beer and pizza, I don't really want to be a political statement but I wind up being that everywhere I go. People will come up and say, "Oh, you guys are so cute" or whatever.

For men who lived in more progressive areas, the increased attention they received because of their family status was described as largely positive—though sometimes intrusive. As Stan alluded to, those men in gay-friendly, progressive communities were often regarded as part of the new gay parenthood "movement" and were therefore treated as political "symbols" even when men did not regard themselves as such.

A few men observed that their feelings of enhanced outness were due not only to their greater visibility as a family unit, but also to the fact that it was "impossible to talk about being a parent without talking about my partner, and therefore outing myself as gay." Specifically, five men explicitly noted that describing their child or their parental status to colleagues, acquaintances,

and strangers was "virtually impossible" without referencing their male partners, and, in turn, revealing their sexuality. For example, the 32-year-old
Trey, a White dermatologist living in a southern city, observed, "I was pretty
out in the sense that that I wasn't hiding anything before. And so certainly it
becomes—you know, I talk about Daria and then I talk about Rufus and so it
does sort of force the issue [out]." For some men, then, their parental status
resulted in shifts in how they represented their families, which had the effect
of revealing something "personal" about their lives—that is, their sexual orientation—which was previously less visible.

The fact that the men's sexuality was more visible and therefore more the
focus of incidental conversations and encounters is somewhat ironic, given
that a number of men whom I interviewed spontaneously highlighted how
their sexuality seemed *less* important now that they were a parent. Thus, at
the same moment, it seemed, that they began to feel less defined by their
sexual orientation (i.e., more "mainstream"), their sexual orientation was
rendered more visible, thereby differentiating them from the mainstream
(Lewin & Leap, 2009). As Jake, a 32-year-old White graduate student who
lived in a West Coast suburb, mused:

> We don't think of ourselves as really gay; first we're parents. For exam-
> ple, if we're out pushing the stroller and, you know, without thinking,
> there's some kind of display of affection, someone is going to say, "Oh
> my gosh, look at them." A thought that would come to my mind would be,
> "Oh please, come on." It's really not important. I don't know; it's hard to
> explain, but being a parent comes first, you know?

"I Feel More Out in Certain Contexts": Outness as Context Dependent

Some of the men described above noted that they felt especially out in certain contexts. In other words, while they felt more "out" in most aspects of
their lives, their sexuality was made especially salient in particular settings.
Six men observed that becoming a parent had outed them at work. They had
maintained a relatively "low profile" with respect to their sexuality prior to
becoming a parent, but upon announcing their adoption intentions or the
fact that they had adopted, they felt as though their homosexuality was made
"much more visible." In this way, these men had shifted from being implicitly out (i.e., not avoiding the truth about their sexual orientation, but not
explicitly referring to themselves as gay men) to being explicitly out at work
(Griffin, 1991). Finn, a 44-year-old White hospital administrator living in a
metropolitan area in the South, revealed:

Even at work, I did not come out at work until we started trying to adopt. I'm sure everyone knew, but no one had ever asked in all the years that I've been there and then I had to come out and say, "Yes, I've been with this guy for now, at that time, about 10 years." And you know, all the sudden now—I'm talking about *everybody* at work, I'm talking about all the nurses and some of the people in administration and I mean just, *everywhere* I go—I do feel like, "Oh my God, I'm the poster child of adoption at this hospital now!" And I have gotten some people who have like, not smiled or not like, asked anything because it's not cool with them so, you know, but I can't help it, you know how gossip is and the grapevine that goes around. . . . And I do feel like, "Oh my gosh, my entire life now is just right out there, I am out and about!"

In Finn's case, announcing his intention to adopt had prompted him to come out explicitly to his colleagues—a decision that he likely made in part to avoid any uncomfortable inquiries or presumptions that might follow. This ultimately rendered him more vulnerable, in that some of his colleagues appeared to be not "cool" with the idea of a gay man adopting. Indeed, although there are many potential psychological benefits of being out (e.g., enhanced integrity and well-being, closer interpersonal relationships), there are also various costs (e.g., the potential of rejection and judgment), which the men became exposed to when they outed themselves (Fuller, Chang, & Rubin, 2009; Herek, 1996; Mallon, 2004; Oswald, Kuvalanka, Blume, & Berkowitz, 2009).

In three cases, it was a baby shower that outed men at work. Because baby showers are implicitly tied to and representative of both heterosexuality and reproduction, these men—and the individuals who were organizing their baby showers—struggled to determine how exactly to acknowledge men's homosexuality and adoptive status without making it a "big deal." As Trey, the 32-year-old White dermatologist, recalled:

It's interesting. At work they had a big baby shower for me, and there were definitely people at work—because it went out to everyone—that didn't know that I was gay. It wasn't a problem that I was, but sort of a little coming-out party in that sense, because I know there was a big discussion with the women who organized it trying to figure out how to balance this. Because she wanted the focus to be on the baby shower and not "The Trey Is Coming Out Party."

Three men noted that they felt more out at church. The 38-year-old Trevor, a White technical support technician living in an urban area on the West Coast, observed:

When we go to church, everybody now knows that Richard and I are a couple and a family. . . . When Sharlene was baptized, every member of the church was there, which is 250 to 300 people. And every single person came out to shake our hand or congratulate us. So it wasn't just feeling more out but feeling more like we are accepted as a couple.

For Trevor, becoming a parent actually seemed to invite greater acceptance by his congregation. Ironically, then, his becoming a parent as a gay man was viewed not as transgressive, but rather as assimilationist, something that in fact made him (and his family) more accessible and congenial to his fellow congregants.

On the other hand, Elliott, a 40-year-old White executive director living in an urban area on the East Coast, expressed some discomfort with his and his partner Nolan's increased visibility at the church they attended, and felt uneasy that his fellow (straight) congregants might think he was trying to make a "statement" with his new family. He observed:

At the church we go to, there's no other gay people, so now we're standing around, me and Nolan with Sam, and so obviously we're the gay couple with the kid and I don't feel like anyone is looking at us in a disapproving way, but I just don't like my business being that vulnerable, you know, just being that sort of like, open and obvious. And I don't want people to think that I'm trying to make a statement or do anything like that.

Far from seeking to resist or challenge heteronormativity, Elliott wished to blend in, and to avoid making waves in his community. In fact, he was uncomfortable with the notion that other people might see him as "trying to make a statement"—that is, as being one of *those* gay men. He preferred instead to be what the communications scholar Jay Clarkson (2008) has referred to as "quietly gay." That is, Elliott did not believe in "shov[ing] [his] sexual orientation in people's faces" and wished to be seen as "one of those 'normal' men living normal lives" (p. 373).

In addition, four men noted that they felt more out in the "straight world"—that is, in contexts dominated by heterosexual couples with children. These men observed feeling more out at soccer games, music classes, community centers, and day care, contexts in which they were one of the few, and perhaps only, gay-parent families. It was in these contexts that men felt that their family status and therefore their sexual orientation were the most "on display." Lars, a 36-year-old White man who lived in a suburb in the South, mused:

There have been a few more opportunities [to come out], you know, like at the soccer games. . . . The first time, when he went to his first soccer game, and I was talking to a woman there named Melissa, and Joshua comes over and Melissa's asking him, "Oh, who's your kid?" And he's like, "It's the same one. It's Evan," and she's like, "Oh. I get it."

Finally, seven men, including two couples, emphasized that their perceived visibility—and, in turn, the level and type of attention they received—was geographically dependent, such that they felt more out in certain geographic areas than others. Their impressions are consistent with research indicating that both visibility and community acceptance of lesbians and gay men vary as a function of geographic location and context (e.g., the Northeast vs. the South; urban areas vs. rural and suburban areas; see Fried, 2008; Fuller, Chang, & Rubin, 2009; Steinbugler, 2005). As one man noted, "It all depends on where you are."

These men often contrasted their experiences in gay-friendly cities with their experiences in the less-gay-friendly suburbs; or they highlighted how their perceived outness varied as a function of whether they were at home (e.g., in more progressive areas) versus traveling (e.g., to the "Deep South" to visit relatives). For example, James, a 41-year-old White man who lived in San Francisco, observed, "When I'm walking around with her or with Brett, we're not terribly unique. In the suburbs, where my sister lives, yeah, we are unique!" Likewise, Luis, a 45-year-old Latino man who lived on the outskirts of a major northeastern city, observed:

When we go shopping to Babies 'R' Us or something like that, we definitely get the most attention, no doubt about it. . . . We can definitely see the curiosity on people's faces. And, you know, it's very geographically dependent. I mean if we're in the city, we're a dime a dozen. But out here in our neighborhood (*laughs*), you know, we're clearly the zebra among the horses.

Likewise, Kevin, 40, who lived in a midwestern city, noted that how people responded to him and his family—and, in turn, how out he felt—varied as a function of geography:

There is a difference when we're out in public, when we were out in California north of San Francisco compared to here. When we were out [in California], people were more likely to approach us and say, "Congratulations, that's wonderful, that's great for you guys," basically treating us as a couple. Whereas here, I think people are more standoffish and trying to figure out the situation. And people are friendly, but they don't really say much or ask much. It is not assumed that we are a couple and they are a little bit more standoffish. I feel like people are trying to sort of figure out what the story is.

Notably, in the latter two cases, men felt more out in the places where they lived. It was only when they traveled outside of their communities that they felt like they were "a dime a dozen" and as though people treated them "as a couple." These experiences highlighted for them how their "queerness"—at least as others perceived it—was contextually dependent.

"People Assume Parenthood Equals
Heterosexuality . . . and So We Feel Less Out"

In contrast to the above group of men, 28 men (including four couples) noted that they actually felt *less* out, and more likely to be mistaken as het-erosexual, now that they were parents—in certain contexts, that is. These men articulated that when they were out with their children, without their partners; or they were out with their children, as well as their partners *and a female friend or sister*, they encountered presumptions of heterosexuality. In this way, gay men were "miscategorized" (Fuller, Chang, & Rubin, 2009) and unintentionally "passed" as heterosexuals, given the presence of "markers" that seemed to indicate their membership in that group (Goffman, 1963).

It is notable that of the 28 men who described feeling less out, almost three-quarters were the primary caretakers of their children (i.e., they were staying at home part-time or full-time) and spent a fair amount of time interacting with the world with their children, but without their partners. Instances of presumed heterosexuality were particularly salient to them, as they seemed to occur fairly often. For example, when asked if he felt more out, David, a 33-year-old White man living in a metropolitan area on the West Coast, who was staying at home with his son full-time, responded, "No, the funny thing is, it is the opposite. People will just start talking to me about my wife. It is weird; it's like [having a child with you] makes people assume that you are heterosexual." Patrick, a 41-year-old White man who resided in a midwestern suburb, provided this example:

Well, I was at a store yesterday with Arianna, and they had this little tiny silk Japanese dress with a collar and I thought, "Oh, she will look great in it." I wasn't sure about the size and I kind of laid it up on her in the stroller to check the size and the guy said, "You know, I can hold that for you if you want to have the wife check it out." And, you know (*sigh*), I told Carter, you can't be an activist every day. You have to pick your battles and at 4:30 in the afternoon after spending all day with the kid out running around, that was the last thing that I wanted to do, was have a sit down with this guy— "Listen, idiot . . . you know. There is no wife in the picture and why are you assuming there is?" I just let it go.

The salesman's offhand comment ("I can hold that for you if you want to have the wife check it out") revealed a set of heteronormative assumptions (e.g., Patrick was presumed to have a wife, and his wife was assumed to hold primary decision-making power where clothing selections were concerned). Although Patrick was annoyed with the salesman's assumption of heterosexuality, his sense of "you can't be an activist every day" overrode his need to correct the salesman. Many men voiced this sentiment—that is, having insufficient energy or desire to correct presumptions of heterosexuality that they viewed as relatively harmless. An additional reason for not speaking up was reluctance to embarrass the speaker: some men expressed that they simply did not want to "make a big deal out of it, so [they] just didn't bother to correct them." Thus these men implicitly rejected the notion that it was their responsibility, on a daily basis, to challenge heteronormativity.

In several cases, the men suggested that they possessed other potential "markers" of heterosexuality (e.g., wedding rings), which, when coupled with the presence of a child, might cue others to presume that they were heterosexually married. As Henry, a 45-year-old biracial man who resided on the outskirts of a major northeastern city with his partner, Luis, and who was staying at home with their daughter, Madison, part-time, reflected:

We live in what I would consider, you know, a middle-class, working-class neighborhood, and people will say to me things like, you know, if you're having your coffee and you're wearing a baseball hat and sitting in the park, they're thinking right away. . . . they say, "Oh, you're giving the little lady a break," or you know, they just say these things. . . . Yeah, people just like right away will say "Who does she look like, does she look like your wife?" You know, I wear a wedding ring, so, you know, there are all those kind of assumptions and stuff.

Similar to Patrick's narrative, Henry's story illustrates how assumptions of heterosexuality were often intertwined with sexism, such that men were presumed not only to be heterosexually married, but also to be "giving the little lady a break." In this way, they were cast as secondary caregivers automatically, based solely on their gender (Mallon, 2004). The frequency with which men fielded inquiries about their supposed female partners also speaks to societal presumptions about the primacy of the mother-child relationship. Strangers frequently noticed, and noted, the absence of a woman. Also notable is Henry's description of a baseball cap as a potential signifier of heterosexuality. He observed, at least implicitly, that gender presentation also functions to determine who will "pass" as heterosexual, such that, for example, men who dress in conventionally masculine clothing are more likely to pass as straight (Fuller, Chang, & Rubin, 2009).

Henry's anecdote also indicates how presumptions of heterosexuality were frequently accompanied by assumptions about biological parenthood, thereby not only erasing men's sexuality but also their adoptive family status. Questions such as "Who does she look like, does she look like your wife?" reveal the power of biologism underlying ideas about family structure and relatedness (Crabb & Augoustinos, 2008; Hargreaves, 2006; Modell & Dambacher, 1997). For example, Jason, a 37-year-old White man who lived in a West Coast suburb and who was staying at home with his daughter part-time, described how "when I take her out. . . . we'll get a lot of people coming up and saying, 'Oh a baby, how cute,' and then of course, naturally assuming that, you know, she has a mommy and a daddy. So I've had those conversations and I've had a number of people say, 'Oh she looks just like you!'"

In most cases, men were only mildly irritated that they were presumed to be heterosexual. In two cases, however, men were "disturbed" by the fact that they were mistaken as heterosexual. They felt that their parental status suddenly made their sexuality invisible. In their eyes, parenthood seemed to prompt an automatic assumption of heterosexuality and a presumption that they were "mainstream"—an identity they rejected vehemently. Such instances reveal the dominance of societal stereotypes of "family" as heterosexual and biologically related (Naples, 2004; Stacey, 1996), discourses that men recognized and resisted. Rufus, a 37-year-old White man who resided in an urban area in the South and who was staying home with his daughter part-time, experienced such assumptions as unnerving, even upsetting:

> For me, there have been times when Trey was gone and I've had Daria. And actually, what's interesting about that, what I don't like, is that I suddenly look like a straight dad, which isn't what I want to look like. Like, suddenly I'll be places where I see some gay people and I'll think, "They don't think I'm gay." And it's not like, you know, it doesn't really matter but there's something really fun about when Trey and I are both together with the baby and so we're sort of both—we're both parents and we're still gay. And when I

walk around as a single person, especially because she's White and she has blue eyes right now and has kind of blond peach fuzz . . . there's just a sense of, "Oh yeah, she must be my natural born child," or "Oh, she looks just like you." . . . So I feel like, I guess I blend in when I'm by myself. And Trey's been gone for a while, so I've been doing a lot of things by myself . . . like with [Gay] Pride. We were going to go alone because he was away . . . and I remember thinking, "Oh, I don't want to be at the parade and have people think, 'Oh, that's so nice, a straight dad brought his daughter!,'" and I was like, "I'm going to find my Pride flag in the basement somewhere and wrap it around her." . . . And I do think about ways I can still make sure that I sort of identify as gay with her because I really end up looking like this straight White guy when I'm alone sometimes.

For Rufus, being mistaken as heterosexual was experienced as unsettling in that he did not feel "recognized" by his own people. His concern about being misjudged as heterosexual by other gay people at a gay pride event was so great that he revealed his intention to wrap his daughter in a rainbow flag, to identify himself as "one of the tribe." In this way, he aimed to resist heteronormativity by clearly identifying himself as a *gay* parent. For Rufus, both his sexual orientation and parental status were viewed as important aspects of his identity, which he therefore sought to communicate to the outside world, particularly other gay people and gay parents.

"People Assume Parenthood Equals Heterosexuality . . . and So We Are Constantly Coming Out"

Of note is that 12 of these 28 men (including two couples) observed that, because they were routinely being misread as heterosexual, they felt compelled to correct this misappraisal. They emphasized that they were actually coming out much more frequently than in the past. These men noted that passersby would often inquire about the whereabouts of their wives, which prompted them, in many situations, to come out. They did this because they were uncomfortable with the idea of "misrepresentation," feeling that it "doesn't do us justice, so to speak." By making "declarative statements" about their sexuality and family structure, they outed themselves and, in doing so, relieved the discomfort associated with not being honest about who they were (Fuller, Chang, & Rubin, 2009; Herek, 1996). For example, the 32-year-old Jake, who lived in a West Coast suburb and who was staying home with his daughter part-time, described how "people embarrass themselves by saying something like, 'How's the mom doing?,' 'Oh well, she has two dads!,' 'Oh, ooh, okay . . . well that's a nice stroller!' (*laughs*) The response is just—they're so taken off guard." Likewise, Carl, a 41-year-old White fund-raising director who lived in suburban California, exclaimed:

> Even just in the hospital, I'd ask people, "Can you press '4' please?" And they'd go, "Oh, that's the delivery room, congratulations, how is your wife doing?" And I would say, "My partner and I, we're adopting, she's not my wife." Even at the first doctor's appointments, they ask, "Is your wife attending?" And you just have to decide in a split second, am I going to say something? Or just say, "No," and not make an issue out of it? But we're both training ourselves well, I think, to just say, "Nope! My partner will be there." And so far, every single person has been like, "Oh, great! Well, we will see you then." It's not an issue at all.

Carl described a scenario where he was mistaken for being a heterosexual father. In contrast to some of the other men in the study, Carl was uncomfortable allowing others to maintain the assumption that he was heterosexual, as such an assumption erased not only his sexual orientation but also his partner's very existence. Thus he responded to such mistaken presumptions of heterosexuality by outing himself, because the psychological costs of denying who he was seemed to outweigh any perceived benefits of passing (Fuller, Chang, & Rubin, 2009). It is interesting that he described a uniformly positive response to his coming out. The fact that he had met a consistently positive reaction to his disclosures likely reinforced his commitment and willingness to engage in discursive acts of resistance to heteronormativity. In other words, his social context can be viewed as facilitating his efforts to challenge heteronormativity. Because he lived in suburban California, his disclosures were likely viewed as understandable efforts to communicate basic facts about his family structure, as opposed to being seen as unnecessarily or purposefully "shocking."

In several cases, the men were explicit that they were insistent on coming out not just for their own sake but for their child's sake as well. They were practicing for the future, when their child would be old enough to pick up on these conversations—and would likely wonder why they were allowing a stranger to maintain an incorrect assumption regarding their family. For example, the 39-year-old Cooper, a multiracial physician assistant living in a metropolitan area on the West Coast, mused:

> [Before we became parents], a lot of times people wouldn't know we are gay. Some couples, it is a little bit more obvious but when we go traveling

together, unless we say something, people will often think we are a couple of good friends. It doesn't come out in the forefront. But with the baby, oh man, it is sort of out there. The first question out of most peoples' mouths when there is two guys traveling with a baby is, "Oh, where's mommy?" Questions come up immediately about home or family and stuff like that. So we try to be really straightforward about it, too. I think that one thing we have decided is that we don't want Benny to grow up thinking it is taboo to talk about it. If he grows up thinking we are ashamed of it or trying to hide it, it is going to affect him in some pretty bad ways. If he grows up thinking that being gay is a bad thing or something, that we have to hide or something, that you are not supposed to talk about it, I think that would come out in some really weird ways. So I definitely feel [more out], and that hasn't always been comfortable for me either.

Although Cooper acknowledged a commitment to be "straightforward" about his familial and relational status, for his child's sake, he noted that this had not always been comfortable for him. In this way, he suggests that he felt compelled to move beyond his personal preference for privacy to consider the implications of remaining silent for his son. Not wishing for his son to grow up believing that his family was shameful, Cooper adopted a stance of openness. Cooper's strategic, reflexive approach to openness, whereby he prioritized the need to model openness and pride over his personal desire for privacy, illustrates how gay men may push back against heteronormativity even when personally fearful of negative repercussions. This example is consistent with prior research on lesbian mothers, who often describe purposeful efforts to model openness and pride in their interactions with outsiders (Bennett, 2003; Gartrell et al., 2000). Lesbian mothers who strive to come out purposefully in public interactions do so in an effort to resist, and hopefully counteract, the shame and homophobia that their children may eventually confront (Goldberg, 2010a; Mezey, 2008).

No Change in Outness

Finally, 18 men, including five couples, noted that parenthood had had little impact on how out they felt. These men asserted that they had always been very out and thus felt no more out now that they were parents. They emphasized that they were "as out as can be," such that "neighbors, people at work, everybody" knew that they were gay, and therefore felt that they "couldn't get any more out!" once they became parents. Most of these men lived in very gay-friendly areas (e.g., San Francisco), which had facilitated their ease in being out (Steinbugler, 2005). They emphasized that their outness had not changed upon becoming parents, given the generally tolerant and supportive climate of their immediate communities. As Brett, a 42-year-old White man in San Francisco, stated, "I don't really know that we have [felt more out], because we were pretty out before. I mean, living where we live, it's so enlightened in that respect, that it's just not a big deal." Likewise, Allan, a 36-year-old White man, reflected that he had not felt more out "because in the Bay Area, it's like, gay families are a dime a dozen." These men did not feel that they "stuck out" any more now than they did when they were just a couple, by virtue of the fact that they lived in areas heavily populated by same-sex couples and lesbian/gay-parent families, which had in turn facilitated their outness prior to becoming parents. Where they lived, gay parenthood was constructed as (relatively) normal, and their own families "blended in" more so than in geographic contexts that lacked an organized or sizable gay parent community. In turn, these men were less likely to feel as though they had to explain or defend their family; their families were, in many cases, already recognized and to some degree accepted as "real" families.

A few of these men, though, lived in areas with few same-sex couples or parents. Yet becoming a parent had not changed their sense of outness or visibility, in that "everyone knew that we were gay before." Prior to parenthood, they had not made any effort to hide their relationship, and were "well-known around town" for being one of the few gay couples in the area. In contrast to the men described above, who reported being very out in gay-friendly communities with a large number of same-sex couples and parents, these men were very out in communities characterized by few, if any, other same-sex couples and parents. Daniel, who lived in the rural Northeast and whose story opened this chapter, asserted, "I've always been out (*laughs*). And it's not so much in a flamboyant way, but even when I lived in Florida, I have always been just me. I don't hide myself." Joshua, a 40-year-old White man who lived in a southern suburb, attested:

> I've been out. It's not been—if someone doesn't know I'm gay it's because they're really stupid or blind (*laughs*). I mean, at work it's like, if you haven't figured it out, it's because you've not been paying any attention. But that's their own problem. If they've not been paying attention, it's nothing on my end (*laughs*). Where we go, the restaurants around here—a lot of the cooks know us. We're obviously a couple wherever we go.

Interestingly, four men who did not feel any more out now than they did before did not attribute this lack of change to already having been very out.

They stated that they simply did not give much thought to their sexual orientation, and paid little attention to how outsiders were responding to them. They claimed that they had encountered few situations or people that had prompted them to "come out." Shane, a 32-year-old White man living in a metropolitan area of the South, mused, "I don't personally think about it, honestly. I never did anyways. I never thought about—I mean, obviously we're a gay couple, but, I don't know, I've always tried to live my life where it's like that's just, secondary to everything." Shane therefore denied that his sexual orientation had been made more salient or visible as a function of becoming a parent.

Adopting Transracially: Creating More "Colorful" Families

Racial differences between parents and children often serve to mark children as "adopted," thereby revealing something private about families and sometimes leading others, including strangers, to inquire about children's adoptive identities (Harrigan, 2009).

Added Visibility, Increased Outness

Eleven men (including three couples) emphasized their perception that their families were made more visible by the multiracial nature of their families. Notably, seven of these men had adopted African American children; in two cases, the adopted child was Latino/a; and in two cases, the adopted child was multiracial. The multiracial nature of their families, these men said, sometimes led people to "do a double take" and occasionally to make statements or ask questions that in some cases revealed racial stereotypes. For example, two men observed that, because their child had noticeably darker skin than they did, they were frequently asked whether they had adopted internationally. Darker skin was equated with international adoption (Richardson & Goldberg, 2010). As Jake, who had adopted a multiracial daughter, described, "Everybody has actually looked at her and said, 'Oh, what country did you adopt from?,' thinking we did an international adoption. . . . And the irony of that is that everyone thinks she's Asian because of her features and she's not Asian at all."

Another stereotype that their child's race seemed to elicit in others was the presumption that because "dark" children are stereotypically poor, from questionable backgrounds, and "unwanted," they were therefore "lucky" to have been adopted by two White men into a middle-class lifestyle (Dorow, 2006; Harrigan, 2009). Two men described encountering this type of assumption. Rett, a 35-year-old White man who had adopted an African American boy with his partner, Barry, in an urban area in the Midwest, explained what he described as outsiders' "racist assumption" that a White middle-class upbringing was inevitably better than whatever upbringing their son's birth parents could have offered him:

> People love his hair, it's a big full head of hair. And, there's this feeling of, it's great that you guys are doing this. It's almost an implication of, because you'll be able to give him such a better life. And I know that, like, if you just look objectively at the circumstances in his case, you know, homeless, mentally ill mother versus a stable middle-class upbringing—like, just on that, on the face of it, yeah, you're right. We're going to be able to give him a stable foundation and life. But there is something that's definitely lost in that. And I get the sense that a lot of times the way White people react, is there's this ongoing racist assumption of how much better the upbringing will be by two White people.

The men also encountered inquiries about their children's hair and skin that were racial in nature. For example, three men—all with African American children—described encounters where a stranger asked them questions about their child's hair or skin. Barry, Rett's partner, noted that "folks will ask about African American hair. . . . So we explain that, you know, we won't wash his hair every day, or we need to oil his skin, those kinds of questions."

Interestingly, nine men (including two couples) explicitly noted that their visibility as a multiracial, adoptive family made them more aware of and sensitive to potential criticism from their child's racial group. These men were aware of the debates surrounding transracial adoption, which often center on the question of whether White parents are capable of providing the kind of racial socialization experiences that children of color need to develop a healthy racial identity (Quiroz, 2008). In turn, these men were aware that some racial minorities, particularly African Americans, might be resistant to transracial adoption, and might be resentful toward them specifically for adopting a member of their racial group. For example, the 34-year-old Robbie, a White man who had adopted a biracial (African American and White) child, observed that "living in [city], it's sometimes more difficult to have an African American child because of the huge population here in [city], and you get the reverse pressure, where it's frowned upon more from people that we know and are friends with in the African American community than it is in the White community."

Six of these nine men described encounters in which they perceived disapproval, avoidance, or resentment from members of their child's racial group. As the 40-year-old Theo, a White man who had adopted an African American girl with his African American partner in a West Coast suburb, stated, "Every once in a while I sense, from Black people, disapproval. Like, when it will be me and Emma alone." Similarly, the 35-year-old Rett described a situation where:

Barry and I were with Christopher in a store, and there was a Black woman who asked if she could look at the baby and so we clipped up the little hood on the car seat and there was Christopher. There was kind of an awkward silence. The initial thing would be to say, "Oh, what a cute baby." But she was really, I think, taken aback at first.

Notably, Rett went on to carefully consider the broader racial dynamics at play and how these influenced this singular woman's reaction to him and his son:

It's just this very micro-situation. But I recognize that in those random encounters there also is this sort of broader impact, the dynamics that are at play and the racial dynamic in particular. . . . So when I see an African American woman react negatively, it sort of reminds me of the fact that, yeah, you're a White man and you're raising a Black child in a White supremacist culture, and it brings to mind the kind of political ramifications of just a very personal choice.

In three of these nine cases, however, men noted that while they had anticipated a negative response from members of their child's racial group, they had not yet experienced it. For example, the 38-year-old Nick, a White man partnered with an African American man who had adopted an African American boy, noted that "one of the things that we'd heard about or talked to people about is sometimes reactions from other African Americans seem more negative. They would prefer to see one of their own being raised by one of their own. [But] I have yet to experience anything like that." Likewise, concerning how African American people had responded to him, his partner, and their African American daughter, Vaughn, who was White, observed:

Funny enough, oddly enough, I'm a little bit more concerned about that than I am about anybody else's reaction. And the few [African Americans] that we've seen here are pretty open and tolerant and accommodating, but

I'll be anxious to see what happens the first time we go down to [nearby city] or something, or someplace like that, and encounter different kinds of people and see what kind of vibe I get from them. . . . But I will definitely, I'm sensitive, so I will pick up a vibe from them. I'll get a sense of where they're at just by how they interact with us.

Finally, three men noted that they felt more visible not only as adoptive families, but also as gay men, insomuch as their multiracial, adoptive status often cued people to consider their sexual orientation. Somewhat ironically, the fact that they deviated in multiple ways from stereotypical representations of family served to cue outsiders that they *were* in fact a family—and signaled details about both men's route to parenthood and also their sexuality. For example, the 36-year-old Thomas, a White man residing in southern suburb, observed that his daughter's race had served as an additional cue to his sexual orientation:

I mean we were pretty out before; we've never hid it anywhere. But we live in a small town, a small country town. We live in the suburbs and so when we go to a restaurant or a café, before it could have been just two buddies having dinner with a little bit of a question. But now it is, "Well, I believe they are a gay couple because they actually also have a Black baby."

Thus men who adopted children whose race was distinctly different from their own were ironically immediately recognized both as gay (i.e., as "outside" the heteronormative nuclear ideal) and also as fathers and partners (i.e., they and their partners and their children were more readily recognized as a family).

Little Added Visibility

Some men, however, described little added visibility as a function of their transracial adoptive status. Eight men (including two couples) attributed this to the fact that their child was biracial or "light-skinned," allowing them to "pass" as biogenetically related. In other words, they observed that their child's light skin often led people to assume that they were biologically related to one of their parents, deflecting inquiries about their race or adoptive status. As Henry, who was biracial (Latino and White), reflected, "They say she looks like me. She's very fair and I'm fair and Luis is more Latin-looking, so they think she looks like me." In several cases, men expressed a sense of relief that their child "blended in" relatively easily, in that they did not feel as visible or scrutinized when out in public, whereas they might have been if they had an "obviously Black child." For example, Paul, a 40-year-old White man who had adopted a biracial male infant with his partner, Miles, who was also White, stated, "She looks totally White and so yeah, when she was born we weren't sure what she was going to look like, you know? But so yeah, does that help? Yes it does, because that was a concern of ours." As the sociologists Maura Ryan and Dana Berkowitz (2009) have noted, racial similarity between parents and children may help gay-parent families to "blend in with other dominant families, releasing them slightly from the effects of heterosexual domination" (p. 165). In this way, gay men who adopt racially similar children arguably have the privilege of conforming, at least ostensibly, with the requirement that a "real" or "normal" family be physically similar. Although actually adoptive, these family members' racial similarity may lead them to be "read" as biogenetically related—the requirement underlying the norm of physical similarity.

A few men noted that, in that they were not readily recognizable as a multiracial family, they were assumed to be biogenetically related to their child and possibly heterosexual, a set of assumptions that left them at a loss regarding whether, when, and how to out themselves. Likewise, the 37-year-old Carter, a White man residing in a midwestern suburb, revealed:

> She looks very Caucasian. I was truly not expecting that. I think Patrick and I would have done well either way. I think it's going to be interesting with her looking so Caucasian, looking so White, I think we are going to get a lot of people assuming that one of us is the biological father. . . . I want to know what people [in this situation] say. What do they do? I don't feel I need to out myself to total strangers every time I say something and to explain this whole situation [but] you pretty much have to do that.

Carter asserted that while he did not feel the need to "out [him]self to total strangers," he recognized that in order to explain "this whole situation" (i.e., his child's adoptive status), he "pretty much [has] to do that." Thus Carter saw no way of explaining that his child was adopted without giving the full story, which involved disclosing that he and his partner were a gay couple.

Seven men (including two couples) similarly noted that because their child was the same race as one of the partners, people assumed that their child was biogenetically related to that parent. This in turn precluded inquiries regarding their child's adoptive status, and also led to assumptions about heterosexuality. Nick, the 38-year-old White man who had adopted an

African American child with his partner, Todd, who was also African American, stated:

> Todd has gotten a lot from his coworkers and some of other folks that he knows, "Wow, he even kind of looks like you." So there's some resemblance between them that I think helps bridge that, the issue of the dramatic difference. . . . I think there are some similarities, and so because then, when Todd and I are there together, people will automatically pick up on the similarities and say, "Oh, okay." They make this natural assumption of, oh, they do resemble each other, so Todd must be his bio-father.

Similarly, the 36-year-old Dashaun, who had adopted an African American child with his partner, Theo, who was White, shared, "I do get that she literally looks like me. People say, 'She looks just like you. That is your daughter.' And I say, 'Yeah.'" In turn, Dashaun acknowledged that when he, Theo, and their daughter, Emma, were out in public, people tended to presume that he was Emma's biological father, whereas Theo was "probably just a friend."

Conclusion

In becoming parents, gay men expose themselves to considerable scrutiny. As the men in this study quickly learned, the presence of a child invited outsiders to make certain assumptions about their family structure. In some cases, the men described feeling more out as parents, such that, as one man said, "there is no more closet door anywhere." These men felt that their interactions as a family (e.g., both men feeding their child at a restaurant) cued people to recognize, and make conclusions about, their family and relational status. Thus the men's sexuality was on display in a new way, such that they no longer possessed the ability to manage their own outness. Other men, though, asserted that they felt less out now that they were parents, in that the presence of a child seemed to invite presumptions of heterosexuality. The men were particularly likely to describe this as their experience if they were the primary caregivers of their children, such that they were frequently out alone with their child. Thus situational context—as well as the presence of other "markers" of heterosexuality, such as wedding rings, or a very masculine gender presentation—may have led outsiders to presume that they were heterosexual. Many of the men described feeling as though their adoptive status was also rendered invisible in public, insomuch as assumptions of heterosexuality and reproduction are deeply intertwined (Ryan & Berkowitz, 2009). Strangers often commented on physical resemblances between the men and their children (or asked whether their children looked like their wives), revealing assumptions about the men's sexuality and (biological) route to parenthood. Finally, some of the men claimed that they did not feel more or less out, which they attributed to the fact that they had already been "very out" in their communities.

The experiences of men who had adopted transracially highlight how race and racial similarity also play into men's experiences of (in)visibility in their communities. Men who had adopted children who were visibly different from them racially found that the multiracial nature of their families was often noted and commented on, in some cases leading strangers to draw an associated range of conclusions about men's sexuality and route to parenthood. These men were subjected to "double visibility," in that neither their sexuality nor their adoptive status was a private matter, but was rendered visible for the world to see and comment on. These men, whose families deviated from the heteronormative nuclear family model in multiple ways, were charged with the task of learning to navigate and respond to strangers' inquiries and comments regarding their child's origins and adoptive status. Men who adopted children who were light-skinned or the same race as one of the partners faced a different set of challenges. These men observed that the adoptive status of their families, or one man's relationship to his child, were often rendered *in*visible, putting the impetus on men to correct strangers' mistaken (heteronormative) assumptions about their family status.

These findings point to the complex set of ideologies that dictate strangers' reactions to gay men as they "step out" as parents and families. They reveal the power of biologism and heteronormativity, as well as the influence of geographic, situational, and relational context, in shaping assumptions about families. In turn, gay fathers are in the unique and often challenging position of having to decide how to navigate public reactions to and questions about their family structure. Do they correct presumptions of heterosexuality and biological relatedness, thereby contesting heteronormativity? Or do they refrain from educating outsiders in the service of protecting the privacy and even safety of their families? As one man pointed out, gay fathers are "walking political statements," even if they don't want to be. They are charged with the task of responding to various questions about and attacks on their families on a daily basis, even if they would prefer to be left alone.

These findings also point to the ways that gay adoptive parents' increasing visibility in society has the potential to further push and expand definitions and ideas about family. The fact that they are parenting with another man, are not biologically related to their children, and are often racially dissimilar from their children—and sometimes their partners—all represent deviations from the heterosexual nuclear family ideal. To the extent that they are recognized for what they are—that is, two men parenting a child—their presence in the world has the capacity to transform what people see as "family." As Jana Wolff (2008), a writer and a heterosexual adoptive mother, observes, "Look-alike families are assumed to belong together, but families like ours—who don't match—are seen as curious groupings of individuals. A White woman holding the hand of a little Black boy prompts guessing: His social worker? His baby-sitter? His Black father's White girlfriend? His mother? (No, couldn't be that.)"

As adoptive families, gay-parent families, and other types of "curious groupings of individuals" become increasingly common and also increasingly vocal about their presence and experiences, societal views about what constitutes a family can and will begin to change. In turn, greater recognition and acceptance by societal institutions (such as schools, religious organizations, and the medical community) will improve the conditions of individuals living in these "diverse families."

CONCLUSION

Gay parenthood represents just one example of the new family forms that are emerging in today's society. Single-parent families, adoptive families, multiracial families, and complex co-parenting arrangements (e.g., a lesbian couple and a gay male couple; a single woman and a gay male friend, who is also the sperm donor) are just a few examples of innovations in family life (Kleinfield, 2011). As we have seen, the stories of the men in this book reveal insights into the "doing of" and the "living in" creative and new family forms, particularly families that deviate from the heterosexual two-parent family ideal, and thus these men face societal opposition. The creativity and resourcefulness that the men demonstrated in the face of challenging circumstances reveal the exciting possibility of the "new family forms." For example, when faced with legal inequities (such as discriminatory adoption and marriage laws), some of the men employed other strategies to both communicate and protect their familial status, such as hyphenating their names and obtaining legal safeguards. Likewise, upon becoming parents, gay men who lacked contact with other gay parents in their immediate social networks sometimes sought out gay parenting groups, or created their own gay parenting groups. These examples highlight the potential for gay fathers and other new family forms to innovate the definitions and enactment of family in complex and creative ways.

* * *

As we saw, the politics of gay parenthood, although a hotly debated topic in the public arena, was often experienced in relatively mundane ways by the men in the study. Occasionally they alluded to their status as "walking political statements." Yet even those men who were attuned to the ways their choice to parent was "political" did not embark on parenthood in order to make a political statement. Like heterosexual men and women, their drive to become parents was grounded in a desire to love, care for, and be responsible for another human being. Unlike many heterosexual couples, however, they encountered numerous obstacles, both structural and ideological, to enacting this desire due to their sexual orientation.

All the men in the study encountered dominant discourses regarding family as heteronormative and biologically related, although there was variability in their response to such discourses. Some men initially questioned whether they could in fact be gay and be a parent, but others claimed that they never regarded their sexuality as a barrier to becoming a parent. Likewise, some men longed for biological children and grappled with the decision to adopt, but others rejected the importance of biological bonds and reached the decision to adopt fairly easily. Further, some men, having made the decision to adopt, intensely desired an infant child, while others felt less strongly about the importance of raising a child from birth.

It is perhaps tempting to view those men who seemed not to struggle with, or who seemed to internalize, heteronormative discourses as somehow less sophisticated, less radical, or less politically aware than those who appeared to resist them, and, further, to dichotomize the men into two distinct groups: "accommodators" and "resisters." But such characterizations would be overly simplistic for several reasons. First, such a dichotomization obscures the variability both within and across the men. Some men conformed to heteronormativity in some aspects of their lives and resisted it in other ways. For example, as we have seen, some couples divided paid and unpaid labor in a fairly segregated manner, with one partner staying home full-time or part-time and the other working full-time, yet these men rarely conceived of themselves and their partners as "mirroring" heterosexual arrangements. Further, couples in which one member was staying at home part-time or full-time were often aware of the ways their work-family arrangement could lead to highly differentiated parenting roles. In response, they worked together to ensure that this did not happen (e.g., by encouraging the full-time-employed parent to contribute as equally as possibly to child care). The men cannot be viewed as simply "accommodating" to heteronormative configurations of work-family roles, inasmuch as their meaning-making processes and enactment of the division of labor often served to disrupt, not uphold, heteronormative scripts.

Second, dichotomizing the men into "accommodators" versus "resisters" would overly politicize men's possible motives, because it seems to suggest that those men whose behavior does not conform to heteronormativity are necessarily acting intentionally and for political reasons. In other words, such a categorization would oversimplify (and ignore the variability in) the motivations for accommodation versus resistance. There were men who were aware that their choices and families could be viewed as political statements, but who resisted such interpretations, wishing to "just blend in" and be left alone. Likewise, some men were aware that instances in which they were recognized as gay parents—or, alternatively, mistaken as heterosexual—offered the opportunity to educate outsiders about their families. But they objected to the notion that they ought to engage in such efforts, preferring just to "live [their] life." They were not ashamed of their status as gay male parents, but at the same time did not feel compelled to challenge heteronormativity in public settings. Similarly, some of the men in the study desired the privileges and rights of marriage, but did not conceptualize this desire as either radical *or* assimilationist. They asserted their wish to be married in uncomplicated, politically neutral terms, perhaps reflecting, as Weeks (2008) described, their desire for simple "recognition for what you are and want to be, for validation, not absorption . . . [a desire for] the ordinary virtues of care, love, mutual responsibility" (p. 792).

Moreover, dichotomizing men into two types is overly simplistic because it fails to acknowledge the social conditions that facilitate conformity versus resistance. As we have seen, some men's geographic advantage and financial privilege facilitated their ability to resist heteronormativity or to circumvent it altogether. Men who lived in liberal locales or who were fairly affluent often conducted extensive research before choosing private domestic adoption agencies with gay-friendly reputations. Gay men who lived in conservative areas or who lacked financial resources were forced to work with their local child welfare system or to choose from a limited number of agencies, thereby rendering them more vulnerable to heterosexism and sexism by agencies, social workers, and the legal system. Another type of privilege pertained to resources, which served to shape men's ability and willingness to resist normativity. Gay men who lived in rural areas and relied heavily on families for support, for example, sometimes accommodated to their parents' and families' racial preferences in order to avoid losing their support. These men were parenting *as gay men* in areas that were not heavily populated by gay men. Though they might be viewed as yielding to familial pressures regarding the race or ethnicity of their future children, they can also be seen as pioneers by virtue of pursuing gay parenthood while living in rural areas. This latter point speaks again to the complexity and impossibility of categorizing men as either challengers or conformists.

Regardless of whether and how the gay men in this study seem to accommodate to or resist heteronormative discourses, *all became parents in the context of same-sex relationships and adopted a child.* Thus one can take the perspective that although they may not (always) resist heteronormativity in their everyday lives, their very existence poses a challenge to heteronormativity. By forming families that are headed by gay parents and that consist of biologically unrelated and sometimes racially dissimilar members, they are functionally destabilizing traditional notions of "the family" as heterosexual and biogenetically related. Their existence has the potential to challenge heteronormativity in their families, communities, and society. For example, gay men may influence their family members' ideas about family, possibly leading their family members to confront and challenge heteronormativity in their own lives. Indeed, even family members who did not fully "accept" them were sometimes pushed to reconsider their basic beliefs and assumptions about family, parenthood, and love. Likewise, gay men's interactions with their community may have the effect of disrupting heteronorms and advancing outsiders' awareness of the growing diversity of "the family."

Gay adoptive fathers' presence in society and their interactions with family, friends, and community members have the potential to alter ideologies about family not only in theoretical but also in practical terms. As gay adoptive fathers engage in the mundane events of everyday living, such as buying groceries, attending religious services, going to the doctor, and so on, they interact with a wide range of individuals whose ideas about families may be minimally or significantly altered. Indeed, gay men who raise adopted children dislodge many basic assumptions about families: that they must be heterosexually parented, that they must be biologically related, and, perhaps, that they must be racially similar. To the extent that these men and their children are recognized for what they are—a family unit—they can help to transform societal understandings of family, gender, sexuality, race, and love.

Implications

This study holds many implications for the work of scholars in fields as diverse as gender and sexuality studies, family studies, social work, and legal studies. Scholars who study families and gender have much to learn from these men, whose work-family roles and parenting arrangements resist simplistic readings or attributions of "mother" and "father," and whose relationships therefore cannot be viewed as "mirrors" of heterosexual relationships. Indeed, the men may draw from gendered or heteronormative meaning systems to make sense of their experiences and roles, but at the same time, they complicate such meaning systems by pointing out ways in which their identities as men, parents, and workers cannot be mapped on, and do not "fit" within, traditional heteronormative scripts. Their disruption of these larger meaning systems highlights the socially constructed nature of categories such as male/female, mother/father, breadwinner/homemaker, gay/straight, traditional/nontraditional, and other binaries.

Scholars of men and masculinity, who often do not explicitly consider the perspectives of gay men and gay parents, might consider how the voices of the gay men in this book serve to complicate dominant notions of "masculinity" and related concepts. The men, for example, often alluded to ways in which parenting in a male-male parental context posed challenges to their subjective sense of masculinity, particularly when valued aspects of masculinity (e.g., breadwinning, careerism) were diminished or absent. At the same time, the men's stories hinted at ways that their definition of masculinity was reshaped by parenthood, such that, for example, they were pushed to revise what it means to be a "man" or to have "accomplished" something. Heterosexual men, particularly those who are highly involved parents, may experience similar shifts in or challenges to their sense of masculinity (Doucet, 2006). And yet heterosexual men who are partnered with women may experience greater constraints on the degree to which they can redefine masculinity, in that the male-female parenting context often "pulls for" particular gendered roles from both men and women. Research that includes both gay male couples and heterosexual couples, in both single- and dual-earner work arrangements, could shed further insight into how men's (re)construction of masculinity is affected by their relational and situational context. For example, such research could enable us to examine how sexual orientation, relational context, work arrangements, and other factors (such as gender ideology and social class) intersect to shape men's ideas about and enactment of masculinity.

Scholars who study heterosexual parenting and families may be encouraged to examine and interrogate more closely the production and reproduction of heteronormativity in the heterosexual family context—and, by extension, to study the ways that heterosexual people and parents resist heteronormativity in their daily lives. Placing heteronormativity at the center of analysis may yield new insights, as researchers examine, for example, the ways heterosexual adoptive couples also deviate from the idealized heterosexual nuclear family model, and how they make sense of and interpret such deviations (Goldberg, Downing, & Richardson, 2009). Examination of how single parents, as well as individuals involved in more complex co-parenting arrangements (e.g., a single woman and a gay male couple), negotiate and respond to heteronormativity in their daily lives would also be informative, as it would reveal how other types of diverse family arrangements are affected by and resist societal discourses about families.

These men's voices offer a variety of practical implications for practitioners, as well as for gay men (and sexual minorities in general) who wish to become parents. Practitioners, such as adoption professionals, who wish to assist gay prospective adopters in their efforts to become parents, are advised to know the laws of their states, and the implications of these laws for gay men who are adopting domestically and internationally. Practitioners should also take pains to ensure that their written materials, training materials, and websites address the needs and perspectives of diverse groups, including gay men. Further, adoption practitioners and agencies should consider offering support groups and trainings specifically aimed at gay men and lesbians who are adopting or seeking to adopt; if this is impractical, they might consider partnering with another agency or organization to offer such resources. Perhaps most important, practitioners should seek to maintain awareness of the ways that heteronormative and gender biases may adversely affect their evaluation of, and ability to serve, gay men effectively.

Practitioners who seek to support gay men in their quest to adopt should also encourage men to talk with their partners (if they are coupled) about the various decisions that they must make both pre- and post-adoption. For example, collaborative discussions about the varied types of adoption, desired child characteristics, racial attitudes, personal strengths and weaknesses, future work-family arrangements, philosophies about parenting, and how to deal with difficult or unsupportive social-network members should be encouraged, given their importance in the adoption and parenting process.

Sexual minorities who wish to adopt can find many points of guidance throughout these pages. For example, the men's stories suggest the importance of working actively to find a gay-friendly (or at least gay-toler-ant) agency, and also the importance of knowing the laws of one's state of residence—as well as the laws of other states—regarding gay adoption. Fur-ther, the men's stories highlight the salience of contextual factors such as geo-graphic location and finances in their parenting decisions and trajectories; such information may be crucial for gay men as they consider parenthood in general and adoption in particular. The men's stories also highlight the importance of evaluating one's social resources—and, ideally, identifying and anticipating social network gaps that might occur upon becoming parents.

The men's stories shed light on the pervasiveness of heteronormativity in society. As we have seen, heteronormativity operates at the ideological, structural, and interpersonal level. At the ideological level, heteronormativ-ity is embedded in basic ideas about what makes a "real" family (heterosexual parents with biologically related children) and who is ideally suited to care for children (heterosexual married parents). Heteronormative ideologies may interfere with gay men's family-building efforts by undermining their confidence, as well as fueling family members'—and sometimes friends'—resistance to their adoption plans. These ideologies also underpin the struc-tural barriers that gay men encounter when they seek to build their families. For example, heteronormative ideologies are institutionalized in the form of adoption-agency discrimination and laws barring gay men from adopting. Indeed, adoption agencies and laws function to uphold heteronormativity by clearly privileging and prioritizing heterosexual married couples as the "ideal" family. When gay men finally do become parents, they may person-ally struggle against heteronormative discourses that presuppose a male and female co-parental unit, and that equate breadwinning with masculinity and child rearing and housework with femininity. They also encounter het-eronormativity in the form of outsiders' assumptions of heterosexuality. In short, gay men are continually faced with occasions—be they felt as burdens or opportunities—to respond to and possibly disrupt heteronormativity.

Indeed, the men's stories also highlight ways that all parents—single or coupled, heterosexual or gay, male, female, or genderqueer—may resist heteronormativity within their immediate social contexts, thus creating the possibility for shifts in beliefs about gender and parenting both within and beyond their proximal environment. For example, some of the men's extended family members were emboldened by their love for their gay fam-ily member to challenge and resist heteronormativity outwardly. All people, heterosexual or not, have the capacity to acknowledge, confront, and resist heteronormativity in their parenting and work roles. Indeed, as Jackson (2006) has pointed out, institutionalized heterosexuality governs not only the lives of those excluded from its boundaries, but also the lives of those who are contained within it. Heterosexual men and women, in addition to sexual minorities, can push against the norms and regulations imposed by institutionalized heterosexuality, and in doing so, potentially lead richer and fuller lives.

Future Research

Much more research is needed that examines how gay men create and maintain their parenting identities over time. This volume provides only a snapshot of the kinds of experiences and changes that gay men who adopt undergo; follow-ups are needed to determine how things unfold in the long term. More research is also needed that explores the perspectives of gay men of color, as well as working-class gay men, concerning adoption and parenthood. Race and social class intersect with gender and sexual orientation in complex ways, and inevitably have implications for gay men's adoption and parenting experiences.

This book raises many questions for future research. For example, how do gay men's social support networks continue to change after the immediate post-placement period? To what extent do family members and friends who struggle initially "come around"? What types of factors or conditions predict whether family members and friends increase their support or remain relatively unsupportive and uninvolved? How do gay men's relationships with their neighborhoods and communities change as their children grow older? What kinds of challenges and experiences do gay men who adopt—particularly those who adopt transracially—encounter in their children's schools and communities, and to what extent are these challenges and experiences shaped by men's geographic location and other contextual factors?

Much more research is needed to explore how gay men conceive of their parenting identities and roles amid the swiftly changing but pervasively heteronormative sociopolitical environment. Researchers must recognize that even though heteronormativity is an ever-present "backdrop" to gay men's daily lives, gay men's parenting configurations and experiences should not be considered as either derivative of or reactions against heteronormativity. As difficult as it is, we must increasingly recognize and study gay men's experiences, beliefs, and roles as complex, messy, and sometimes contradictory—and resistant to easy classification and categorization. Further, researchers as well as society at large must recognize both the practical and theoretical usefulness of supplanting the "destructive sanctity of the family with respect for diverse and vibrant families" (Stacey, 1996, p. 126). By fully recognizing and including gay men and their families as part of the mosaic of family diversity, we can begin to dismantle heteronormativity from the center to the sidelines.

APPENDIX A

The Larger Study

The data for this project are derived from a larger study that follows gay, lesbian, and heterosexual couples across the transition to adoptive parenthood. In this project, my graduate students and I interview couples pre-adoption (before they are placed with a child) and post-adoption (three or four months after they are placed with a child). I began this study in 2005 and it is still underway, given that we continued to recruit new couples for the study until 2009; indeed, some couples have not yet adopted, precluding completion of the post-adoptive placement interview.

The larger study from which these data are drawn focused on many domains. Most of these domains are included in this book: namely, the rich qualitative data in the study address men's motivation for parenthood (chapter 1), perceived barriers to adopting (chapter 2), experiences of balancing work and family (chapter 3), social support experiences (chapter 4), and experiences interacting with the broader community (chapter 5). These data were gleaned largely from men's responses to the open-ended interview questions. But the larger study is a mixed-methods endeavor, meaning that I gather both qualitative and quantitative data from participants. In addition to exploring big, open-ended questions such as "Why do gay men seek to become parents?" and "What challenges do they face in their efforts to become parents?," I also seek to examine, using questionnaire-based, quantitative measures, how various dimensions of men's lives and adjustment change across the transition to parenthood. For example, I have used these quantitative measures to examine changes in perceived parenting skill across the transition to parenthood (Goldberg & Smith, 2009), as well as changes in couples' relationship quality (Goldberg, Smith, & Kashy, 2010) and mental health (Goldberg & Smith, 2011). In sum, this book represents an examination of many but not all of the topics that I address in the larger study.

Procedure

The Interviewers

The 70 gay male participants who are described in this book were interviewed by me or my graduate student research assistants (all doctoral students in clinical psychology) during the years 2005–2009. All interviewers
underwent a rigorous training process. First, they listened to several taped
interviews. Then they sat in on a "live" interview; that is, they were in the
room with the interviewer while she interviewed the participant over the
telephone (with the participant's permission). Next the interviewers partici-
pated in one or two "mock" interviews. Interviewers were given substantial
feedback on their mock interviews, in terms of their mastery of the interview
protocol, their knowledge of when to probe, the effectiveness of their probes,
their rapport-building skills, and the overall smoothness of the interview. At
this point, they were ready to conduct participant interviews.

Transcription Procedures

All participant interviews were tape-recorded and later transcribed. Both
undergraduate and graduate research assistants transcribed the interviews.
As Bailey (2008) and others have noted, "Representing audible talk as written words requires reduction, interpretation and representation to make the
written text readable and meaningful" (p. 127). Undergraduate and graduate
student research assistants were trained to employ a number of transcription conventions to aid later interpretation. Namely, because the meanings
of utterances are shaped by the way something is said in addition to simply
what is said (Bailey, 2008), transcribers were trained to indicate key details in
the text. For example, changes in volume or speed were indicated in parentheses (e.g., softly; loudly; voice gets softer). Adjectives were also inserted
in parentheses to indicate how something was said (e.g., in an exasperated
tone; wistfully; emphatically). Finally, pauses (including a note about the
approximate length) and laughter were also included in parentheses (Rubin
& Rubin, 2005). Inaudible remarks by the participant were indicated with

question marks, as in "I never knew that my partner was so ?? to become a parent, but I later learned that this was something he really wanted to do."

In the interest of protecting participants' confidentiality, transcribers were trained never to transcribe identifying details of participants. For example, in the place of proper names, appropriate placeholders were used (e.g., participant's sister; participant's partner; participant's child). Likewise, the names of employers were never transcribed, nor were highly specific details associated with the participant's story of their child's adoption.

Interview Questions

The data discussed in this book are derived from a number of closed- and open-ended interview questions. The questions listed here are those that most typically evoked the themes and narratives described in this book.

Chapter 1

QUESTIONS FROM THE TIME 1 INTERVIEW:
Why do you want to become a parent? (Prompt: What drew you to be a parent? Did you always want to become a parent?)
Why do you want to become a parent now?
How did you decide to adopt? (Prompt: Tell me the process by which you came to adopt, as opposed to pursuing surrogacy, etc.?)
Did you attempt to have a biological child (e.g., via surrogacy)? Tell me about this process.
What type of adoption are you pursuing?
Why did you choose this type?

Chapter 2

QUESTIONS FROM THE TIME 1 INTERVIEW:
What type of adoption are you pursuing?
Why did you choose this type?
Are you adopting as a couple or is one of you adopting as a single parent?
If one partner is adopting as a single parent: How did you make the decision about who would be the official adoptive parent?
What are your feelings about adopting as a single/primary? What has been hard/difficult about this?
Tell me about the adoption process so far. How has it been for you?
What aspects of the adoption process have been the most challenging?
Do you feel like you've faced certain barriers or challenges because you are a same-sex couple?

How satisfied are you with your agency?
Were there things that they did that were helpful?
Were there things that they did that were unhelpful?

Questions from the Time 2 interview:

If open adoption: Did you meet the birth mother/birth parents?
Do you know if they specifically looked for a gay couple?
Did you encounter any problems or surprises with the adoption process?
How was the agency helpful?
How was the agency unhelpful?
Did you adopt as a couple, or is one of you currently identified as the "primary" parent or official legal adoptive parent?
If only one parent is primary/legal parent: What has that been like? (Prompt: Have you experienced any legal insecurities? Feelings of invisibility during the process?)
Have you pursued a second-parent adoption? If no, why?
Do you have any concerns about the effect that not having certain legal protections like marriage will have on your family? Explain.
Would you like to be able to get married? Why or why not?

Chapter 3

QUESTIONS FROM THE TIME 1 INTERVIEW:
Tell me about your job.
What is your job title?
Are you self-employed?
Do you work at home?
How many hours per week do you work?

Questions from the Time 2 interview:

Are you back at work? How many hours are you working?
What has it been like for you, trying to balance work with parenthood and also your relationship with your partner? (If applicable: What strategies have you used?)
Do you feel you have sacrificed job opportunities for family? Sacrificed aspects of family life for work? Explain.
What is your current child-care arrangement?
How did you decide on this arrangement?

If one parent is staying home/now working part-time: How did you decide who would stay at home/cut down work hours?

If interviewee is the one staying home: What has been like for you, to be at home? (Prompt: What has it been like to go from working to being a stay-at-home-parent?)

Has your experience attaching to your child been different from your partner's experience attaching to him/her? Have you and your partner bonded differently to your child? Explain.

If one parent is at home part-time or full-time: How has the fact that one of you has been home more with the child influenced things (e.g., attachment, the division of child care)?

Chapter 4

QUESTIONS FROM THE TIME 1 INTERVIEW:

What level of support did you receive from your family with regard to your decision to adopt as gay parents? Explain.

If unsupportive: Why are they unsupportive?

What level of support did you receive from your partner's family with regard to your decision to adopt as gay parents? Explain.

If unsupportive: Why are they unsupportive?

What level of support did you receive from your friends with regard to your decision to adopt as gay parents? Explain.

If unsupportive: Why are they unsupportive?

QUESTIONS FROM THE TIME 2 INTERVIEW:

How supportive and involved has your family of origin been since you became parents?

Are they more supportive and involved, less supportive and involved, or about the same, compared to before you had children? Explain.

How supportive and involved has your partner's family of origin been since you became parents?

Are they more supportive and involved, less supportive and involved, or about the same, compared to before you had children? Explain.

How supportive and involved have your friends been since you became parents?

Are they more supportive and involved, less supportive and involved, or about the same, compared to before you had children? Explain.

Have there been any changes in who you are spending time with and relying on for support?

Chapter 5

QUESTIONS FROM THE TIME 2 INTERVIEW:

Have you felt more "out" since you became parents? Explain/give examples.

How have people responded to the fact that you are two men raising a child?

If child is of a different race/ethnicity: Tell me about your decision to adopt a child of a different race. How do you expect this to affect your family? Are there any unique issues you foresee in the future?

If child is of a different race/ethnicity: Tell me about how people have reacted to the fact that you are two men raising a child of a different race.

If child is of a different race/ethnicity: Have you felt accepted by members of your child's race/culture? Explain.

APPENDIX D

Participant Demographic Table

Fam #	Names	Race	Age	Occupation	Adoption Type	Child Name	Child Race	Child Age	Child Sex	Region
1	Robbie	White	34	IT Manager	Private Domestic	Travis	Biracial	Newborn	Boy	South, Urban
	Finn	White	44	Hospital Administrator						
2	Carter	White	37	Teacher	Private Domestic	Arianna	Biracial	Newborn	Girl	Midwest, Suburb
	Patrick	White	41	Associate Professor						
3	Russell	White	41	Executive Director	Private Domestic	Noam	Latino	Newborn	Boy	West Coast, Urban
	David	White	33	Massage Therapist*						
4	Nathan	White	38	Asst. Director of Museum	Private Domestic	Leah	White	Newborn	Girl	East Coast, Suburb
	Ray	White	37	Pharmaceutical Representative						
5	Dennis	White	40	Business Owner	Public Domestic	Judah	White	Toddler	Boy	West Coast, Urban
	Justin	White	42	Computer Programmer						
6	Chuck	White	38	Web Developer	Intern'l	Micah	Guatemalan	Newborn	Boy	East Coast, Suburb
	Donovan	Latino	42	Engineer						
7	Allan	White	36	Public Relations Manager	Private Domestic	Lewis	White	Newborn	Boy	West Coast, Suburb
	Drew	White	33	Retail Manager						
8	Gerard	White	48	Architect	Private Domestic	Tara	White	Newborn	Girl	East Coast, Urban
	Scott	Latino	47	Physician						
9	Henry	Biracial	45	Physical Therapist	Private Domestic	Madison	Biracial	Newborn	Girl	East Coast, Urban
	Luis	Latino	45	Surgeon						
10	Frank	White	39	Physician	Private Domestic	Benny	White	Newborn	Boy	West Coast, Urban
	Cooper	Multiracial	39	Physician Assistant						

Fam #	Names	Race	Age	Occupation	Adoption Type	Child Name	Child Race	Child Age	Child Sex	Region
11	Trevor	White	38	Technical Support Technician	Private Domestic	Sharlene	White	Newborn	Girl	West Coast, Urban
	Richard	White	37	Urban Planner						
12	Theo	White	40	Chef	Public Domestic	Emma	African American	Toddler	Girl	West Coast, Suburb
	Dashaun	African American	36	Mental Health Technician						
13	Carl	White	41	Fund-Raising Director	Private Domestic	Carrie	White	Newborn	Girl	West Coast, Suburb
	Jason	White	37	Teacher						
14	Chris	White	45	Research Scientist	Private Domestic	Quinn	Latino	Newborn	Boy	West Coast, Urban
	Eric	Latino	40	Marketing Executive						
15	Nick	White	38	Public Relations Manager*	Private Domestic	Emmett	African American	Newborn	Boy	West Coast, Urban
	Todd	African American	46	Marketing Communications Specialist						
16	Bill	White	38	Director of Programs	Private Domestic	Joey	White	Newborn	Boy	West Coast, Urban
	Darius	White	41	Graduate Student*						
17	Timothy	White	41	Sales Manager	Public Domestic	Ross	White	School-Aged	Boy	East Coast, Suburb
	Jim	White	36	Cook						
18	Rufus	White	37	Computer Programmer	Private Domestic	Daria	White	Newborn	Girl	South, Urban
	Trey	White	32	Dermatologist						
19	Ryan	White	37	Engineer	Public Domestic	Solomon	White	School-Aged	Boy	West Coast, Urban
	Harvey	Asian	41	Sales Representative						
20	Lars	White	36	Human Resources Officer	Public Domestic	Evan	Biracial	Toddler	Boy	South, Suburb
	Joshua	White	40	Administrative Assistant						
21	Brian	White	52	Sales Manager	Intern'l	Aiden	Vietnamese	Toddler	Boy	East Coast, Suburb
	Gregory	White	40	Graduate Student						
22	Xavier	White	39	Software Developer	Public Domestic	Colin	White	Toddler	Boy	West Coast, Urban
	Doug	White	37	Bank Manager*						
23	Miles	White	40	Consultant	Private Domestic	Dylan	Biracial	Newborn	Boy	East Coast, Suburb
	Paul	White	40	Administrative Assistant						

Fam #	Names	Race	Age	Occupation	Adoption Type	Child Name	Child Race	Child Age	Child Sex	Region
24	Stan	White	32	Asst. Professor	Private Domestic	Caitlyn	White	Newborn	Girl	West Coast, Urban
	Dean	Asian	30	Asst. Director, Nonprofit Organization						
25	Daniel	White	38	Graduate Student	Private Domestic	Miri	African American	Newborn	Girl	East Coast, Rural
	Vaughn	White	39	Consultant						
26	Will	White	37	Marketing Manager	Public Domestic	Emeline	White	Infant	Girl	West Coast, Urban
	Charlie	Asian	32	Operations Manager						
27	Rett	White	35	Graduate Student	Public Domestic	Christopher	African American	Toddler	Boy	Midwest, Urban
	Barry	White	35	IT Manager						
28	Thomas	White	36	Real Estate Agent	Private Domestic	Lillian	African American	Newborn	Girl	South, Suburb
	Devon	White	47	Administrative Assistant						
29	Derek	White	32	Software Consultant	Private Domestic	Lucia	White	Newborn	Girl	East Coast, Urban
	Roger	White	36	Business Owner						
30	Elliott	White	40	Executive Director	Public Domestic	Sal	White	School-Aged	Boy	East Coast, Urban
	Nolan	White	36	Teacher						
31	Sam	White	36	Financial Analyst	Private Domestic	Hannah	Multiracial	Newborn	Girl	West Coast, Urban
	Jake	White	30	Graduate Student						
32	Shane	White	32	Sales Representative	Private Domestic	Dominick	White	Newborn	Boy	South, Urban
	Corey	White	31	Journalist						
33	Brett	White	42	Lawyer	Private Domestic	Rachel	Latina	Newborn	Girl	West Coast, Urban
	James	White	41	Urban Planner*						
34	Kevin	White	40	Psychologist	Private Domestic	Brody	Latino	Newborn	Boy	Midwest, Urban
	Brendan	White	43	Graduate Student						
35	Carlos	Latino	30	Sales Representative	Private Domestic	Damian	Multiracial	Newborn	Boy	West Coast, Urban
	Michael	White	33	Psychiatrist						

NOTES

NOTES TO THE INTRODUCTION

1. Most men who were gay who were also fathers during this time had become fathers in the context of heterosexual marriages and later came out as gay following a divorce (Barrett & Robinson, 1990; Goldberg, 2010a).

2. Intentional parenthood was still considerably more common among lesbians than among gay men at this point in history, in part because of the greater acceptability of lesbian motherhood as compared to gay fatherhood, and because of the greater number of options available to lesbians wishing to become a parent (alternative insemination, performed either at home or by medical professionals, was the most common way that lesbian women chose to become mothers in the 1980s and 1990s; see Littauer, 2004).

3. Please see the participant demographic table in appendix D for descriptive data on the gay male couples in this study.

4. Some gay couples may pursue surrogacy abroad (e.g., in India). Transnational surrogacy is less expensive, but this practice of "reproductive outsourcing" has racial, economic, and gender implications (Jones & Keith, 2006; Riggs & Due, 2010).

5. Pleck (1981, 1995) and others (e.g., Mahalik, Talmadge, Locke, & Scott, 2005) have argued that men who confront and actively challenge/disengage from traditional gender role standards and stereotypes about masculinity may receive psychological benefits. For example, a man who is emotionally expressive may experience relationships that are more supportive and emotionally connected (Rochlen, Suizzo, McKelley, & Scaringi, 2008).

6. Children were of varying ages at the time of placement (see "The Men in the Study" section, below).

7. A home study is a report written by a social worker who has met with the prospective adoptive parents on several occasions. In addition to interviewing the prospective adoptive parents, the social worker also visits the adoptive parents' home and investigates their health, medical, criminal, and family background. The purpose of the home study is to help the court determine whether the adoptive parents are qualified to adopt a child, based on the criteria established by state law. It is only when the home study is completed, and the prospective adoptive parents are officially "approved" as qualified to adopt, that they are eligible to be placed with children.

8. As discussed in appendix A, I also included quantitative measures in this study, but the results of these are not reported here. For reports of these quantitative data, see Goldberg and Smith (2009), Goldberg, Smith, and Kashy (2010), and Goldberg and Smith (2011).

9. Occasionally, each partner was interviewed by a different person. For example, I would interview one partner, and one of my research assistants would interview the other

partner. But more often than not, the same person interviewed both partners. To ensure that each partner felt comfortable, the interviewer always reminded the participant to find a private room where their conversation would not be overheard.

10. *SD* stands for standard deviation, a measure of the dispersion of a set of data from its mean. The more spread apart the data (i.e., the more variability), the higher the deviation. Standard deviation is calculated as the square root of the variance.

11. The median is the middle of a distribution: half the scores are above the median and half are below the median. The median is less sensitive to extreme scores than the mean, and this makes it a better measure than the mean for highly skewed distributions. The median income is usually more informative than the mean income, for example.

12. There were 10 interracial couples in the study (i.e., 10 couples in which partners were of different racial backgrounds), which represented 29% of the sample.

13. Again, I define "heteronormativity" broadly to include the presumption that heterosexuality is the default and "natural" position in the social world, social institutions, romantic relationships, and familial relationships, and also the related presumption that there are two sexes that are "naturally" gendered.

NOTES TO CHAPTER 1

1. For an account of early gay parenthood, see Mallon (2004), who interviewed 20 gay men who became parents in the 1980s. His book describes the challenges and hurdles experienced by these early pioneers, and it provides insight into how the pursuit and experience of gay parenthood has changed over the past several decades.

2. Some of the material discussed in this section—that is, on factors affecting the timing of parenthood—is also discussed in Goldberg, Downing, and Moyer (2012).

3. Commercial surrogacy involves significant costs, including the cost of the egg donor's participation; in vitro fertilization; physician services; health insurance to cover all procedures and the pregnancy; legal services for agreements among all parties; the services of the egg-donor agency; and the services of the surrogacy agency (Bergman, Rubio, Green, & Padron, 2010).

4. Openness is increasingly becoming "the norm" in private domestic adoption (Pertman, 2000). Openness in adoptions falls along a continuum: some adoptive families exchange letters, photos, and e-mails with their children's birth parents; others have occasional visits with their children's birth parents; and still others agree to regular visits.

5. Some of the material in this section—that is, the factors that influence gay men's decision making about what adoption route to pursue—is discussed in Downing, Richardson, Kinkler, and Goldberg (2009).

NOTES TO CHAPTER 2

1. Historically, second-parent adoptions have been used most often by heterosexual stepparents (typically stepfathers) who wish to adopt their spouse's children (Connolly, 2002a), but they are now increasingly being used by to ensure legal recognition of the nonlegal adoptive lesbian or gay partner, in cases in which only one partner can legally adopt (e.g., in international adoption and certain U.S. states). But judges may deny a second-parent adoption to a same-sex partner based on the lack of an official, legal, or institutionally defined relationship between the two partners (Richman, 2002). In this way, individual judges may actively uphold or resist heteronormativity, depending on how they choose to interpret the law.

2. Gay couples who live in states that permit same-sex partners to co-adopt cannot necessarily adopt their child jointly. If they match with a birth mother who lives and gives birth in a state that does not permit adoptions by same-sex couples, they will need to complete two separate adoptions of the same child (a primary and secondary adoption). The Interstate Compact on the Placement of Children (ICPC) requires the state in which the child is born to approve the adoption, and if the state's law explicitly prohibits adoption by same-sex couples, the couple will not be able to gain said approval. But the couple will be able to obtain ICPC approval from the state in which the child was born for *one* of them to adopt in their home state, and once that adoption is completed, the (first, legal) adoptive parent will then have the authority to consent to his/her partner adopting their child by way of a "second parent" adoption, assuming that this is permitted in their home state. By completing these two adoptions of the same child, both partners can become full legal parents (Wald, 2010).

3. Only two couples in this study had access to marriage or civil unions in their home state at the time of the interviews. One couple lived in Massachusetts, where same-sex marriage was legal, but they had decided to wait until after the adoption was completed before marrying. They made this decision based on the advice of their adoption agency, who had warned them that by getting married, they were legally bound together as a couple, which limited their options in the adoption process (e.g., they would not be able to match with a birth mother in a state where co-parent adoption by gay men was illegal). One couple lived in Vermont and had completed a civil union.

4. Several states (e.g., California, Washington, Oregon) have passed legislation that provides rights and responsibilities to registered domestic partners. These rights include power of attorney, inheritance without a will, and hospital visitation on the same terms as a spouse. Importantly, domestic partnerships do not reach the same legal threshold as civil unions or civil marriages (Pawelski et al., 2006).

REFERENCES

Allan, G. (2008). Flexibility, friendship, and family. *Personal Relationships, 15,* 1–16.

Almack, K. (2005). What's in a name? An exploration of the significance of the choice of surnames given to the children born within female same sex families. *Sexualities, 8,* 239–254.

———. (2008). Lesbian parent couples and their families of origin negotiating new kin relationships. *Sociology, 42,* 1183–1199.

Anderson, S. C., & Holliday, M. (2004). Normative passing in the lesbian community: An exploratory study. *Journal of Gay & Lesbian Social Services, 17,* 25–38.

Armstrong, E. A. (2002). *Forging gay identities: Organizing in San Francisco, 1950–1994.* Chicago: University of Chicago Press.

Bailey, J. (2008). First steps in qualitative data analysis: Transcribing. *Family Practice, 25,* 127–131.

Barclay, L., Everitt, L., Rogan, F., Schmied, V., & Wyllie, A. (1997). Becoming a mother—an analysis of women's experience of early motherhood. *Journal of Advanced Nursing, 25,* 719–728.

Barrett, R. L., & Robinson, B. E. (1990). *Gay fathers.* Lexington, MA: Lexington.

Baxter, J., Hewitt, B., & Haynes, M. (2008). Life course transitions and housework: Marriage, parenthood, and time on housework. *Journal of Marriage & the Family, 70,* 259–272.

Ben-Ari, A., & Livni, T. (2006). Motherhood is not a given thing: Experiences and constructed meanings of biological and nonbiological lesbian mothers. *Sex Roles, 54,* 521–531.

Bennett, S. (2003). International adoptive lesbian families: Parental perceptions of the influence of diversity on family relationships in early childhood. *Smith College Studies in Social Work, 7,* 73–91.

Bergen, K. M., Suter, E. A., & Daas, K. L. (2006). "About as solid as a fish net": Symbolic construction of a legitimate parental identity for nonbiological lesbian mothers. *Journal of Family Communication, 6,* 201–220.

Bergman, K., Rubio, R. J., Green, R. J., & Padron, E. (2010). Gay men who become fathers via surrogacy: The transition to parenthood. *Journal of GLBT Family Studies, 6,* 111–141.

Berkowitz, D. (2009). Theorizing lesbian and gay parenting: Past, present, and future scholarship. *Journal of Family Theory & Review, 1,* 117–132.

Berkowitz, D., & Marsiglio, W. (2007). Gay men: Negotiating procreative, father, and family identities. *Journal of Marriage & the Family, 69,* 366–381.

Bernstein, M. (2002). Identities and politics: Toward a historical understanding of the lesbian and gay movement. *Social Science History, 26,* 531–581.

Biesen, W. (December 31, 2010). Commentary: Top 10 LGBT events that made 2010 a memorable year. *San Diego Lesbian & Gay News.* Retrieved on January 17, 2011, from http://sdgln.com/commentary/2010/12/31/ commentary-top-10-lgbt-events-made-2010-memorable-year.

Blankenhorn, D. (1995). *Fatherless America: Confronting our most urgent social problem.* New York: HarperCollins.

Bogdan, R. C., & Biklen, S. K. (2003). *Qualitative research for education: An introduction to theories and methods.* Boston: Allyn & Bacon.

Bost, K. K., Cox, M., Burchinal, M. R., & Payne, C. (2002). Structural and supportive changes in couples' family and friendship networks across the transition to parenthood. *Journal of Marriage & the Family, 54,* 517–531.

Bowlby, J. (1969). *Attachment and loss: Attachment* (vol. 1). New York: Basic.

Brandon, P. D. (1999). Income-pooling arrangements, economic constraints, and married mothers' child care choices. *Journal of Family Issues, 20,* 350–370.

Brickell, C. (2000). Heroes and invaders: Gay and lesbian pride parades and the public/private distinction in New Zealand media accounts. *Gender, Place, & Culture, 7,* 163–178.

Brinamen, C. F., & Mitchell, V. (2008). Gay men becoming fathers: A model of identity expansion. *Journal of GLBT Family Studies, 4,* 521–541.

Brind, K. (2008). An exploration of adopters' views regarding children's ages at the time of placement. *Child & Family Social Work, 13,* 319–328.

Brodzinsky, D. M. (2003). Adoption by lesbians and gay men: A national survey of adoption agency policies, practices, and attitudes. Retrieved on September 6, 2009, from http://www.adoptioninstitute.org/whowe/Gay%20and%20Lesbian%20Adoption1.html.

Brodzinsky, D., Patterson, C., & Vaziri, M. (2002). Adoption agency perspectives on lesbian and gay prospective parents: A national study. *Adoption Quarterly, 5,* 5–23.

Brooks, D., & Goldberg, S. (2001). Gay and lesbian adoptive and foster care placements: Can they meet the needs of waiting children? *Social Work, 46,* 147–157.

Brown, D., Ryan, S., & Pushkal, J. T. (2007). Initial validating of the Open Adoption Scale: Measuring the influence of adoption myths on attitudes toward open adoption. *Adoption Quarterly, 10,* 179–196.

Brown, J. (2010). Can friendship survive parenthood? Retrieved June 17, 2010, from http://www.parents.com/parenting/relationships/friendship/can-friendships-survive-parenthood.

Bumpass, L., & Lu, H. H. (2000). Trends in cohabitation and implications for children's family contexts in the U.S. *Population Studies, 54,* 29–42.

Calhoun, C. (1997). Family outlaws: Rethinking connections between feminism, lesbianism, and the family. In H. L. Nelson (Ed.), *Feminism and families* (pp. 131–150). New York: Routledge.

Carberry, J., & Buhrmester, D. (1998). Friendship and need fulfillment during three phases of young adulthood. *Journal of Social & Personal Relationships, 15,* 393–409.

Carrington, C. (1999). *No place like home: Relationships and family life among lesbians and gay men.* Chicago: University of Chicago Press.

Centers for Disease Control and Prevention. (2009). NCHS data brief: Delayed childbearing: More women are having their first child later in life. Retrieved on May 27, 2010, from http://www.cdc.gov/nchs/data/databriefs/db21.htm.

Chambers, D. (2000). Representations of familialism in the British popular media. *European Journal of Cultural Studies, 3,* 195–214.

Charmaz, K. (2006). *Constructing grounded theory: A practical guide through qualitative analysis.* London: Sage.

Chauncey, G. (2005). *Why marriage? The history shaping today's debate over gay equality.* New York: Basic.

Cherlin, A. (1992). *Marriage, divorce, remarriage.* Cambridge, MA: Harvard University Press.

———. (2010). Demographic trends in the United States: A review of research in the 2000s. *Journal of Marriage & the Family, 72,* 403–419.

Clarke, V. (2001). What about the children? Arguments against lesbian and gay parenting. *Women's Studies International Forum, 24,* 555–570.

Clarke, V., Burns, M., & Burgoyne, C. (2008). "Who would take whose name?" Accounts of naming practices in same-sex relationships. *Journal of Community & Applied Social Psychology, 18,* 420–439.

Clarkson, J. (2008). The limitations of the discourse of norms: Gay visibility and degrees of transgression. *Journal of Communication Inquiry, 32,* 368–382.

Cohen, P. N., & Bianchi, S. M. (1999). Marriage, children, and women's employment: What do we know? *Monthly Labor Review, 122,* 22–31.

Colberg, M. (1997). Clinical issues with gay and lesbian adoptive parenting. In S. K. Roszia, A. Baran, & L. Coleman (Eds.), *Creating kinship* (pp. 115–123). Portland, OR: Dougy Center.

Cole, S. A. (2005). Foster caregiver motivation and infant attachment: How do reasons for fostering affect relationships? *Child & Adolescent Social Work Journal, 22,* 441–457.

Coltrane, S. (1996). *Family man: Fatherhood, housework, and gender equity.* New York: Oxford University Press.

———. (2000). Research on household labor: Modeling and measuring the social embeddedness of routine family work. *Journal of Marriage & the Family, 62,* 1208–1233.

Connell, R. W. (1995). *Masculinities.* Cambridge, UK: Polity.

Connell, R. W., & Messerschmidt, J. W. (2005). Hegemonic masculinity: Rethinking the concept. *Gender & Society, 19,* 829–859.

Connolly, C. (2002a). Lesbian and gay parenting: A brief history of legal and theoretical issues. *Studies in Law, Politics, & Society, 26,* 189–208.

———. (2002b). The voice of the petitioner: The experiences of gay and lesbian parents in successful second-parent adoption proceedings. *Law & Society Review, 36,* 325–346.

Cooper, M. (2000). Being the "go-to guy": Fatherhood, masculinity, and the organization of work in Silicon Valley. *Qualitative Sociology, 23,* 379–405.

Crabb, S., & Augoustinos, M. (2008). Genes and families in the media: Implications of genetic discourse for constructions of the "family." *Health Sociology Review, 17,* 303–312.

Cronenwett, L. R. (1985). Parental network structure and perceived support after birth of first child. *Nursing Research, 34,* 347–352.

DeBoer, D. (2009). The psychosocial context of gay men choosing fatherhood. In P. Hammack & B. Cohler (Eds.), *The story of sexual identity: Narrative perspectives on the gay and lesbian life course* (pp. 327–346). Oxford: Oxford University Press.

DeJordy, R. (2008). Just passing through: Stigma, passing, and identity decoupling in the work place. *Group & Organization Management, 33,* 504–531.

Deutsch, F. (1999). *Halving it all: How equally shared parenting works.* Cambridge, MA: Harvard University Press.

Dillaway, H., & Pare, E. (2008). Locating mothers: How cultural debates about stay-at-home versus working mothers define women and home. *Journal of Family Issues, 29,* 437–464.

Dorow, S. (2006). Racialized choices: Chinese adoption and the "white noise" of blackness. *Critical Sociology, 32,* 357–379.

Dorow, S., & Swiffen, A. (2009). Blood and desire: The secret of heteronormativity in adoption narratives of culture. *American Ethnologist, 3,* 563–573.

Doucet, A. (2006). *Do men mother? Fathering, care, and domestic responsibility.* Toronto: University of Toronto Press.

———. (2009). Dad and baby in the first year: Gendered responsibilities and embodiment. *annals of the American Academy of Political & Social Science, 624,* 78–98.

Doucet, A., & Merla, L. (2007). Stay-at-home fathering: A strategy for balancing work and home in Canadian and Belgian families. *Community, Work, & Family, 10,* 455–473.

Downing, J. B., Richardson, H. B., Kinkler, L., & Goldberg, A. E. (2009). Making the decision: Gay men's choice of an adoption path. *Adoption Quarterly, 12,* 247–271.

Downs, A. C., & James, S. E. (2006). Gay, lesbian, and bisexual foster parents: Strengths and challenges for the child welfare system. *Child Welfare, 85,* 281–298.

Drentea, P., & Moren-Cross, J. L. (2005). Social capital and social support on the web: The case of an Internet mother site. *Sociology of Health & Illness, 27,* 920–943.

Edwards, M. R. (2007). An examination of employed mothers' work-family narratives and perceptions of husbands' support. *Marriage & Family Review, 42,* 59–89.

Ehrensaft, D. (1990). *Parenting together: Men and women sharing the care of their children.* Chicago: University of Illinois Press.

Ericksen, K. S., Jurgens, J. C., Garrett, M. T., & Swedburg, R. B. (2008). Should I stay at home or should I go back to work? Workforce reentry influences on a mother's decision-making process. *Journal of Employment Counseling, 45,* 156–167.

Erwin, E. J., & Kontos, S. (1998). Parents' and kindergarten teachers' beliefs about the effects of child care. *Early Education & Development, 9,* 131–146.

Evan B. Donaldson Adoption Institute. (2002). The 2002 National Adoption Attitudes Survey. Retrieved July 22, 2009, from http://www.adoptioninstitute.org/survey/survey_intro.html.

Evans, A., Barbato, C., Bettini, E., Gray, E., & Kippen, R. (2009). Taking stock: Parents' reasons for and against having a third child. *Community, Work, & Family, 12,* 437–454.

Ewick, P., & Silbey, S. (1998). *The common place of law: Stories from everyday life.* Chicago: University of Chicago Press.

———. (2003). Narrating social structure: Stories of resistance to legal authority. *American Journal of Sociology, 108,* 1328–1372.

Family Research Council. (2011). The slippery slope of same-sex marriage. Retrieved on January 17, 2011, from http://www.frc.org/get.cfm?i=bc04c02.

Fischer, L. R. (1988). The influence of kin on the transition to parenthood. *Marriage & Family Review, 72,* 201–219.

Fitch, C. A., & Ruggles, S. (2000). Historical trends in marriage formation, United States, 1850–1990. In L. Waite, C. Bachrach, M. Hindin, E. Thomson, & A. Thornton (Eds.), *Ties that bind: Perspectives on marriage and cohabitation* (pp. 59–88). Hawthorne, NY: Aldine de Gruyter.

Folgero, T. (2008). Queer nuclear families? Reproducing and transgressing heteronormativity. *Journal of Homosexuality, 54,* 124–149.

Fried, J. (2008). *Democrats and Republicans—rhetoric and reality: Comparing the voters in statistics and anecdotes.* New York: Algora.

Friedman, C. (2007). First comes love, then comes marriage, then comes baby carriage: Perspectives on gay parenting and reproductive technology. *Journal of Infant, Child, & Adolescent Psychotherapy, 6,* 111–123.

Fuller, C. B., Chang, D. F., & Rubin, L. R. (2009). Sliding under the radar: Passing and power among sexual minorities. *Journal of LGBT Issues in Counseling, 3,* 128–151.

Gallup (2010). Gay and lesbian rights. Retrieved June 17, 2010, from http://www.gallup.com/poll/1651/Gay-Lesbian-Rights.aspx.

Gameiro, S., Boivin, J., Canavarro, M. C., Moura-Ramos, M., & Soares, I. (2010). Social nesting: Changes in social network and support across the transition to parenthood in couples that conceived spontaneously or through assisted reproductive technologies. *Journal of Family Psychology, 24*, 175–187.

Gartrell, N., Banks, A., Hamilton, J., Reed, N., Bishop, H., & Rodas, C. (1999). The National Lesbian Family Study: 2. Interviews with mothers of toddlers. *American Journal of Orthopsychiatry, 69*, 362–369.

Gartrell, N., Banks, A., Reed, N., Hamilton, J., Rodas, C., & Deck, A. (2000). The National Lesbian Family Study: 3. Interviews with mothers of five-year-olds. *American Journal of Orthopsychiatry, 70*, 542–548.

Gates, G., & Ost, J. (2004). *The gay and lesbian atlas.* Washington, DC: Urban Institute.

Gattai, F. B., & Musatti, T. (1999). Grandmothers' involvement in grandchildren's care: Attitudes, feelings, and emotions. *Family Relations, 48*, 35–4

Gergen, K. J. (1985). The social constructionist movement in modern psychology. *American Psychologist, 40*, 266–275.

Glaser, B. G., & Strauss, A. L. (1967). *The discovery of grounded theory: Strategies for qualitative research.* Chicago: Aldine.

Gianino, M. (2008). Adaptation and transformation: The transition to adoptive parenthood for gay male couples. *Journal of GLBT Family Studies, 4*, 205–243.

Goffman, E. G. (1963). *Stigma: Notes on the management of spoiled identity.* Englewood Cliffs, NJ: Prentice Hall.

Goldberg, A. E. (2006). The transition to parenthood for lesbian couples. *Journal of GLBT Family Studies, 2*, 13–42.

———. (2009a). Lesbian parents and their families: Complexity and intersectionality from a feminist perspective. In S. Lloyd, A. Few, & K. R. Allen (Eds.), *The handbook of feminist family studies* (pp. 108–120). Thousand Oaks, CA: Sage.

———. (2009b). Lesbian and heterosexual preadoptive couples' openness to transracial adoption. *American Journal of Orthopsychiatry, 79*, 103–117.

———. (2010a). *Lesbian and gay parents and their children: Research on the family life cycle.* Washington, DC: American Psychological Association.

———. (2010b). Studying complex families in context. *Journal of Marriage & the Family, 72*, 29–34.

Goldberg, A. E., & Allen, K. R. (2007). Imagining men: Lesbian mothers' ideas and intentions about male involvement across the transition to parenthood. *Journal of Marriage & the Family, 69*, 352–365.

Goldberg, A. E., Downing, J. B., & Richardson, H. B. (2009). The transition from infertility to adoption: Perceptions of lesbian and heterosexual preadoptive couples. *Journal of Social & Personal Relationships, 26*, 938–963.

Goldberg, A. E., Downing, J. B., & Sauck, C. C. (2007). Choices, challenges, and tensions: Perspectives of lesbian prospective adoptive parents. *Adoption Quarterly, 10*, 33–64.

———. (2008). Perceptions of children's parental preferences in lesbian two-mother households. *Journal of Marriage & the Family, 70*, 419–434.

Goldberg, A. E., Kinkler, L. A., & Hines, D. A. (2011). Perception and internalization of adoption stigma among lesbian, gay, and heterosexual adoptive parents. *Journal of GLBT Family Studies, 7*, 132–154.

Goldberg, A. E., Downing, J. B., & Moyer, A. M. (2012). Why parent, and why now? Gay men's motivations for pursuing parenthood. *Family Relations, 61*, 157–174.

Goldberg, A. E., & Perry-Jenkins, M. (2007). The division of labor and perceptions of parental roles: Lesbian couples across the transition to parenthood. *Journal of Social & Personal Relationships, 24*, 297–318.

Goldberg, A. E., & Smith, J. Z. (2009). Perceived parenting skill across the transition to adoptive parenthood among lesbian, gay, and heterosexual couples. *Journal of Family Psychology, 23*, 861–870.

———. (2011). Stigma, social context, and mental health: Lesbian and gay couples across the transition to adoptive parenthood. *Journal of Counseling Psychology, 58*, 139–150.

Goldberg, A. E., Smith, J. Z., & Kashy, D. A. (2010). Pre-adoptive factors predicting lesbian, gay, and heterosexual couples' relationship quality across the transition to adoptive parenthood. *Journal of Family Psychology, 24*, 221–232.

Griffin, P. (1991). From hiding out to coming out: Empowering lesbian and gay educators. *Journal of Homosexuality, 22*, 167–196.

Gross, M. J. (July 23, 2009). Gay is the new Black? *The Advocate*. Retrieved October 21, 2011, from http://www.advocate.com/printArticle.aspx?id=43252.

Guendouzi, J. (2006). "The guilt thing": Balancing domestic and professional roles. *Journal of Marriage & the Family, 68*, 901–909.

Haddock, S. A., & Rattenborg, K. (2003). Benefits and challenges of dual-earning: Perspectives of successful couples. *American Journal of Family Therapy, 31*, 325–344.

Hargreaves, K. (2006). Constructing families and kinship through donor insemination. *Sociology of Health & Illness, 28*, 261–283.

Harrigan, M. M. (2009). The contradictions of identity-work for parents of visibly adopted children. *Journal of Social & Personal Relationships, 26*, 634–658.

Hayden, C. P. (1995). Gender, genetics, and generation: Reformulating biology in lesbian kinship. *Cultural Anthropology, 10*, 41–63.

Heller, K. S. (1993). "Silence equals death: Discourses on AIDS and identity in the gay press, 1981–1986." PhD diss., University of California.

Henwood, K., & Procter, J. (2003). The "good father": Reading men's accounts of paternal involvement during the transition to first-time fatherhood. *British Journal of Social Psychology, 42*, 337–355.

Herek, G. M. (1996). Why tell if you're not asked? Self-disclosure, intergroup contact, and heterosexual's attitudes toward lesbians and gay men. In L. Garnets & D. C. Kimmel (Eds.), *Psychological perspectives on lesbian, gay, and bisexual issues* (pp. 270–298). New York: Columbia University Press.

———. (2006). Legal recognition of same-sex relationships in the United States: A social science perspective. *American Psychologist, 61*, 607–621.

Hicks, S. (2006a). Maternal men—perverts and deviants? Making sense of gay men as foster carers and adopters. *Journal of GLBT Family Studies, 2*, 93–114.

———. (2006b). Is gay parenting bad for kids? Responding to the "very idea of difference" in research on lesbian and gay parents. *Sexualities, 8*, 153–168.

Hiller, D., & Philliber, W. (1986). The division of labor in contemporary marriage. *Social Problems, 33*, 191–201.

Holcomb, B. (1998). *Not guilty: The good news about working mothers.* New York: Scribner.

Howes, C. (1990). Can the age of entry into child care and the quality of child care predict adjustment in kindergarten? *Developmental Psychology, 26*, 292–303.

Human Rights Campaign. (2010). Parenting laws. Retrieved June 3, 2010, from http://www. hrc.org/documents/parenting_laws_maps.pdf.

Huston, T. L., & Melz, H. (2004). The case for (promoting) marriage: The devil is in the details. *Journal of Marriage & the Family, 66*, 943–958.

Jackson, S. (2006). Interchanges: Gender, sexuality, and heterosexuality: The complexity (and limits) of heteronormativity. *Feminist Theory, 7*, 105–121.

Johnston, D. D., & Swanson, D. H. (2003). Undermining mothers: A content analysis of the representation of mothers in magazines. *Mass Communication & Society, 6*, 243–265.

———. (2006). Constructing the "good mother": The experience of mothering ideologies by work status. *Sex Roles, 54*, 509–519.

Jones, C. A., & Keith, L. G. (2006). Medical tourism and reproductive outsourcing: The dawning of a new paradigm for healthcare. *International Journal of Fertility & Women's Medicine, 51*, 251–255.

Kahn, J. S., Holmes, J. R., & Brett, B. L. (2011). Dialogical masculinities: Diverse youth resisting dominant masculinity. *Journal of Constructivist Psychology, 24*, 30–55.

Kaiser Family Foundation. (2001). *Inside out: A report on the experiences of lesbians, gays, and bisexuals in America and the public's view on issues and politics related to sexual orientation.* Menlo Park, CA: Author.

Kindregan, C. P. (2008). A family law revolution: Changing attitudes about parentage in nontraditional families' use of collaborative reproduction. *Legal Studies Research Paper Series, Research Paper No. 08-39*, 16–23. Retrieved on May 25, 2010, from http://papers. ssrn.com/sol3/papers.cfm?abstract_id=1304284.

Kleinfield, K. (June 19, 2011). Baby makes four, and complications. *New York Times.* Retrieved June 26, 2011, from http://www.nytimes.com/2011/06/19/nyregion/an-american-family-mom-sperm-donor-lover-child.html.

Kluwer, E. S., Heesink, J. A. M., & van de Vliert, E. (2002). The division of labor across the transition to parenthood: A justice perspective. *Journal of Marriage & the Family, 64*, 930–943.

Kroska, A. (2003). Investigating gender differences in the meaning of household chores and child care. *Journal of Marriage & the Family, 65*, 456–473.

Kurdek, L. (2005). Reflections on queer theory and family science. In V. Bengtson, A. Acock, K. Allen, D. Klein, & P. Dilworth-Anderson (Eds.), *Sourcebook of family theory and research* (pp. 160–166). Thousand Oaks, CA: Sage.

Landau, J. (2009). Straightening out (the politics of) same-sex parenting: Representing gay families in US print news stories and photographs. *Critical Studies in Media Communication, 26*, 80–100.

Lannutti, P. J. (2005). For better or worse: Exploring the meanings of same-sex marriage within the lesbian, gay, bisexual and transgendered community. *Journal of Social & Personal Relationships, 22*, 5–18.

Lassiter, P. S., Dew, B. J., Newton, K., Hays, D. G., & Yarbrough, B. (2006). Self-defined empowerment for gay and lesbian parents: A qualitative explanation. *Family Journal, 14*, 245–252.

Lease, S. H., & Shulman, J. L. (2003). A preliminary investigation of the role of religion for family members of lesbian, gay male, or bisexual male and female individuals. *Counseling & Values, 47*, 195–209.

Letherby, G. (1999). Other than mother and mothers as others: The experience of motherhood and non-motherhood in relation to "infertility" and "involuntary childlessness." *Women's Studies International Forum, 22*, 359–372.

Lev, A. I. (2004). *The complete lesbian and gay parenting guide.* New York: Berkley Books.

Levitt, M. J., Weber, R. A., & Clark, M. C. (1986). Social network relationships as sources of maternal support and well-being. *Developmental Psychology, 22,* 310–316.

Lewin, E. (1993). *Lesbian mothers: Accounts of gender in American culture.* Ithaca, NY: Cornell University Press.

———. (2009). *Gay fatherhood: Narratives of family and citizenship in America.* Chicago: Chicago University Press.

Lewin, E., & Leap, W. (2009). *Out in public: Reinventing lesbian/gay anthropology in a globalizing world.* Malden, MA: Blackwell.

Littauer, A. H. (2004). Same-sex parenting. In *Encyclopedia of children and childhood in history and society, 2004.* Retrieved May 27, 2010, from http://www.encyclopedia.com/doc/1G2-3402800355.html.

Logan, J., & Sellick, C. (2007). Lesbian and gay fostering and adoption in the United Kingdom: Prejudice, progress, and the challenge of the present. *Social Work & Social Sciences Review, 13,* 35–47.

Lupton, D., & Schmied, V. (2002). "The right way of doing it all": First-time Australian mothers' decisions about paid employment. *Women's Studies International Forum, 25,* 97–107.

Mahalik, J. R., Talmadge, W. T., Locke, B. D., & Scott, R. P. J. (2005). Using the Conformity to Masculine Norms Inventory to work with men in a clinical setting. *Journal of Clinical Psychology, 61,* 661–674.

Mallon, G. P. (2004). *Gay men choosing parenthood.* New York: Columbia University Press.

Martin, K. (2009). Normalizing heterosexuality: Mothers' assumptions, talk, and strategies with young children. *American Sociological Review, 75,* 190–207

Matthews, J. D., & Cramer, E. P. (2006). Envisaging the adoption process to strengthen gay- and lesbian-headed families: Recommendations for adoption professionals. *Child Welfare, 85,* 317–340.

Maurer, T. W., Pleck, J. H., & Rane, T. R. (2001). Parental identity and reflected-appraisals: Measurement and gender dynamics. *Journal of Marriage and Family, 63,* 309–321.

Merla, L. (2008). Determinants, costs, and meanings of Belgian stay-at-home fathers: An international comparison. *Fathering, 6,* 113–132.

Mezey, N. J. (2008). The privilege of coming out: Race, class, and lesbians' mothering decisions. *International Journal of Sociology of the Family, 34,* 257–276.

Miller, N. (2006). *Out of the past: Gay and lesbian history from 1869 to the present.* New York: Alyson.

Modell, J., & Dambacher, N. (1997). Making a "real" family: Matching and cultural biologism in American adoption. *Adoption Quarterly, 2,* 3–33.

Morrow, S. (2005). Quality and trustworthiness in qualitative research in counseling psychology. *Journal of Counseling Psychology, 52,* 250–260.

Murdock, G. P. (1960). *Social structure.* New York: Macmillan.

Naples, N. A. (2004). Queer parenting in the new millennium. *Gender & Society, 18,* 679–684.

Oswald, R. (2002). Who am I in relation to them? Gay, lesbian, and queer people leave the city to attend rural family weddings. *Journal of Family Issues, 23,* 323–348.

Oswald, R., Blume, L., & Marks, S. (2005). Decentering heteronormativity: A model for family studies. In V. Bengtson, A. Acock, K. Allen, D. Klein, & P. Dilworth-Anderson (Eds.), *Sourcebook of family theory and research* (pp. 143–165). Thousand Oaks, CA: Sage.

Oswald, R. F., & Culton, L. S. (2003). Under the rainbow: Rural gay life and its relevance for family providers. *Family Relations, 52*, 72–81.

Oswald, R. F., Goldberg, A. E., Kuvalanka, K., & Clausell, E. (2008). Structural and moral commitment among same-sex couples: Relationship duration, religiosity, and parental status. *Journal of Family Psychology, 22*, 411–419.

Oswald, R. F., Kuvalanka, K. A., Blume, K. B., & Berkowitz, D. (2009). Queering "the family." S. Lloyd, A. Few, & K. R. Allen (Eds.), *The handbook of feminist family studies* (pp. 43–55). Thousand Oaks, CA: Sage.

Patterson, C. J., Hurt, S., & Mason, C. D. (1998). Families of the lesbian baby boom: Children's contact with grandparents and other adults. *American Journal of Orthopsychiatry, 68*, 390–399.

Patterson, C. J., Sutfin, E. L., & Fulcher, M. (2004). Division of labor among lesbian and heterosexual parenting couples: Correlates of specialized versus shared patterns. *Journal of Adult Development, 11*, 179–189.

Pawelski, J. G., et al. (2006). The effects of marriage, civil union, and domestic partnership laws on the health and well-being of children. *Pediatrics, 118*, 346–364.

Peel, E., & Harding, R. (2004). Civil partnerships: A new couple's conversation. *Feminism & Psychology, 14*, 41–46.

Pertman, A. (2000). *Adoption nation: How the adoption revolution is transforming America.* New York: Basic.

Pew Research Center. (2006). Survey report: Pragmatic Americans liberal and conservative on social issues. Retrieved October 8, 2009, from http://people-press.org/report/283/pragmatic-americans-liberal-and-conservative-on-social-issues.

———. (2007). Survey report: Trends in political values and core attitudes: 1987–2007. Retrieved May 27, 2010, from http://people-press.org/reports/pdf/312.pdf.

Planck, C. (2006). Connection and community: How the Family Pride Coalition supports parents and children of GLBT families. *Journal of GLBT Family Studies, 2*, 39–48.

Pleck, J. H. (1981). *The myth of masculinity.* Cambridge, MA: MIT Press.

———. (1995). The gender role strain paradigm: An update. In R. F. Levant & W. S. Pollack (Eds.), *A new psychology of men* (pp. 11–32). New York: Basic.

Poncz, E. (2007). China's proposed international adoption law: The likely impact on single U.S. citizens seeking to adopt from China and the available alternatives. *Harvard International Law Journal, 48*, 74–82.

Ponterotto, J. G. (2005). Qualitative research in counseling psychology: A primer on research paradigms and philosophy of science. *Journal of Counseling Psychology, 52*, 126–136.

Quinn, S. M. F. (2009). The depictions of fathers and children in best-selling picture books in the United States: A hybrid semiotic analysis. *Fathering, 7*, 140–158.

Quiroz, P. A. (2008). U.S. Rainbow Families online: Emblems of diversity or expansion of whiteness? *International Journal of Sociology of the Family, 34*, 277–299.

Rabun, C., & Oswald, R. F. (2009). Upholding and expanding the normal family: Future fatherhood through the eyes of gay male emerging adults. *Fathering, 7,* 269–285.

Reimann, R. (1997). Does biology matter? Lesbian couples' transition to parenthood and their division of labor. *Qualitative Sociology, 20,* 153–185.

Richardson, H. B., & Goldberg, A. E. (2010). The intersection of multiple minority statuses: Perspectives of White lesbian couples adopting racial minority children. *Australian & New Zealand Journal of Family Therapy, 31,* 340–353.

Richman, K. (2002). Lovers, legal strangers, and parents: Negotiating parental and sexual identity in family law. *Law & Society Review, 36,* 285–324.

Rickey, C. (July 22, 2010). Hollywood paints an updated portrait of the American family. *Philadelphia Inquirer.* Retrieved October 21, 2011, from http://articles.philly.com/2010-07-22/news/24968853_1_donor-portrait-family.

Ridgeway, C. L., & Correll, S. R. (2004). Unpacking the gender system: A theoretical perspective on gender beliefs and social relations. *Gender & Society, 18,* 510–531.

Riggs, D. W. & Due, C. (2010). Gay men, race privilege, and surrogacy in India. *Outskirts: Feminisms along the Edge, 22.* Retrieved on May 4, 2011, from http://www.chloe.uwa.edu.au/outskirts/archive/volume22/riggs.

Riggs, J. M. (1997). Mandates for mothers and fathers: Perceptions of breadwinners and care givers. *Sex Roles, 37,* 565–580.

Risman, B. J. (1998). *Gender vertigo: American families in transition.* New Haven, CT: Yale University Press.

———. (2004). Gender as social structure: Theory wrestling with social transformation. *Gender & Society, 18,* 429–450.

Rochlen, A. B., Suizzo, M. A., McKelley, R. A., & Scaringi, V. (2008). "I'm just providing for my family": A qualitative study of stay-at-home fathers. *Psychology of Men & Masculinity, 9,* 193–206.

Rodger, S., Cummings, A., & Leschied, A. W. (2006). Who is caring for our most vulnerable children? The motivation to foster in child welfare. *Child Abuse & Neglect, 30,* 1129–1142.

Rosenfeld, R. A. (2001). Employment flexibility in the United States. In J. Baxter and M. Western (Eds.), *Reconfiguration of class and gender* (pp. 105–130). Stanford, CA: Stanford University Press.

Ross, L. E., Epstein, R., Goldfinger, C., & Yager, C. (2008). Lesbian and queer mothers navigating the adoption system: The impacts on mental health. *Health Sociology Review, 17,* 254–266.

Ross, L. E., Steele, L., & Sapiro, B. (2005). Perceptions of predisposing and protective factors for perinatal depression in same-sex parents. *Journal of Midwifery & Women's Health, 50,* 65–70.

Rostosky, S. S., Riggle, E. D. B., Brodnicki, C., & Olson, A. (2008). An exploration of lived religion in same-sex couples from Judeo-Christian traditions. *Family Process, 46,* 389–403.

Roxburgh, S. (2006). "I wish we had more time to spend together . . . ": The distribution and predictors of perceived family time pressures among married men and women in the paid labor force. *Journal of Family Issues, 27*, 529–553.

Rubin, H. J., & Rubin, I. (2005). *Qualitative interviewing: The art of hearing data.* Thousand Oaks, CA: Sage.

Ryan, M., & Berkowitz, D. (2009). Constructing gay and lesbian parent families "beyond the closet." *Qualitative Sociology, 32*, 153–172.

Ryan, S. D., Pearlmutter, S., & Groza, V. (2004). Coming out of the closet: Opening agencies to gay and lesbian adoptive parents. *Social Work, 49*, 85–95.

Saad, L. (2008). Americans evenly divided on morality of homosexuality. Retrieved on October 8, 2009, from http://www.gallup.com/poll/108115/Americans-Evenly-Divided-Morality-Homosexuality.aspx.

———. (2010). Americans' acceptance of gay relations crosses 50% threshold. Retrieved on January 17, 2011, from http://www.gallup.com/poll/135764/americans-acceptance-gay-relations-crosses-threshold.aspx.

Sanchez, F. J., Greenberg, S. T., Liu, W. M., & Vilain, E. (2009). Reported effects of masculine ideals on gay men. *Psychology of Men & Masculinity, 19*, 73–87.

Schacher, S. J., Auerbach, C. F., & Silverstein, L. B. (2005). Gay fathers expanding the possibilities for us all. *Journal of GLBT Family Studies, 1*, 31–52.

Schieman, S., Glavin, P., & Milkie, M. (2009). When work interferes with life: Work-nonwork interference and the influence of work-related demands and resources. *American Sociological Review, 74*, 966–988.

Seidman, S. (2002). *Beyond the closet: The transformation of gay and lesbian life.* New York: Routledge.

Solomon, S. E., Rothblum, E. D., & Balsam, K. F. (2004). Pioneers in partnership: Lesbian and gay male couples in civil unions compared with those not in civil unions, and married heterosexual siblings. *Journal of Family Psychology, 18*, 275–286.

Spencer, L., & Pahl, R. (2006). *Rethinking friendship: Hidden solidarities today.* Princeton, NJ: Princeton University Press.

Stacey, J. (1996). *In the name of the family: Rethinking family values in the postmodern age.* Boston: Beacon.

———. (2006). Gay parenthood and the decline of paternity as we knew it. *Sexualities, 9*, 27–55.

Stacey, J., & Biblarz, T. (2001). (How) does the sexual orientation of parents matter? *American Sociological Review, 66*, 159–183.

Stein, A. (2005). Make room for Daddy: Anxious masculinity and emergent homophobias in neopatriarchal politics. *Gender & Society, 19*, 601–620.

Steinbugler, A. C. (2005). Visibility as privilege and danger: Heterosexual and same-sex interracial intimacy in the 21st century. *Sexualities, 8*, 425–443.

Stoller, E. P. (2002). Theoretical perspectives on caregiving men. In B. Kramer & E. Thompson (Eds.), *Men as caregivers: Theory, research, and service implications* (pp. 51–68). New York: Springer.

Stone, P., & Lovejoy, M. (2004). Fast-track women and the "choice" to stay home. *annals of the American Academy of Political & Social Science, 596*, 62–83.

Stossel, J., & Binkley, G. (September 15, 2006). Gay stereotypes: Are they true? Retrieved June 17, 2010, from http://abcnews.go.com/2020/story?id=2449185&page=1.

Stychin, C. F. (2005). Being gay. *Government & Opposition, 40*, 90–109.

Sullivan, M. (1996). Rozzie and Harriet? Gender and family patterns of lesbian coparents. *Gender & Society, 10*, 747–767.

———. (2004). *The family of women: Lesbian mothers, their children, and the undoing of gender.* Berkeley: University of California Press.

Sullivan, M. K. (2003). Homophobia, history, and homosexuality: Trends for sexual minorities. *Journal of Human Behavior in the Social Environment, 8*, 1–13.

Sullivan, M. K., & Wodarski, J. (2002). Social alienation in gay youth. *Journal of Human Behavior in the Social Environment, 5*, 1–17.

Suter, E. A., Daas, K. L., & Bergen, K. M. (2008). Negotiating lesbian family identity via symbols and rituals. *Journal of Family Issues, 29*, 26–47.

Tan, S. J. (2008). The myths and realities of maternal employment. In A. Marcus-Newhall, D. F. Halpern, & S. J. Tan (Eds.), *The changing realities of work and family: A multidisciplinary approach* (pp. 9–24). Malden, MA: Wiley-Blackwell.

Taywaditep, K. J. (2001). Marginalization among the marginalized: Gay men's anti-effeminacy attitudes. *Journal of Homosexuality, 42*, 1–28.

Teman, E. (2009). Embodying surrogate motherhood: Pregnancy as a dyadic body-project. *Body & Society, 15*, 46–69.

Thornton, A. (1989). Changing attitudes toward family issues in the United States. *Journal of Marriage & the Family, 51*, 873–893.

Thornton, A., & Young-DeMarco, L. (2001). Four decades of trends in attitudes toward family issues in the United States: The 1960's through the 1990's. *Journal of Marriage & the Family, 63*, 1009–1037.

Townsend, N. W. (2002). *The package deal: Marriage, work, and fatherhood in men's lives.* Philadelphia: Temple University Press.

Troxel v. Granville (2000). 530 U.S. 57.

Tyebjee, T. (2003). Attitude, interest, and motivation for adoption and foster care. *Child Welfare, 82*, 685–706.

Van Balen, F., Verdurmen, J., & Ketting, E. (1997). Choices and motivations of infertile couples. *Patient Education & Counseling, 31*, 19–37.

Voydanoff, P. (2005). Towards a conceptualization of perceived work-family fit and balance: A demands and resources approach. *Journal of Marriage & the Family, 67*, 822–836.

Wald, D. (2007). A legal perspective on gay surrogacy. Retrieved September 30, 2009, from http://gaylife.about.com/od/gayparentingadoption/a/gayparent.htm.

———. (2010). Gay adoption issues: Choosing an LGBT friendly attorney. Retrieved June 4, 2010, from http://adoption.about.com/od/gaylesbian/a/gayadoptissues.htm.

Weeks, J. (2008). Regulation, resistance, recognition. *Sexualities, 11*, 787–792.

Weeks, J., Heaphy, B., & Donovan, C. (2001). *Same-sex intimacies: Families of choice and other life experiments.* London: Routledge.

Wegar, K. (1997). In search of bad mothers: Social constructions of birth and adoptive motherhood. *Women's Studies International Forum, 20*, 77–86.

West, C., & Zimmerman, D. H. (1987). Doing gender. *Gender & Society, 1*, 125–151.

Weston, K. (1991). *Families we choose: Lesbians, gays, kinship.* New York: Columbia University Press.

Whitley, B. E. (2009). Religiosity and attitudes toward lesbians and gay men: A meta-analysis. *International Journal for the Psychology of Religion, 19*, 21–38.

Wiesman, S., Boeije, H., van Doorne-Huiskes, A., & den Dulk, L. (2008). "Not worth mentioning": The implicit and explicit nature of decision-making about the division of paid and domestic work. *Community, Work, & Family, 11*, 341–363.

Wolff, J. (July 1, 2008). Family resemblance in transracial adoption. Retrieved on June 26, 2011, from http://www.rainbowkids.com/ArticleDetails.aspx?id=601.

ABOUT THE AUTHOR

ABBIE E. GOLDBERG is Associate Professor of Psychology at Clark University in Worcester, Massachusetts, and a senior research fellow at the Evan B. Donaldson Adoption Institute. She is the author of *Lesbian and Gay Parents and Their Children: Research on the Family Life Cycle*, which was published in 2010 by the American Psychological Association.